Batá Drumming

*The Instruments, the Rhythms,
and the People Who Play Them*

The Oru Seco

by
Don Skoog

and

Alejandro Carvajal Guerra
Escuela Nacional de Arte, Havana, Cuba

www.contemporarymusicproject.com

© 2010. By Donald Skoog. All rights reserved.

Published by:

The Contemporary Music Project
P.O. Box 1366
Oak Park, IL 60304
708 524-8605

www.contemporarymusicproject.com

First Edition

Second Edition, June, 2011

Third Edition June, 2015

ISBN 978-0-9962263-2-5

This book is a work of independent scholarship. Please do not photocopy it or allow others to do so. When you encourage people to support an author's efforts, you empower him to continue his work, which will benefit everyone.

Contents

Introduction 1

Section One: The People

Chapter One. Sugar and Slaves

    Introduction: The New World 8
    Cuba Before Columbus 10
    The Spanish Conquest 11
    The Early Slave Trade 12
    Sugar Wars and Coffee Plantations 13
    Abolitionists and Slave Traders 14

Chapter Two. Slavery and Society

    Introduction: The Creole World 18
    The Native Americans 19
    The Spanish 20
    The French 20
    The Chinese 20
    The Africans 21
    Meta-Ethnic Denominations
        1) The Congos 23
        2) The Carabalí 24
        3) The Arará 24
        4) The Lucumí 25

Chapter Three. Slave Life in Cuba

    Introduction: The Preplantational and Plantational Eras 27
    Rural Slavery 28
    Urban Slavery 29
    Cabildos and Cofradías 30

Chapter Four. The Transculturation of Cuba

    Introduction: Fernando Ortiz and Cuban Anthropology 34

Transculturation 35
When, How Many, Where, and Who 37
    1) The time factor 38
    2) Relative number of slaves 38
    3) The different societies of Cuba and the United States 39
    4) The differing ethnic backgrounds of the slaves 40

Chapter Five. Afro-Cuban Religion and Drumming

Introduction: Common Traits in West African Religion 42
Trance and Possession 45
Animism 49
Syncretization 50
Afro-Cuban Religions and Drumming Groups 53
    Reglas de Congo 53
        Makuta Drums 54
        Yuka Drums 55
        Palo Drums 56
    Regla Arará 57
    Abakuá 59
        The Legend of Tanze 61

Chapter Six. Santeria

Introduction 64
Olodumare 67
The Orishas 68
Sacred Stories 74
Beliefs and Practices 76
The Oracle of Ifá 78
The Égun 79

Photographs 81

Section Two: The Music

Chapter Seven. The Batá Drums

Introduction 82
Drums That Talk 83

    History of the Batá Drums 84
    General Information 85
    The Acheré 87
    The Temporal Line and Clave 88
    Adapting to Cuban Teaching Styles 89
    Batá Drumming, Gender, and Sexual Orientation 91
    Abuse 92

Chapter Eight. Musical Form and Structure

    Introduction 94
    What is a Toque? 95
    The Oru Seco 96
    The Oru Cantado 97
    The Oru Égun 99
    Calls, Conversations, Transitions, and Variations 100

Chapter Nine. The Oru Seco

    Introduction 103
    On Transcribing Music 104
    Playing Techniques 108
    One Last Warning About Time Feel 109
    Notation Key 110
    Final Thoughts 111

Chapter Ten. Musical Transcriptions of the Oru Seco

    1. La Topa 113
    2. Ogundere 117
    3. Agueré Ochosi 119
    4. Imbaloke 123
    5. Inle 126
    6. Iyakotá 128
    7. San Lazaro 129
    8. Osain 130
    9. Ósun 133
    10a. Rezo de Obatalá 135
    10b. Obatalá 136
    11a. Dadá 141

    11b. Óke 143
    12. Agayú 145
    13a. Titilaro 148
    13b. Meta 151
    14. Orisha Oko 156
    15. Ibeyi 159
    16. Yeguá 160
    17. Oyá 163
    18. Aro 168
    19. Rezo de Ochún 176
    20. Obba 178
    21. Orunla 181
    22. Oduwa 182

Chapter Eleven. Epilogue: Music and Change 185

References Cited and Other Resources 188

Discography 199

Introduction

> To arrive at the point where one sees the life of another culture as an alternative is to reach a fundamental notion of the humanistic perspective, and to accept the reality of one's actions to the people who live there is to understand that one has become part of their history. This insight can become a pathway to responsibility and an opening towards one's own human love.
>
> John Miller Chernoff

Dann Sherrill and I stood, two small white faces, in a sea of dancing, singing black people. Three *batá* drummers spun the elegant rhythms of *santería*, striking the hourglass-shaped drums, horizontal in their laps, with both hands. The air was damp and thick, rich with the smells of food and people. Another man sang in a language I could not understand, and the crowd around us, swaying in time, sang the responses.

We had traveled across Havana to an area called Regla, following the drummers to an initiation ceremony dedicated to the goddess, Ochún. Leaving the road, we wound our way up a hillside through an interlaced network of paths to a busy, festive house. The furniture had been cleared away to accommodate a crowd and the living room was decorated for a party. Dann and I were completely lost and in the hands of strangers, who treated us as honored guests, happy we were there and graciously solicitous of our well-being. Never have I felt so welcome into the lives of strangers.

As the ceremony began, the drummers went into a side room, playing a series of salutes, first to Eleguá, the gatekeeper of the spiritual pathways, then to others, asking for their attention and attendance at the ceremony about to begin. Back in the living room, they were joined by a singer, whose haunting, melodic calls were answered by the chorus around us. Women kissed the drums and put money in a dish, prostrating themselves on the ground in front of the drummers. Later, one of the drummers gave me two of his pesos, which I still cherish.

The ceremony lasted for four hours, the song and drum never slowing. But for me time seemed to stop in a universe of melody and rhythm that had no beginning or end, only a tightly woven fabric of interrelated parts that together made one. The sound of the drums changed. Where I first heard separate rhythms I now only heard one. Where I first heard many voices I now only heard one. Where I came, striving to study, I was now content to just be.

Suddenly, a man became possessed by his guardian, the god entering his body, present in the room through him. Eyes fluttering, he extended his arms toward the ceiling, and his body shook as he surrendered it to the god. Friends held him upright to keep him from falling, then helped him from the room. Later, he returned dressed all in yellow, and a cry of delight rose from the crowd. Here was Ochún, present to receive the allegiance of those who had dedicated their lives to her (Ochún is female but perfectly capable of possessing a man's body). He went from one person to the next, giving each a hug and a kiss, and when it was my turn I looked in his eyes. They were wells of love and deep joy. He was indeed entranced.

Another man became possessed, then a woman. The drummers played louder and the singer, inspired, led the chorus in a harmony of the spirit. They all danced as one. Four more became possessed together and the room became a blur of movement and sound, building like a wave to a roaring climax, and just at the peak, when it could go no higher, the lights went out! Instantly we were in a world of warm, dark, moist quiet. Nothing else existed. Finally, a light bulb on a wire was carried in, and Dann and I, backs to the wall and stiff as boards, found ourselves surrounded by the drummers who howled with laughter when they saw our faces, a little bit whiter than when we came in. This was our introduction to Afro-Cuban drumming.

I will probably never have another experience quite like that one. It fired my imagination and focused my work, leading me to explore a music, a people, and a world that is complex and beautiful, whose stories are amazing and little known. It led me first to a teacher's side, then to the bookshelf of ethnomusicology and through the back door into anthropology and history. While I have never penetrated to its spiritual heart, I have come to respect and, to some extent, understand those who have. And I have come to appreciate the effect it has had on my life. But, above all, I have come to admire those who faced death to preserve their identity and faith in the unrelenting face of displacement and oppression.

This book, the result of those explorations, is a collaboration with master drummer and *babalawo*, Alejandro Carvajal Guerra. The focus is on one set of drums from one Afro-Cuban tradition: the batá of the *lucumí*.

It started out as a very different book. On my first trip to Cuba in 1994, I was shocked at the bewildering variety and sheer number of drumming traditions on the island. Not only did I know nothing about all those strange looking drums, but nobody else I knew did either. I started taking notes and, with the help of María Vinueza, began to gather Cuban anthropology and musicology books. My goal was to write an overview, sorting the drums by ethnic tradition and collecting a few transcriptions for each. I couldn't understand why it hadn't been done before: transcribe some examples and write up some background on each drum, right? Sounds like an easy project. The problem was, the more I researched the field the more complicated it became. What started as a closed-end project turned into a trackless quagmire. The book kept getting bigger but no closer to being finished.

I returned to Cuba at least once a year, gathering the literature and taking lessons with many drum teachers. By this time the book was out of hand. It was obvious that I needed help, so I brought my bad first draft to María who read it and promptly had a meltdown. "*Me diste una fiebre!*" she cried. You gave me a fever! She told me I had no understanding of the subject, couldn't think for myself, and that if it was ever published I should not use her name anywhere in the text. I was mortified. Then, after calming herself down, she sat with me, attempting to show me how it fell short and how I could begin to repair the damage.

I walked out of her house later that day, shattered. I took my manuscript back home and shelved it while I licked my intellectual wounds. Eventually, I decided to continue the project, but it was obvious that I needed to educate myself first, then clarify my goals before I began to write again. The manuscript stayed on the shelf for several years while I read everything I could find on anthropology and musicology, first in English and only later in Spanish, once I felt I had enough background to understand what I was reading. I collected the literature and studied it, trying to think more clearly and write more accurately.

The original concept now seemed incredibly naive. As I regrouped, I began seeking a way to re-conceive it. The manuscript was huge and completely unfocused. I would stare at it, not knowing where to begin. I needed a spark to rekindle the flame.

My students discovered Alejandro before I did. One of them told me he had set up a group batá lesson with some guy, would I like to come? At first I was cautious about getting back into something that I knew required years of commitment, so I went just to watch.

I had taken batá lessons on several occasions during earlier trips but had come away frustrated. The teachers were often confrontational, angry with our lack of comprehension. Their methods didn't work well with foreign students. For instance, one refused to let us write out the patterns, so we came away with nothing. Another insisted that new students play only the smallest drum. Another continually tried to borrow money from us. So lessons with Alejandro came as a pleasant surprise.

He is a very patient, organized teacher. He has adapted the traditional teaching methods to accommodate Cubans who study with him at the *Escuela Nacional de Arte* and again for the foreigners who study with him privately. He understood our need to notate the rhythms. But it is hard to play and write at the same time. Since I was the fastest transcriber, I began writing out the patterns while my students played. Alejandro didn't allow me to stay in that role for long. During the course of our lessons, he realized that I had some playing experience and he gently maneuvered me into using it. To my dismay, I was again picking up a drum I thought I had put down for good. But as my interest in the batá reignited, so did my determination to master, or at least encompass, the repertoire.

Here, at last, was my spark. I tore into the old manuscript, extracted every usable word, restructured the outline, and started over.

Section One is text. Chapter One is a short history of the slave trade. Chapter Two examines the ethnic makeup of the Cuban people. Chapter Three explores slave life in Cuba and its effect on their society. Chapter Four is the first part of a discussion about the processes that shaped the island's people. Chapter Five outlines how those processes affected Afro-Cuban religion. Chapter Six focuses on one of those religions, Santeria.

In Section Two, Chapter Seven describes the batá drums of Santeria. Chapter Eight explains their musical form, structure, and function in Santeria ceremonies. Chapter Nine examines the Oru Seco, contains playing techniques, a notation key, and performance notes. Chapter Ten contains twenty-two musical transcriptions for the Oru Seco, a set of drumming salutes which comprise the first part of some Santeria ceremonies.

Cuban music is a huge field. There are many little-known traditions on the island that are not well understood by foreigners. The depth and variety of these musics are directly linked to the many peoples who brought their cultures to the New World, and are inseparable from the wealth of their religious and secular traditions, drawn mainly from Africa and Europe, but different in many ways from both.

There is a daunting quantity of literature on Cuban history, religion, and music, mostly written in Spanish. There are many studies that explore specific aspects of the various traditions and several good performance guides to learning the music. But many scholarly works do not provide usable examples and none of the performer's guides include the historical and cultural context needed to understand the music. It is impossible to successfully perform music with no concept of where it comes from, who created it, and why.

I have not attempted to write an ethnomusicology text. To do so, I would need to tighten my focus and concentrate on just one aspect of the subject. I would rather consider this book as journalism, a general treatment of a larger field written for the average reader, rather than an enlargement of fine details written for academic specialists. I have tried to eliminate all the specialized vocabularies of the various sources I consulted, while retaining the terminology that applies directly to Afro-Cuban music and the people who make it. Intradisciplinary jargon is often seen by others as a private code for the initiated—a way of keeping others out—and I wish to make these concepts accessible to everyone who is interested.

Needless to say, there is far more missing here than included. There are other drumming traditions on the island that are not included, or touched on only briefly, and the range of popular music styles that developed partially from these roots is another subject deserving its own separate treatment.

One reason many North American scholars shy away from the study of Cuban music is simply that the Cubans got there first. The island has deeply reasoned, thoughtfully articulated disciplines of anthropology and musicology with viewpoints of their own. Foreigners approaching the field will be, by necessity, students who must assimilate the Cuban perspective first before they can make any informed contribution. Cuban musicologists are comfortable contemplating their European, African, Asian, and American roots because they grew up with them. They are not studying "the other" but themselves and their advantage is instinctive as well as earned by thoughtful labor. In the fruits of that labor we can find many good ideas that shed as much light on our part of our shared culture as it does on theirs. The real experts, both musicians and scholars, live on the island, and any unwary outsider who comes bringing light to the darkness may well wind up with it pointing at himself.

Ethnomusicology and anthropology are riddled with problems. Long-standing questions of cultural bias remain unanswered. Think of the minefield a British musicologist must walk through when working in Jamaica. Despite the best efforts of sympathetic scholars, cultural differences and gender issues still haunt the house. When a woman researcher wants to play batá in a ceremony she is trying to alter the religion to suit her needs. It can be a shock to realize that certain aspects of Afro-Cuban religion are open only to men and that this must be understood. A researcher writing about nonwestern art is considered a specialist, yet the people he documents are the true experts and he is usually just another slow student who speaks the language badly. So we need to consider the financial and cultural exploitation of the people from whom we are learning. Scholars build their careers by mining the heritage of others and must at least avoid exploiting them by giving credit where it is due.

All these thorny considerations and more apply to the study of Cuban music by outsiders. Americans working in Cuba quickly become aware that the Cubans view themselves (and us) in a different light. So if one of them cares enough about you to enlighten your political and musical ignorance it will be a mind expanding, if somewhat uncomfortable, experience.

While Cuban scholars may argue gleefully over this or that detail, they all agree that their tradition is more than the sum of its parts. Although its roots are mostly African and European, their tapestry of culture and art is, in Ortiz's elegant conception, transculturated (see Chapter 4). The oppressors and the oppressed brought their inheritances to the island and created something new, something Cuban. And their children are not done yet. Both the process and the scholarship continue.

Cuban researchers are working to augment and refine their understanding of the traditions, producing new and more detailed work, especially the monumental *Instrumentos de la Música Folclórico-Popular de Cuba* compiled by the interdisciplinary team at *Centro de Investigación y Desarrollo de la Música Cubana* (CIDMUC) in Havana. One of my goals is to re-present some of this new information not yet available in English.

But the main goal of this book is to transcribe Alejandro's version of the Oru Seco and to record his thoughts on the music. As an older tradition in a modern world, Santeria must accommodate change while struggling to remain true to its spiritual roots. Alejandro shepherds his heritage through the maze of contemporary Cuba, knowingly adapting to the economic and political pressures that are inevitably changing the religion and its music. His understanding of this process, especially when it differs from mainstream scholarship, will be invaluable to those trying to gain insight into Santeria today.

I have attempted to place Alejandro's testimony within its historical, religious, and artistic context by reading the literature, then interpreting it through my experiences as a participant. While the bibliography is reasonably comprehensive, each book only represents that writer's viewpoint, knowledge, and orientation. My hope is to present their understanding through the filter of my own. You should read this book in the same spirit. Approach it with a skeptical mind, then use it as a springboard for your own researches.

One problem I encountered while navigating this maze of times and cultures is that of spelling. Both African and Afro-Cuban words have been subject to various spellings, and scholars frequently make different choices from a range of options. Spelling variations arise from the traditions and languages of the original authors, and should be respected as such, but they can create confusion. In most cases, I have tried to use the spelling most commonly employed in contemporary Cuban scholarship. But even so, different authors use different spellings so my choices cannot be definitive. I have tried to spell each word the same way every time but have left the original spellings when quoting others. I have tried to use the clearest word or name in each context. Even so, simplifying something complex is the best way to distort it, so I have tried to present these complexities as best I understand them without doing them damage.

As a work that attempts to synthesize various aspects of musicology, history, and sociology from different intellectual traditions, I worry that it will not do justice to any of them. But in the interplay between history, religion, and culture you can find meaning in art. To understand how it came to be, you need a sense of the unfolding drama in the lives of the people who created it. My hope is that in these large outlines the reader will find meaning and spirit in the stories of so many people through hundreds of years and over thousands of miles, meaning that might be lost in a more narrowly focused book.

Acknowledgments

I would especially like to thank Maria Elena Vinueza Gonzáles of Casa de las Americas, who first showed me where to look, guided my way, then kicked my butt around the block when I brought her a poorly reasoned, incomplete first draft. Her uncompromising love of all that is true has (I hope) lighted my way ever since.

This book could not have been completed without the help of Alejandro Carvajal, my partner, teacher, and guide, who reopened his world for me, then led me along its confusing pathways. Through my studies with him, I have collected the transcriptions in this book. But, although he has checked them, any inadequacies or errors still left in the examples are mine.

Many thanks to John Amira, Mikael Ringquist, Carolyn Brandy, and Michael Spiro (who also made suggestions on the transcriptions) for reading and commenting on the text. Their contributions are indicated in parenthesizes in the appropriate spots in the text.

To my Cuban mentors: Dr. Olavo Alén Rodríguez, Roberto Vizcaino, "Don Pancho" Terry, José Eladio, Emilio Vega, Enrique Pla, José Quintana, Tomás Ortiz, Pedro Izquerdo, Pedro Pablo, the staff of La Escuela Nacional de Arte, Ana Casanova Oliva and the other scholars at CIDMUC, and Tulio Raggi Gonzáles for his great stories.

To all the people who gave me institutional support in the United States: Alisa Froman of Plazacuba, Ruby and Melissa, Thor and Jane Anderson of Caribbean Music and Dance, Ann Murray of the International Music Foundation

To the fellow travelers whose shared interests fueled my inspiration, guided my steps, and evolved into lifelong friendships: Dann Sherrill, Wayne Wallace, John Ramsay, John Calloway, Ruben Alvarez, Mike McLaughlin, Ted Hogarth, and Don Gronberg.

A very special thank you to Bob Murphy for his excellent, thoughtful editing and encouragement. This book would be far less literate without his help.

Section One

The People

Chapter One

Sugar and Slaves

From the fifteenth century on through the latter part of the nineteenth, an enormous black wave swept out of Africa. The effect was like dropping a pebble into a still lake, then following it with another and another and another. But this wave rippled out into the sea, faster and faster and more turbulent, until it became a seamless rush, a powerful black tide, that mounted and curled and finally broke up against the farther shore of the Atlantic with a silent but incredible force.

George Brandon
Santeria from Africa to the New World

The still-unfinished music building is called *el gusano* (the worm) by everyone at *La Escuela Nacional de Arte* (ENA). Its winding hallway slinks around the perimeter and off into the fields where no one goes. Normally, I take my batá lessons at a nearby house, but this time we are forced to move to the worm because the owner's neighbors were complaining about the noise. From the worm I can see the Hotel Palco through a curtain of foliage. That is where I stay, just across the street, yet far from the lives of the students who practice here.

I prefer the open-air hallway to the enclosed classrooms, whose curved walls meet the vaulted ceiling at small windows, barred like jail cells. To me, they feel like the dungeons of some ancient Spanish castle—striking but not comfortable. It is a new building, some forty years old, which has aged before its time. To walk its halls is to live its story and I love taking my lessons here.

Alejandro sits on the low, stone wall, smoking a cigarette while I unfold a ten-page batá score. I have taped the pages together and anchor the edges with my water bottle and backpack so it won't blow away in the breeze. He always smiles when I am fussing with my papers. He knows I need them but he just can't seem to take it seriously. He teaches me patterns—calls and responses—not technique. To him, the melodies of the drums are echoes of the divine. To me, they are a puzzle to be solved. He imparts them to me as language, but I perceive them as rhythm, so there is impediment in the exchange. He hears the words from the beginning of the sentence, but I hear the rhythm from the beginning of the measure. It is always a problem, and so we must compromise.

My other problem is that I am trying to write out the toques while still learning them. Since my understanding is limited my notation is inaccurate, but as I encompass each rhythm the paper becomes more meaningful. Alejandro is interested in the process too. It is foreign to the way he learned them, but he has become both accustomed to and invested in the idea. After all, both student and teacher should learn from the lesson.

Sometimes, I bring other students to study with him. It helps him, them, and me. He makes some money, they learn some batá, and I get to watch him teach. They struggle with the same issue. While he starts at the beginning of the melodic exchange, they try to start at the downbeat, which is often in the middle of the underlying phrase. Or they start in the middle, thinking it is the beginning. The misunderstanding makes everyone crazy because they don't know why it is a problem, and it is hard to explain. As I watch my countrymen suffering through the lesson, I am struck by how much everyone has learned just to be able to bridge the gap. And while we will never be Cuban, or he American, together we mold an understanding that creates common ground.

Alejandro is a tall man. When he teaches, he leans over you, playing the drum, backwards for him, from the other side. He stares you in the eye like a snake charmer. It is hard to look away. You can tell how well you are doing by the expression on his face. At times, he will wrinkle his nose at you (the Cuban sign for "what?") as if you just spoke Chinese on his talking drum. He is very patient, correcting mistakes and guiding you back onto the groove until the patterns lock together and the melody begins to sing. Then, and only then, he smiles.

I wonder at Alejandro's facility for guiding his heritage through the realities of modern Cuba. It cannot be easy to adapt these traditions to the requirements of life on the island while trying to retain the legacy that was passed down to him by his father. In fact, those traditions have been in constant flux from the time the first slave arrived in Cuba. The impositions of the Spanish, the changing politics of the Caribbean, and even the different physical environment in the New World, have all conspired to force these transplanted belief systems to evolve away from their African roots. Yet much remains and that which is new has its own story to tell.

The discovery of the New World forever altered the flow of history for Europe, Africa, and the Americas. This fact, like the sun's rise each morning, is so important that its significance is often missed. The wealth of the Americas was an irresistible opportunity for Europeans, igniting a desperate race. Lured by silver, adventurers flocked to seize new riches. Growing sugar, coffee, tobacco, and other crops, colonists stayed to build new lives. This economic potential fueled international campaigns to conquer and settle the Americas, and the profits helped fund the Industrial Revolution. The European imperative to exploit this potential led to the collapse of Native America and sparked the resurgent slave trade that played a critical role in shaping the character of the modern world.

The story of the Americas is the legacy of a man who was actually seeking Asia—a man who never understood that he had stumbled upon two continents unknown, at least to western civilization—and whose discovery was a pivotal event in history. Christopher Columbus landed in Cuba on October 27, 1492. This first contact literally uncovered a world new to the Europeans and exposed the old to the peoples of the Americas. As Fernando Ortiz explains, the Europeans brought a wealth of knowledge: new systems of law and tradition, as well as iron, gunpowder, the wheel, the horse, the ox, money, capital, wages, the letter, the printing press, and the book. They also brought an already senile and cruel feudalism and a destructive mercantile capitalism. In short, they brought the world of the Renaissance. While the peoples of the Americas contributed riches unknown to the Europeans—potatoes, corn, chocolate, peppers, tobacco, and more—their biggest contribution was millions of square miles of fertile, virgin land to replace the worn, tired soil of the Old World.

Cuba Before Columbus

There were three major indigenous peoples in the Antilles when Columbus landed: the Arcaicos, Arawaks, and the Caribes.

The Arcaicos, also called *guanajabibes* or *ciboneyes*, were a less developed, Paleolithic people who probably had emigrated from Florida. The term *ciboney* might be derived from the Taíno word *ciba* (stone or mountain) and may mean cave dweller, as indeed the Ciboneys were. The Ciboneys had no metal, ceramics, or agriculture. They lived by fishing and hunting, and little remains of their implements and other artifacts or their language, which was distinct from other native tongues. Little is known of their social structure. The Ciboneys were early inhabitants of Cuba who were later invaded by the more advanced Arawaks who came to the island from Haiti.

The Arawaks were usually referred to as *taínos*, which the Spanish derived from the word *nitayno*, an Arawak expression of honor or gentility. It was the Arawaks that met Columbus when he landed in Cuba. They were a Neolithic people, sailors and warriors, who had also brought agriculture and ceramics to the island.

The third group, the Caribes, were a warlike, aggressive people who, like the Arawaks, had emigrated north from South America. They were conquering the Antilles but had not yet reached Cuba at the time of the European discovery.

It is believed that some 100,000 Native Americans lived in Cuba at the time of Columbus's landing. Within fifty years there were no more than 2000 left.

The Spanish Conquest

The New World offered opportunity to thousands of poor people trapped in the stale, class-bound world of imperial Europe. But the first Spaniards crossed the Atlantic to be bosses, not workers. Their intention was to use Native Americans to dig the mines and work the fields, but it proved unworkable because the Indians made bad slaves. They died by the millions, and the church fought to keep them from being exterminated. Columbus had brought the first Africans as servants, but it was a cleric, Bartolomé de las Casas, who in 1511 first supported a Dominican proposal to import Africans as a way of protecting the remaining Native Americans. It seemed the only way to supply the labor to extract the wealth needed by the governments of Europe. This wealth stimulated the European economy and, combined with new technologies, led to the industrial revolution, heralding the modern world and producing the goods, mostly textiles, that were sent to Africa to purchase more slaves. These, in turn, were sent to the Americas to help produce the gold, sugar, coffee, cotton, pepper, and tobacco so highly valued in Europe and so necessary to its economic and political expansion. And it was the industrial capitalism which developed from this trade that eventually ended slavery in the New World.

This, of course, is a generalization painted in broad strokes. The slave trade was not so simple, and the histories of the Caribbean and North and South America developed along different but connected pathways. The relationship between Europe and Africa was always very complex, and the lives and stories of the mestizo cultures of the New World were far more varied, far more important, than the worth of the goods they sent to Europe. But the underlying dynamic was there, and it is important to keep this in mind when attempting to understand why the Americas evolved as they did.

Spain took early advantage of its opportunities, creating colonies in the sixteenth century in North, Central, and South America, as well as in the Caribbean, and the wealth of this empire gave the Spanish capabilities well beyond the reach of other European powers. But Cuba, with limited resources and few precious metals, was a backwater in the empire, its main advantage being its location. In the mid-fifteen hundreds, Havana was the rendezvous for two convoys, the *flota* from Mexico carrying silver, cochineal, and other goods, and the *galeones* which picked up Peruvian silver from way stations in Panama. The combined fleets would then sail back to Seville by late summer or early autumn. This was Cuba's role in the early Spanish empire, as a meeting and resupply point for convoys and their warship escorts. It was the mines of Mexico and Peru that financed Spain's vision of empire, and they were desperately short of labor.

The Early Slave Trade

In a period of no more than fifty years after the European discovery, the estimated Native American population of 40 million in Spanish America was reduced to maybe a tenth of that number. Thus began the process of repopulation mostly by the Spanish, and by Africans brought as slaves to supply the workforce depleted by the loss of the Native Americans. While the Portuguese had imported slaves into Europe as early as 1441, the Caribbean slave trade, initiated by the Spanish, did not begin until 1503. But as Spain's rivals began colonizing the New World, challenging Spanish hegemony, Spain discovered that it was at a disadvantage in the slave trade. Having given up its right to establish African outposts as part of the Treaty of Alcacovas in 1479, Spain had developed a system of *asientos*, or monopoly contracts, with foreign merchants to supply the slave needs of its American colonies. Although most European countries had trading interests in Africa by the mid-eighteenth century, Spain did not. By relying completely on the asientos, Spain limited the number of slaves that could be brought to Cuba, which also put it at the mercy of the unstable political and military alliances of Europe.

On August 13, 1762, an English expedition captured Havana from Spain. The British occupation, although brief, helped spark Cuba's sugar industry by opening its markets and by allowing more slave importation. The Spanish government, fearing rebellion and wary of large slave populations, had limited the size of the Cuban slave market, much to the chagrin of the labor-hungry planters. But the British opened Cuba to many forms of international trade and this lifting of restrictions stimulated the island's economy and agriculture. And the newly-opened market was now able to supply the slaves needed for expansion. It has been estimated that there were approximately 32,000 slaves in Cuba before the invasion. Hugh Thomas writes that within eleven months some 4,000 more were sold there (1998: 50, 52) but Herbert Klein puts the number at 10,700 in only five months (87). But both agree that by 1789 a probable 60,000 to 70,000 more were sold on the island, although many were undoubtedly taken elsewhere.

Once Spain recovered Cuba, it did not reimpose the same commercial restrictions, but actually began encouraging investment, immigration, and exploration of the island's interior. This led to a further economic expansion that required even more labor, and Cuba became the destination for more than half the slaves sent to the Spanish colonies after 1770.

By the mid-seventeen seventies, Spanish and Cuban merchants were making their first attempts to engage directly in the slave trade. Two active trading stations on the West African islands of Fernando Po and Annobon were purchased from Portugal in

1778 and a trading company was formed, but the Spanish government was still reluctant to release control, bowing finally to the planters' demands only in 1788. Then in 1789 Spain opened all of its American colonies to trade with any nation, but Spanish merchants still found it difficult to enter the slave trade.

Thomas writes that *La Cometa*, the first Spanish slave ship sent to Africa, did not set sail until 1792 (1998: 68, 70), and the Castellanos team's research indicates that the first direct expedition arrived in Havana from Senegal in 1798 (1988: 24). The British abolished their trade in 1808, cutting off an important slave source, but the Cubans were already developing their own market and by 1810 were launching about thirty successful voyages each year. The end result was that Cuba was better prepared for further expansion when the opportunity arose.

Sugar Wars and Coffee Plantations

The Haitian slave revolt of 1791 changed the nature of the sugar economy in the Caribbean and presented Cuba with just such an opportunity. Columbus himself had carried the first sugar cane to the Caribbean on his second voyage in 1493, but it was in Haiti, not in Cuba, that the sugar industry flourished first. At the end of the eighteenth century the island of Hispañola was the largest sugar producer in the world. Haiti, at the western end, had been colonized by the French who, in the aftermath of the French Revolution, passed legislation giving the free colored of the West Indies the right to vote. This was rejected by both Haitian planters and the governor of the island, creating open conflict among whites and between whites and mulattos. In the midst of this fight, a slave revolt erupted, and in the ensuing months a thousand sugar plantations were destroyed, 2,000 whites and 10,000 slaves were killed, and the French were driven from the island. In the next few years, the ex-slaves fended off invasions by the French, British, and Spanish, surviving to declare independence and emancipation in 1804. But by this time the country was in ruins. Within a decade Haiti would drop completely out of the sugar market.

The result of the revolution and thirteen years of war was the elimination of the world's largest sugar producer, and Cuba was one of the countries ready to take advantage of the expanded market and higher prices for both sugar and coffee. But among whites the Haitian revolt also reignited the ever-present fear of slave rebellion, resulting in a tightening of slave laws and a crackdown on the rights of free blacks that lasted for years, a bitter setback that remained in some societies until final emancipation. Among slaves everywhere, the Haitian revolution was also a beacon of hope that they too might eventually win their freedom.

So Cuba underwent a major social and economic transformation in the 1790s. From being simply a port of call for Spanish fleets, it grew into a flourishing colony whose sugar harvest filled the void left by the destruction of Haiti's economy during its revolution. The needs of this new boom required the importation of larger numbers of African slaves.

Cuban coffee farming also experienced a period of growth in the late eighteenth century, spurred partially by the influx of Franco-Haitian coffee growers fleeing the revolution. It was the newly-arrived French who organized the *cafetal* (coffee plantation) system that enabled Cuba to enter the international market. By 1827, the number of coffee plantations reached 2,000, producing 20,000 tons a year, and by the 1830s over 50,000 slaves worked on cafetales. But despite coffee's rapid rise, its rivalry with sugar was short-lived. Higher production costs and lower profits than sugar, a series of bad harvests caused by hurricanes, and competition from Brazil combined to lower the crop's value, and by the 1840s many cafetales were being bought up and converted to sugar production.

Cuba's profits from, and dependency on, sugar continued to grow until, by the late 1820s, it was the richest colony and largest sugar producer in the world. By 1840 Cuba was exporting over 161,000 tons each year, about 21 percent of the world's production, and by 1870 it accounted for 41 percent, producing over 702,000 tons. It ultimately became the largest slave colony in Spanish America, as well.

The wealth of the colonies was essential to the governments of Europe, not only to finance their wars, but also to fuel the process of industrialization that was reshaping European life. The triangle trade (Europe to Africa, Africa to the colonies, the colonies to Europe) and the East India trade were the decisive forces in the industrialization of Europe. But it was as yet unforeseen that the forces that drove the slave trade would, in the end, help to undo it.

Abolitionists and Slave Traders

World events were overtaking the Cuban planters. The abolitionist movement of the eighteenth century was spearheaded by French Enlightenment thinkers and protestant reformers, especially the Quakers, who, in 1761, excluded from membership all persons engaged in the slave trade. The abolitionists began as a small intellectual and clerical elite, but their theories on the moral, economic, and political problems of slavery began slowly to affect society on both sides of the Atlantic. By the 1770s, Portugal, England, and France had all abolished slavery within their borders, and the states of Vermont, Pennsylvania, Massachusetts, Rhode Island, and Connecticut were the first in the United States to do the same.

Reformers focused first on the slave trade, and it was Britain that took the lead in the fight to limit and eventually abolish it. Many of the finest minds in England spoke out against the trade, including Daniel Defoe, Alexander Pope, William Cowper, Adam Smith, Samuel Johnson, and Edmund Burke, among many others. In 1787 the Society for the Abolition of the Slave Trade was formed to sway public opinion and urge legislation to limit the trade. Britain and the United States abolished their trade in 1807, then began an active and eventually successful effort to get France, Spain, and Portugal to do the same. In 1820 the British navy began patrolling the coasts of Africa to intercept slave expeditions. The French, under British pressure, ended their trade in 1815, but Spain and Portugal held out until the 1850s.

As international efforts to stop the slave trade began to choke off the supply, European and American abolitionists concentrated on ending slavery itself. This turned out to be a long and bitter fight, as the legal, political, and economic foundations of many countries were built on it. Owners fought back to protect their investments and livelihoods, and only slowly did abolition begin to take hold. Britain ended slavery in its colonies in 1834, France and Denmark in 1848, and the Dutch followed in 1863. The now independent ex-colonies of Bolivia, Venezuela, Columbia, and Ecuador all abolished slavery in the 1850s.

Another important factor in the decline of the slave economy was that the industrial capitalism made possible by the slave trade eventually made slavery itself less profitable. The new factories of Europe, financed largely by revenues from the colonies, made more money. Slavery was running its course. But that does not mean that the efforts of the abolitionists were wasted. Basil Davidson writes:

> (It) is not that the work of the abolitionists was of little importance: on the contrary, it was crucial. But it could be crucial only because the abolitionists were able to address an audience whose interests and attitudes were no longer the same as those that had prevailed in earlier years (84).

So the increasing difficulties of the triangle trade and the lower profits of the commercial capitalism that it made possible (and the ever tightening noose of moral indignation) combined to hasten slavery towards its inevitable end.

But as the legal slave trade was curtailed, it also became more lucrative for smugglers. The demand for slaves rose in Cuba because of their scarcity, and the price dropped in Africa as the official markets dried up. In 1835 a slave could be purchased in Africa for as little as $16 and sold in Havana for $360 or more. Profits like these, and Cuba's labor shortage, guaranteed the continuance of the trade long after it was legally abolished.

One consequence of this was that the soon-to-be-emancipated slave populations of

Cuba, Brazil, and Haiti were closer to their African roots than the slaves of other New World countries. Chile had abolished slavery as early as 1823, and Mexico freed the last of its slaves in the 1830s. Even Brazil ended its slave trade in 1850, although emancipation did not come until 1888. Cuba had formally banned the slave trade in 1820, but continued to smuggle slaves through the 1850s, averaging between 10,000 and 13,000 a year or approximately 200,000 people in all. But Manuel Moreno Fraginals estimates that at least 442,000 slaves were landed in Cuba between 1817 and 1860 (Davidson: 96).

The last known slave landings happened between 1865 and 1870, but there may have been others, unrecorded. Jesús Gaunche, citing Pérez de la Riva, notes smuggling as late as 1873 (50). This late influx of slaves might help to explain why Cuba retains so much of its African heritage. It is logical to speculate that, because so many nineteenth century Cuban slaves were actually born in Africa, they contributed a more markedly African cultural heritage to contemporary Cuban society than would the descendants of Africans in countries whose black populations, separated by time and distance from Africa, were more *creole* in character.

With the closure of most markets and the Union navy assisting the long-standing British effort, the slave trade was effectively brought to an end in the 1860s. The end of the trade exacerbated Cuba's labor shortage and raised the price of slaves, thus hastening the decline of the sugar industry and making emancipation inevitable. In the aftermath of the American Civil War, Cuban intellectuals began to realize that slavery was doomed. In 1870, Spain passed the Moret law that freed all slaves born after its enactment, or over the age of sixty-five. But Cuba, in the midst of a rebellion, refused to comply, at least in rebel held areas. Once the rebellion was defeated, the Moret law was applied and the number of slaves began to decline rapidly from 228,000 in 1878 to under 100,000 in 1883. In November 1879, the Spanish Prime Minister, General Martínez Campos, abolished slavery in Cuba effective in 1888. Rather than compensating Cuban slave owners there would be an eight-year *patronato* (trusteeship) for all ex-slaves. By 1886 there were only 25,000 slaves still held under the patronato, and on October 7th they were also freed, ending slavery in Cuba two years early.

Because of poor record keeping and much smuggling, it is difficult to estimate the number of Africans brought to the New World, let alone to Cuba, but scholars surmise that between eleven and twelve million people were landed alive during the time of the Atlantic slave trade. Of those, between 520,000 and 800,000 came to Cuba. To sum up the effect Cuba's slave trade history had on its black population, Hugh Thomas says:

> The tribal origins of the Cuban Negroes are not very easy to resolve and since
> for so many years the planters depended upon non-Spanish shippers, it would seem

> that the Cuban Negro population derived from the whole range of African slave ports from Senegal in the north to the Congo and Angola in the south. The Dutch and Portuguese shippers of the seventeenth century had concentrated on the Gold Coast and Angola; the British in the eighteenth century concentrated on the Slave Coast (Dahomey and Lagos), with their wares usually shipped from Jamaica; the Spaniards and Portuguese of the early nineteenth century concentrated to begin with in the Cameroons but afterwards returned to the Niger Delta, the Slave Coast and Angola. They also went to East Africa. Most Cuban Negroes descend from the nineteenth-century imports of slaves and since a wide variety of slaves were shipped even then it would be rash to say that a larger proportion were Yoruba or Ashanti, Carabalí or Popo; but it seems likely that the Congolese and the Yoruba cultural influences were in the long run the strongest (1998: 183).

So Spain's lack of direct access to slave ports and its reliance on outside suppliers contributed to the diversity of African cultures represented in the Cuban slave population. Who were these Cuban slaves? Brought continuously for four centuries from many different places and diverse, evolving cultures, the various slaves of Cuba were representatives of different traditions, customs, and beliefs (separated by time as well as by distance) that would never have come together in such cramped, confused proximity had they been left in Africa. Uprooted, they began the task of reintegrating their lives, and in the process created rich, hybrid cultures that, while related to the old, were unique to the island, and which influenced the character of Cuban society as a whole. This process occurred all over the New World between Native Americans, Europeans, and Africans, among others. But because of differences in local conditions, historical forces, and varying racial and ethnic mixes, a wide range of new American cultures were born. That of Cuba is one of the richest.

Chapter Two

Slavery and Society

> And to work the mills and plantations thousands and thousands of miserable wretches were killed or enslaved: Negroes from Africa, Indians from Yucatán, Mongolians from China. For the profit of the sugar plantation whole communities were dragged from their homes, blood flowed like sugar from the cane, and all races suffered the lash, the stocks, and the prison cell.
>
> Fernando Ortiz
> *Cuban Counterpoint*

The people of Cuba are the children of immigrants. Their forebears brought the languages, customs, religions, and arts of the world to the island. And in continual procession, they carried four hundred years of ideas to this nexus of time and place. As Fernando Ortiz so famously wrote, these were transformed, not in a homogeneous melting pot but into a heterogeneous stew (1991: 14) of many ingredients, each flavored by the others but still retaining its own taste. This cultural stew has become something new, more than the sum of its parts, born in the Americas, a creole people.

To understand Afro-Cuban culture you must see it within the creole panorama of the country as a whole. Afro-Cuba is one pole, Euro-Cuba is the other. They must be understood in relation to each other. If they are viewed as poles, then one can see a continuum and a continual interchange of ideas, beliefs, words, and DNA between them. This is the fundamental dynamic of Cuban society, but there were other influences as well:

> With the whites of Europe, arrived the blacks of Africa and to us they contributed bananas, plantains, yams and their cooking techniques. And later the Asians with their mysterious oriental spices; and the French with their ponderation of flavors that softened the causticity of the wild pepper; and the Anglo-Americans with their domestic machines that simplified the kitchen and who wanted to metallize and convert to their standard the earthen pot that we were given by nature, together with the tropical fire to heat it, water from its skies for the broth and water from its seas for the splash of the saltshaker. With all this has been made our national stew (1991: 14).

Cuba's neighbors to the north and south, immigrants from the west, and the natives who walked its beaches long before sailing ships appeared on the eastern horizon—all affected the magnetic pull of the Afro/Euro poles. But it was the land itself that was the clay pot, and the island's size, which was large enough to hold so many, in "the fire of the tropics." So let us consider the peoples who were cooked in the Cuban stew.

The Native Americans

First, as always, were the Native Americans. As mentioned in Chapter One, there were two native groups in Cuba at the time of European discovery. The first, the Arcaicos, were hunter-gatherers, located mostly near the western coast of the island. The second, the Arawaks, were more numerous and developed, with permanent settlements, elaborate social structures, and agriculture.

The Arawaks contributed many of the indigenous words and traditions still found in Cuba today. For example, their rulers were called *caciques*, a term still in use, and one type of dwelling, a four sided hut called a *bohío*, can still be seen on the island. Some words—canoe, hurricane, and hammock—for example, have even passed into English.

But their most enduring contribution was the cultivation of tobacco, a plant that would have a great symbolic and financial impact on the island. While tobacco was grown in many places in the New World, it was from Cuba that it was first imported back to Europe. It was in Cuba that the practice of curing and rolling tobacco became an art form that is still associated with the island today. The best cigars in the world still come from Cuba, and on the island the cigar still represents all that is truly Cuban. However, Europe's growing addiction to tobacco, sugar, and coffee had a powerful effect on Cuba's relations with the Old World—an effect, as we shall see, that was not always in Cuba's best interest.

Of course, the original inhabitants were not around to see any of these developments because most of them were dead within fifty years of the first European contact. Many of the survivors were forced into "*pueblos indios*" while others fled to the hills, establishing the first *palenques*, fugitive settlements that would be shared with, and later passed on to, escaped slaves (CIDMUC: 12).

Ortiz believed that most of the Native American traits present in Cuba today are remnants of Indian slaves brought from Mexico rather than traces of the original indigenous population (1991:104). Although later scholarship indicates a much-diluted Arawak presence on the island today, most of what we know about them is based on archeology. So, while a few Cubans can claim at least some Native American ancestry, nothing survives of their music or dance.

The Spanish

The Spanish conquest put an end to Native American Cuba. The Spanish were the most dominant foreign influence on the island. Various Iberians from distinct areas: Castilians, Asturians, Catalans, Gallegos, Andalusians, Vascos, Basques, and Canary Islanders, as well as the Portuguese and others, brought their customs to Cuba. The island's language, civil apparatus, food, clothing, and more have been contributed largely by the Spanish.

Above all, the Spanish brought Catholicism, the official religion so closely tied to the Spanish crown and to Rome. It was the tenets of Catholicism, and the financial needs of the monarchy, that shaped Spain's policies toward Cuba. The Catholic church greatly influenced the development of Afro-Cuba, acting not only as an intermediary between master and slave but, as we will explore later, it helped define the legal and social rights of the slaves. Also, church policy enabled, or at least tolerated, the slave organizations that preserved African religion and art, which allowed for their incorporation, although in altered form, into the culture of the island.

The French

The French have always had some interaction with Cuba due to the proximity of both Haiti and Louisiana, but after the French Revolution, as we have seen, there was an influx of displaced French planters (and their slaves) who established a lucrative system of coffee plantations in eastern Cuba. The French contributed to the social refinement of the island and, while their ascendancy was fairly brief, they made a lasting and still visible impact on Cuban culture. Also, this first wave of French slaves brought the religious beliefs and musical structures that would eventually become *vodú*, and later surges of Haitian immigration would bring a more formalized version of that religion and its music to Cuba.

The Chinese

As the slave trade declined, the supply dropped and prices rose, worsening the country's labor shortage. Cuba responded by importing laborers from other countries, including China, India, and the Philippines. Exact estimates differ, but over a hundred thousand Chinese were brought to Cuba during the nineteenth century. They were imported as indentured servants, but their lives were worse than that of the slaves. Contracted to work for eight years, they also had to pay back the costs of their passage and their living expenses. Since they would work for only a few years they were of less value than the slaves who were a permanent labor force. The Chinese were treated badly. The work was hard and the conditions difficult, and very few women were imported, so many men went back once their indentureship was over. By the time of the 1877 census, only 40,261 Chinese remained in Cuba (Thomas 1998: 188). But they had a lasting effect on the Cuban people and can still be found in the population today, and one of their instruments, the *trompeta de china*, is still used in *comparsa* musical groups.

While European and Asian immigrants made fundamental contributions to Cuba's cultural stew, the island's continual interaction with its neighbors allowed it both to absorb and influence the formation of New World culture as we know it. Cuba had and has relations with the various countries of Central and South America, the islands of the Caribbean, Canada, and, of course, a stormy but inseparable link to the United States. Cuba has both history and culture in common with its neighbors. Throughout its history, Cuba has dealt with, and often fought back from, pressures put on by its large neighbor to the north. Thanks to the United States, Cuba had a railroad system before Europe did, making it easier to transport both people and products, and the U.S. helped bring steam power to the island, a critical improvement in the refinement of sugar cane. However, Cuba's relations with the United States have often been difficult. I would not be the first to point out that most U.S. interventions in Cuba are seen to be more in the United States' own self-interest than in the interests of the Cuban people. This view is widely and justifiably held by many Cubans today. The two countries' interactions are still strained and still inextricably intertwined. So Cuba's varied relationships with its neighbors have changed it and them, and in this way the island has become an integral part of the Pan-American community, as much of the New World as of the Old.

The Africans

So at one pole we have Euro-Cuba: the Spanish, French, English, Irish, Portuguese, and others who left indelible marks on the people of Cuba. We also have various Asians and Native Americans on the island, and the influences of neighboring countries to consider.

At the other pole we have the Africans. It is important to understand that Africans are not monolithic—that is, there are many different kinds of them—so to consider Africans as one people would be as inaccurate as thinking that all Europeans are alike. The anthropological quest for an accurate understanding of Cuba's African roots has been one of the most remarkable success stories in Cuban scholarship, but it is a complicated history, as we shall see.

Time is another consideration when dealing with any ethnicity. Even if a certain people come from one geographical area, the culture they bring with them—language, food, clothing, religion, music—will change over time. So the Franco-Haitian slaves who came to Cuba at the beginning of the nineteenth century would have brought different beliefs than those Haitians who migrated to Cuba in the 1980s. Even if their roots were the same, their cultures, already far from home, would have developed differently through time and geographical separation.

Also, there has been some confusion regarding the ethnic identities of the various African peoples brought to the New World. People of different ethnic backgrounds were often referred to by one name, and people of the same ethnicity were sometimes referred to by different names. Also, the names people gave themselves were often different from the names others used when referring to them. Cuban scholars use a precise approach to this problem (Gaunche, 1996: 48) that I have not seen mentioned in English-language anthropology. (The closest I know of are the well-known concepts of "emic" and "etic" mentioned in Murphy: 127.) It is worth delving into briefly in order to sort the various names into their proper categories. It should be noted here that María Vinueza attributes the following concepts to R. Lopez Valdés (Vinueza, 1988: 23) while CIDMUC credits Yulián Bromlei (CIDMUC: 19).

In Cuban scholarship, an *etnónimo* (ethnonym, Brown: 14) is the name a people call themselves. The problem with using the etnónimo to identify an ethnicity is that, since Africans did not write, all records were kept by whites who had little interest in accuracy. Consequently, names were spelled different ways, ignored, or perhaps lost over time.

A *denominación étnica* (ethnic denomination) is a name given to a people by others. Ethnic denominations often refer to groups of related peoples who are identified together, confusing one ethnicity with another. In the case of Cuba, people of different ethnicities who were distantly related, neighbors, or those who happened to be shipped through the same transit points, could end up in the same ethnic denomination. To make matters worse, the people in those groups eventually adopted these ethnic denominations while often retaining their etnónimos as well.

So an ethnic denomination is better identified as a *denominación metaétnica* (meta-ethnic denomination)—that is, a group containing more than one ethnicity. By identifying the ethnic roots of the various peoples within each meta-ethnic denomination, scholars can both trace them back to Africa and identify their place in Cuban society.

In Cuba today, there are four main meta-ethnic denominations: *congo, arará, carabalí,* and *lucumí.* The Congo and Lucumí traditions are the most influential and are found all over the island. The Arará and Carabalí are less numerous. The Carabalí were centered mostly in Havana and Matanzas, while the last Arará temples are found only in Matanzas. Although related to the Lucumí, the Arará have retained their own traditions separately as well, and while the Carabalí arrived in fewer numbers, they have made lasting contributions to the island's language, dance, and music.

There are also remnants of other meta-ethnic denominations that still exist in some form, and still more which have been lost or absorbed into the larger groups. (The *macuá, mandinga, gangá,* and *mina* still survive. For a more comprehensive history of the meta-ethnic denominations and a listing of the many African peoples who contributed to them, see CIDMUC: 20, and Castellanos and Castellanos, 1988: 37).

Here is an overview of the most important meta-ethnic denominations, their religions, and religious drumming:

Denominaciónes	**Religion**	**Drum Groups**
Congo	Regla de Palomonte (also called Palo)	palo yuka makuta
Carabalí	Abakuá	conjunto biankomeko
Arará	Regla Arará	arará (or hun)
Lucumí	Regla de Ocha (also called Santería)	batá bembé iyesá chequeré

This list is incomplete and simplified—an outline only. There are subdivisions in the denominations, variants in each of the religions, and more drumming groups than I have listed here. But I wanted to start with a clear outline for those who are new to the field. Memorize these four groups, their religions, and drumming groups, then fill in the many blanks as you delve further into each.

The Congos

Congo is the meta-ethnic denomination for those Africans brought from between the mouth of the Congo River and the southern area of Angola. Their etnónimos, the names they gave themselves, include *bacongo, ambundu, bambala, bangui, kuba, mongo, loango, macuba, mayombe, mondongo* and *musundi* peoples, among others. They were bantu speakers.

Dominated by the Portuguese, the Congo River area was one of the most important and productive slave trading centers from the sixteenth through the eighteenth centuries. Since Cuba participated very early in the slave trade, there was a steady traffic of Congo slaves to the island until the beginning of the nineteenth century, and they remained a large part of the slave population after that time. Because of their long history in Cuba and their sheer numbers, these slaves became a fundamental influence in the development of Cuban culture.

The Carabalí

The slaves brought to Cuba from the area between the mouths of the Niger and Calabar rivers were known as the Carabalí. This area is now in Cameroon and Nigeria. They were from different peoples, including the *ibó, iyo, ekoi, ibibio* and *hausa*, among others, who lived in the region of the Calabar river.

Their influence is very important in modern Cuba. Many Cuban words and concepts have their roots in Carabalí culture and their music and dance styles are a major influence in rumba, especially in the *columbia*. They were brought mainly to the areas of Havana, Matanzas, and Cárdenas where they worked, often as porters, in the shipyards.

The Arará

The slaves who came from the *ewe* and *fon* peoples living between the Volta and Niger rivers in the central and southern regions of today's Benin, Togo, and Nigeria were known in Cuba as *arará*. (Amira says that the *mahi* people should also be included in the Arará.) At the time of the slave trade this area was the kingdom of Dahomey and in Cuba they were often referred to as *dahomeyanos*. Dahomey was a "child of the African-European connection," as Basil Davidson puts it, emerging in the early seventeenth century when the *fon* drew together to protect themselves from both the slave collecting *yorubas* and from coastal raiders, as well. In order to obtain the firearms it needed to defend itself against Oyó, Dahomey also entered the slave trade, becoming a powerful slaver, whose exports reached 20,000 captives a year by 1727, only to drop off rapidly after that (241).

Many Dahomeyan slaves were brought to the New World by the French, which explains their presence in the French colonies of Haiti and Louisiana as well as in Cuba. As was already mentioned, the Haitian slave revolt of 1791 sent many French colonists and their slaves fleeing to Cuba, and more emigrated after Napoleon's sale of Louisiana to the United States in 1812 (Alén, 1994: 14).

The Lucumí

The slaves brought from the regions of today's Nigeria, Benin, and Ghana around the mouth of the Niger River were known in Cuba as the Lucumí. They were from the *yoruba, edo, nupe, mosi, iyesá,* and *wari* peoples, among others, and were related by language, culture, history and geography as subjects or neighbors of the Oyó empire,

Beginning its rise to power during the fifteenth century, Oyó dominated much of the area until the end of the 1700s. It was a strong confederation of interrelated city-states, often at war with each other and their neighbors. Yoruban culture was perhaps the most advanced in West Africa. Its centers of power were the political capital, Oyó, governed by a ruler called the Alafin, and the religious center, Ifé, ruled by the Oní. There were other smaller Yoruban city-states as well, that formed the Oyó confederation, but they did not consider themselves as one people. According to Harold Courlander "the name *yoruba* was applied to all these linguistically and culturally related peoples by their northern neighbors, the Hausa" (185), although they do call themselves *yóruba* today. (Note that Africans generally pronounce the word with the accent over the "o" rather than the "u.")

Oyó participated actively in the slave trade, selling captives mostly from the peoples around them. The Ewe and Fon, and the Nupe, who became identified with the Lucumí in Cuba, as well as others, were sold from Oyó ports at Lagos and Badagrí. But Oyó also sold numbers of their own people into slavery, ostensibly for debts owed to or crimes committed against the government. Also, the nearby kingdom of Dahomey, Oyó's sometime tributary but constant enemy, sold large numbers of Yoruban slaves from its ports at Juda and Whydad. Even after the slave trade was declared illegal, and in spite of constant efforts by England, the demand for, and traffic in, slaves continued to grow through the first half of the nineteenth century. It was at this time that the Oyó empire hastened its decline, caused initially by an invasion of the *fulani* from the north, and later, by warfare and revolt from within.

The Oyó empire began to unravel in the 1820s. Because of a Moslem uprising in 1817, in which a slave rebellion played an important part, Oyó had lost control of many of its smaller principalities and towns and by 1830 it had collapsed, making Dahomey a free state. Oyó's neighbors began to take advantage of its loss of power, selling larger numbers of its people to European slave traders.

The decline of the Oyó empire triggered a wave of Lucumí slaves coming to Cuba at the beginning of the nineteenth century. Brought mostly to Havana and Matanzas provinces, these new arrivals profoundly altered the makeup of Cuban slave society.

María Vinueza describes the main streams of African influence in Cuba as a *T* structure, the vertical base of which is Congo, running deep into the roots of society and back towards its beginnings. But the horizontal beam is Lucumí, coming late but in large numbers and retaining much of its culture intact. Lucumí traditions do not go to the foundations of Afro-Cuban culture but can be considered as a thick veneer laid over the older Congo roots (Vinueza,1996a). However, the Lucumí traditions are central to any understanding of Cuban culture since their relatively late arrival and significant numbers profoundly altered the trajectory of Afro-Cuba's formation.

So if genetic diversity makes for a healthy population, then the people of Cuba are strong, indeed:

> The unique pot of our land, as the one of our stew, had to be of clay and very open. Then a fire of ardent flame and a fire of dull embers, to divide in two the cooking; in such a way it occurs in Cuba, always the fire of the Sun but with the rhythm of two seasons, rainy and dry, hot and mild. And into it go the essences of the most diverse kinds and origins (Ortiz, 1991: 14).

Like light through a prism the people of Cuba glow in different colors. They spread through time as well as place, sometimes stopping the clock to protect their memories of home. They were a human spectrum stretched across centuries, all migrating to an island nexus, an alchemist's crucible, where an astonishing convergence turned them into something new. That is the story we take up next.

Chapter Three

Slave Life in Cuba

> The negroes brought with their bodies their spirits (bad business for the plantation owners!), but not their institutions, nor their instruments. A multitude of negroes came with a multitude of origins, races, languages, cultures, classes, sexes, and ages, confused in the boats and barracks of the trade and socially equalized in the same regimen of slavery. They arrived uprooted, wounded, and broken like cane in the sugar mill, and like it they were ground and pressed to extract from them the juice of their work.
>
> Fernando Ortiz
> *Estudios Etnosociológicos*

Cuba was shaped by both time and place. Its historical imperatives and geographical realities intertwined, driving the social and economic needs of African slave and European master, and impelling their contributions into the formation of a new people whose unique character was defined by the indomitable forces that molded the country.

Historically, the slave era was divided into two phases: the Preplantational Period, from the sixteenth to the mid-eighteenth century, and the Plantational Period, from the mid-eighteenth century to the end of slavery in 1886. During the former, there were fewer slaves on the island, the nature of their work more artisanal, and their relations with their owners were more personal. The Plantational Period required many more slaves for the arduous tasks in the cane fields and mills. The work was harder, the treatment more brutal, and the relationship between owner and slave more distant. The Preplantational Period allowed the slaves to establish a place in Cuban society, a relationship with the Catholic church, and a growing population of free blacks. The Plantational Period became a frenzy of production which led to large-scale slave importation during the nineteenth century. It was also a time of nightmarish cruelty that led inevitably to rebellion, abolition, and to freedom for these new citizens of the island.

Geographically, Cuban slaves lived either in the country or in town, where the lives they led and the institutions they developed were directly controlled by the conditions where they lived. African traditions lost in the cities were preserved on the plantations, but the roles slaves created for themselves in town allowed them to protect themselves culturally while influencing Cuban society as a whole. The effects of the rural and urban settings were different, yet each impacted the trajectories of Cuban religion, art, and music.

Rural Slavery

During the Preplantational Period, there were relatively few slaves living in the countryside. Rural slaves were generally housed in the same type of huts, called bohíos, the Native Americans had originally used. These huts were small and relatively comfortable, and they enabled the slaves to live in nuclear families. They were also allowed to work small garden plots called *conucos*. These were important because they gave the slaves some autonomy and an opportunity to create income and perhaps buy their freedom. In other words, they provided a sense of hope. During the Plantational Period, sugar production became industrialized, with newer equipment and methods that demanded more slaves and longer working hours, so the gardens, along with their sense of self-sufficiency, were gradually abandoned, and the slaves were fed on provisions bought by the plantation owners.

The sugar plantation required larger numbers of slaves whose lives became harder and their treatment more inhuman. This led to more active resistance and frequent rebellions which in turn led to harsher suppression by the slave owners. The bohíos were replaced by slave barracks, *barracones*, large, often windowless, buildings which could hold more slaves more securely. Life in these dark, airless barracks was miserable and unhealthy.

As their living conditions deteriorated and the work became more dangerous, the mortality rate among slaves began to rise. The plantation owners began to view them as an expendable commodity, investing little effort or money on their clothing and food, and none on their education. Although the law required plantation owners to provide Sunday mass, religious instruction, and the sacraments for the slaves, in practice they made little effort. This lack of religious indoctrination would be a major factor in the preservation of African religious rites in rural Cuba.

Locked in their barracks and hidden from their owners, the slaves began to re-form their identities, reshaping their languages and beliefs into a new culture, blending their old world with the new in an effort to survive. This culture of resistance gave them strength. As the slave population grew and their lives became more unbearable, the number of revolts increased, resulting in both brutal crackdowns and a wave of escapes. This led to a rise in the number of *palenques,* escaped-slave communities whose fugitive inhabitants, called *cimarrones*, were able to preserve their religious and artistic traditions with less interference from white society. Indeed, there are a number of firsthand accounts of palenque life, for example, the *matiabo* sect of the congos who worked to retain their heritage during the Ten Years' War, and whose religious practices were similar to those of today's *paleros*. The power of the palenques was not lost on the slave owners who fought to contain their influence. Ortiz wrote that the authorities would prohibit the playing of drums in the slave compounds to stop the dangerous dialogue between the slaves and cimarrones (1991: 103).

While the sugar plantations industrialized, many coffee and tobacco plantations stayed much as they were in the early days. Because of the nature of the product, they used fewer slaves who often worked alongside their owners. Still living in bohíos, some slaves continued working their conucos to raise food and perhaps a little income in hope of eventually buying their freedom. While the life of a rural slave was never easy, those few who raised coffee or tobacco lived in relative comfort compared to the many condemned to the brutal and dangerous work in the sugar mills.

Urban Slavery

Life in town was very different than in the country. Slaves who worked as domestics, living in the houses of wealthy Cubans, were often treated like members of the family. Others were artisans, craftsman whose skills generated income for their owners and for themselves. During the Preplantational Period when there were fewer slaves and less fear of rebellion, these artisans often lived in relative autonomy, publicly offering their services as silversmiths, furniture makers, or in other trades, then paying a percentage back to their owners. This ability to create income gave them opportunities less accessible in the countryside. They were able to interact with the larger society around them, if not as equals then as workers whose skills made them more valuable to the community. They formed relationships with the whites among whom they lived, learning the system and using that knowledge to move up within it.

Self-purchase (*coartación*) was an important aspect of slave life in Preplantational Cuba. Slaves were given the opportunity to purchase themselves in installments from their masters and, once the first payment was made, a slave could not be legally sold or moved from his residence. He also had access to the legal system to protect his claims against his master. Practiced widely in Latin America, self-purchase was an innovation on the Roman-based Iberian legal codes and was indicative of Spain's approach to slave rights. The recognition that a slave had some legal standing helped lay the foundation for the acceptance of free blacks in society, and self-purchase enabled many slaves to join their ranks.

Manumission, the release of slaves by their masters, was another road to freedom, especially for urban blacks. This practice was widely followed during the Preplantational Period when slaves had closer, more personal relationships with their owners. Urban slaves were more likely to purchase or receive their freedom than rural slaves, since they were in a better position to produce their own income through their artisanal skills. They also had more access to legal mechanisms and knew their rights better than their rural counterparts. Self-purchase and manumission were important because they allowed for the creation of a sizable, growing population of free blacks. Their numbers increased from 54,000 in 1792 to 272,000 in 1878, to over half a million at the time of final emancipation (Klein: 222). These free blacks actively worked to purchase the freedom of slaves, and created organizations which not only helped their less fortunate brethren but allowed them to protect their religion and art as well.

It is worth noting, however, that during the height of the Plantational Period the rate of manumission and self-purchase declined as the price of slaves rose. The percentage of the free-black population leveled off as the need for more slaves increased, and those free blacks who had used their skills to create wealth and influence saw their rights and privileges eroded during the panics sparked by more frequent slave uprisings.

While manumission and self-purchase were more common in the cities than in the country, there is evidence that rural slaves had some access to them as well. And, as the island prepared for abolition and the fear of revolt receded, the construction of new slave barracks all but stopped, and many slaves returned to living in bohíos. So as emancipation became inevitable, the treatment of the slaves improved somewhat, and the number of blacks purchasing their freedom, and the population of free blacks, began to rise again.

Cabildos and Cofradías

While the barracks sheltered both the slaves and their traditions in rural Cuba, in the cities two related institutions, the *cabildos* and *cofradías*, helped them protect themselves and their heritage.

Cabildos were social organizations centered around people of the same ethnic group. Their purpose was to protect and aid people of the same cultural and territorial ancestry. They also helped to maintain the various rites, practices, religious beliefs, and artistic traditions of their members. All the ethnic denominations had their own cabildos. It is possible to trace the roots of the cabildos back to Spain where the existence of separate slave and Gypsy cabildos were recorded by Ortiz de Zúñiga in the late fourteenth century in Seville (Ortiz, 1992: 4). Gypsies and slaves occupied low positions in Spanish society, so it is not surprising that they organized to protect their members. Fernando Ortiz says that it was these sevillian slaves who brought the cabildo tradition to Cuba (6). The Cuban cabildo's organization was based on European models. Each had a king and queen as well as a hierarchy of other positions. The title of king within the cabildo was not just ceremonial. He was responsible for the cabildo and the actions of its members and represented them in dealings with the government.

The term *cabildo* has had a number of definitions at different times and places. One standard meaning is as a town hall or seat of municipal government, or as a cathedral chapter, but Ortiz says that it was also used in Spain in reference to slave organizations called *cabildos de negros*. He states that in Cuba the *de negros* was unnecessary as all the cabildos were of black origin (1975: 99,100).

There was a religious aspect to many, if not all, cabildos and, since the authorities prohibited them from displaying symbols of African deities, each adopted a Catholic saint, transferring the identity and powers of an African deity to the new patron. Likenesses of these saints were often depicted on the flags they carried when marching in processions. Even though the church at times encouraged the blending of African and Catholic beliefs, the civil authorities often tried to suppress expressions of slave religion and culture. This applied also to public processions. Regulated by various decrees, all public demonstrations by the cabildos were limited to specific days and hours. The Decree of 1792 banned processions altogether but proved unenforceable. Later decrees required that the slaves obtain government permission to march their flags through the streets. The toleration of the cabildo by the slave owners was more than just a humanitarian gesture. They believed the cabildos would help maintain and encourage tribal differences and thus de-unify the slave population. This would make slave uprisings less dangerous. However, they were, at times, suppressed. In 1844, some cabildos in Matanzas helped organize *La Escalera* slave conspiracy. After its defeat, Afro-Cuban religious ceremonies were banned for a time.

The most important of the cabildo processions were the Day of Kings parades held every January 6 during Epiphany. The term *Día de Reyes*, or Day of Kings, a shortening of *La Adoración de los Reyes Magos*, is also known as Twelfth Day, being the twelfth after the birth of Christ and also after the observance of the winter solstice. The slaves and free blacks of Cuba celebrated the Day of Kings by using the opportunity to display their various heritages, each cabildo electing a king and queen, then parading through the streets in elaborate costumes, dancing, drumming, and singing as they went. Slave festivals and processions were held in various parts of Cuba, other Caribbean islands, and in both South and North America, but the center of the Cuban celebration was in Havana. The different processions would converge on the Governor's Palace in the Plaza de Armas where crowds of whites watched from the balconies and sidewalks as each group performed. The king of the cabildo would then ask for a holiday bonus. According to Ramón Meza:

> Later they left the Palacio to make space for others and were parading, in perfect order, the Congos and Lucumís with their large feathered hats, blue striped shirts and pants of red percale; theArarás with their cheeks full of scars from cuts and white hot iron, replete with snails, fangs of dog and caiman, beads of bone and

> strung glass and their dancers inserted up to the waist in a big roll formed with a hoop covered in vegetable fibers; the Mandingas, very elegant with their wide pants, short jackets and turbans generally of blue or rose silk, and bordered with *marabú*; and so many others, in conclusion, of intricate name and capricious dress that were not made entirely in African style, but were reformed or modified by civilized industry (Ortiz, 1992: 27, 30).

We cannot be certain exactly when the black parades of the Day of Kings began, but they may have originated in the relative freedom the slaves were given on that day and because of the holiday gifts of money the owners bestowed on them. The slaves paraded to the Plaza de Armas to receive their bonuses, marching under the flags of the cabildos that represented them in society and this procession was their best chance to display the costumes, music, and dance of their, or their forefathers', homelands. It also helped preserve those traditions. In Africa, the wearing of costumes and parading noisily through the streets is a way of driving out demons or bad spirits, so it is possible that the slaves were using the opportunity to clean house spiritually as well.

The Day of Kings festivities not only preserved African traditions but also blended them with European and Asian influences as well. It is possible that the custom of electing a king and queen for the festival was passed from the Greeks to the Romans and was kept alive in Europe and eventually carried to Cuba by the Spaniards. And the Chinese trumpet seen in today's *comparsa* groups bears testament to the Asian contributions to these Cuban traditions and to the island's ongoing formation.

The Decree of December 19, 1884, finally banned processions during Epiphany so that year's festival was the last, and the African parades of the Day of Kings passed into history. But, as a vehicle for preserving suppressed African traditions, their significance remained and their influence can still be seen in the music of Cuba today.

The elimination of the Day of Kings parades was not the end of the cabildos, but by this time they were in a state of decay. Their decline was partially due to an inability to adapt to changing legal codes and a growing feeling among blacks that they carried a social stigma left over from the days of slavery. In fact, the end of African importation and the increasingly creole nature of Cuban society rendered them less necessary. Also, the government, as Ortiz puts it, "made war on the cabildos," and on the secret societies of *abakuá* whom the authorities believed were involved in criminal practices (1992: 16, 17). Indeed, there is evidence that the Abakuá went through a criminal phase at the end of the nineteenth century. New members, as part of their initiation rite, were sometimes required to kill the first passerby they saw, there was organized theft, and also warfare between the various chapters of the societies. This phase ended around the turn of the century (Thomas, 1998: 522).

Cofradías were mutual aid societies organized within, or with close ties to, the

Catholic church. Although sometimes linked to a cabildo, they had a more distinctly religious character, sponsoring group prayer and festival processions. They were also encouraged by the church to undertake celebrations of black-related religious figures. Although the cofradías were structured much like the cabildos, their religious connection allowed them even more opportunity to preserve their African beliefs while syncretizing them with those of the Catholic church. They were not the only institution that fostered religious syncretism, but the cofradías were one of the most important. Within the outwardly Christian facade, the *rey* might also be a Lucumí or palero priest whose congregation worshiped deities unknown to the church that watched over them.

Eventually, the cabildos and cofradías ceased to exist, but their effect on the people of Cuba endured and their legacy continues today. Castellanos and Castellanos write:

> the cabildos became important centers of cultural resistance: in whose breast were conserved alive for decades and for centuries, all that the negroes were able to save from the great ruin: the residuals of their original language, of their oral literature, and their religion (myths, legends, stories, orations, rites, ceremonies, liturgical costume) and in this way also their art, their music and their dances (1988: 113).

These religious and artistic traditions survived through the abolition of slavery, evolving to reflect the tumultuous history of the island and changing lives of its people. For over sixty years, the guardians of Afro-Cuban culture protected and adapted it as the island fought war after war to secure its independence. Yet as we shall see, Cuba itself was slow to value this part of its heritage, but Afro-Cuba found a champion in a man whose efforts created the framework for its acceptance. This man's intellectual journey reflects the country's reluctant need to embrace the African aspect of its roots, and his personal story symbolizes his country's quest to heal its racial wounds. Next, we turn to Don Fernando Ortiz.

Chapter Four

The Transculturation of Cuba

> In the history of Cuba sugar represents Spanish absolutism; tobacco, the native liberators. Tobacco was more strongly on the side of national independence. Sugar has always stood for foreign intervention.
>
> Fernando Ortiz
> *Cuban Counterpoint*

On May 30, 1937, the sounds of song and drum reverberated through the hall of the Campoamor Theater in Havana. The great anthropologist, Fernando Ortiz, was presenting a demonstration of Lucumí art through a performance of Santeria songs, dance, and batá drumming. This was the first academic presentation of Afro-Cuban culture and the first recognition of its contribution to Cuban society. This presentation was not only a defining moment in Cuban anthropology, but was perhaps a crystalizing moment for Ortiz himself, a man whose efforts had freed himself from the racist preconceptions of his time to become a white voice for a black people. His journey mirrors that of the nation.

Born on July 16, 1881, Fernando Ortiz lived and went to school both in Europe and Cuba, earning a series of law degrees from the University of Barcelona, the University of Havana, and the Central University of Madrid. As an academic, Ortiz had a wide range of interests, but among his early researches were studies of the Afro-Cuban underworld and its crime. His first book on the subject, *Los negros brujos,* was published in 1906. It was met, as he put it, "with silent disgust" among "people of color" (García-Carranza: 11). Undeterred, he wrote a parade of books and articles, often published at his own expense, on Afro-Cuban topics: *Los negros esclavos* in 1916, *Los cabildos afrocubanos* in 1921, *Un catuaro de cubanismos* in 1923, *Glosario de afronegrismos* in 1924, *Contrapunteo cubano del tabaco y del azúcar* in 1940, *El engaño de las razas* in 1946, *Africanía de la música folklórica de Cuba* in 1950, *Los bailes y el teatro de los negros en el folklore de Cuba* in 1951, and *Los instrumentos de la música afrocubana* in 1952, as well as many other works on law, native studies, race, and art. During this time he taught, lectured, published and edited magazines, organized international conferences, and founded academic societies. He even tried his hand at hosting a radio show, *Hora Ultra*, in 1939.

Born before the end of slavery, Ortiz grew up in a society where political and economic power and access to education were reserved for whites. As a product of that society, his early opinions reflected its biases, but his researches required him to deepen his understanding. Over time he outgrew his preconceptions, replacing them with a sympathetic regard for Afro-Cuba's contributions to the island's *cubanidad*. A chronological reading of his works reveals his growing understanding and leaves the reader with a profound respect for the power and originality of his thoughtful, poetic prose. The racist orientation found in Ortiz's early books has drawn criticism from later authors, but he was simply a product of his times and society. His intellectual transformation not only reflected the nation's journey but helped to guide it. He was first among those who sought to value and understand the African contribution to Cuban society, and he was the first to see the people of Cuba as the result of a new and truly American social process.

Transculturation

Ortiz coined the term, *transculturación*, in *Contrapunteo cubano del tobaco y del azúcar*. This fascinating book is essential reading for anyone who wishes to understand the complex dynamics that shaped the economics, history, and people of Cuba. By juxtaposing the symbols of tobacco (indigenous, empowering, and qualitative) and sugar (imported, imperialist, and quantitative), Ortiz explains the interplay of forces that both drove and suppressed the development of the Cuban identity—forces that would transform the various peoples of the island from Europeans, Africans, and others into a people of the Americas, whose unique character was formed in the New World.

Transculturation is a basic tenet of both Cuban musicology and anthropology, but until recently the concept was almost unknown in Europe or the United States, which emphasized deculturation and acculturation. Deculturation is a process of economic exploitation that roots out the culture of a group to facilitate their use as inexpensive labor. The process of deculturation removes those traits that would interfere with the established system of exploitation while leaving intact only those aspects of culture that can contribute to its purposes. Acculturation is the transfer of culture from one people to another. In the process, the people absorbing the new culture lose some of their own.

But deculturation and acculturation were only part of the process which created the national culture of Cuba. Ortiz's concept of transculturation provides a more balanced view of what happened:

> I am of the opinion that the word *transculturation* better expresses the different phases of the process of transition from one culture to another because this does not consist merely in acquiring another culture, which is what the English word *acculturation* really implies, but the process also necessarily involves the loss or uprooting of a previous culture, which could be defined as deculturation. In addition it carries the idea of the consequent creation of new cultural phenomena, which could be called neoculturation (1995: 102).

What Ortiz calls neoculturation is the formation of a distinct people. The Indians and Europeans, the Africans and Asians, brought their cultures to Cuba, whose story is the "history of its intermeshed transculturations" (98). And from these, a new culture was born. This new culture, which the Cubans say is more than the sum of its parts, is the social cradle of the cultural traditions, religious beliefs, and musical practices at the heart of this book. The music is a manifestation of the religion, and the religion is a manifestation of the people who were formed in this ongoing transculturation. To understand the music we must try to understand the forces which molded the people who make it.

The fact that Cuban anthropology has developed its own structures to explain the processes which formed its people indicate that the processes themselves are different from those of other areas. This can be seen by comparing the Euro-American discipline with that of Cuba, and by comparing a few of the historical, demographic, and geographical contrasts between Cuba and the United States.

The difference between transculturation and deculturation is as much one of perspective as of substance, which goes a long way toward explaining why it is so important to Latin American scholars and so often ignored by Anglo academia. The concept of deculturation, while it has been expanded to accommodate some ebb and flow, is by nature eurocentric. European and North American scholars could not help but put their culture at the matrix (after all, that is where anthropology was created), and this orientation is inherent in the concept of deculturation. They implicitly assumed that European culture would be dominant then continued on to describe "the other's" process of assimilation. This is far less true today:

> Ethnography in the service of anthropology once looked out at clearly defined others, defined as primitive, or tribal, or non-western, or pre-literate. or non-historical—the list, if extended, soon becomes incoherent. Now ethnography encounters others in relation to itself, while seeing itself as the other (Clifford, 1986: 23).

Today's anthropologists work hard to recognize and limit these biased viewpoints, but this skewed perspective was a very real factor in the relations between scientist and subject and needs to be considered when reading texts from previous eras.

For Latin American scholars, the European tradition is important, but the eurocentric viewpoint itself is sometimes seen as "the other" simply because, historically at least, it is the Latinos who have been put on the outside. They do not perceive Latin-American thought from a European perspective. A look at a Cuban weather map shows you where they see the center—in Cuba. Transculturation, a New-World concept, removes this Euro-American bias and leaves a much clearer picture, not only of the processes that shaped the culture, but of how Latin Americans view themselves. They are no longer the pretenders at the fringe, trying to win Euro-American approval, but are revealed as thoughtful beings with an understanding of their own character who place the subject, themselves, at the center, no longer viewed from a far away citadel (see Gómez: 12, 14).

Ortiz has never really received his due recognition from the Euro-American anthropological community, but in the end he did not need it. The Cubans themselves know him as the father of the various disciplines which, even today, continue more precisely to define the character of the nation. And Ortiz himself was as transculturated as the people he wrote about. As he shed light on them, they shed light on him. If his European-trained mind explored the Cuban people, they in turn gave something to his work that is rarely found in anthropology—poetry:

> Sugar is to be found in the cradle, in the kitchen, and on the table; tobacco in the drawing-room, the bedroom, and the study. With tobacco one works and dreams; sugar is repose and satisfaction. Sugar is the capable matron, tobacco the dreaming youth. Sugar is an investment, tobacco an amusement; sugar enters the body as nourishment, tobacco enters the spirit as a cathartic. The former contributes to the good and the useful; the latter seeks beauty and personality (1995: 46).

So it is in the metaphor of sugar and tobacco that we can see the outlines of transculturation in Cuba as a whole. While our goal is to understand the effect transculturation had on the African contributions to Cuban music, we had to see it in this larger context first, since the slaves were but one component in the process. Exactly how that process shaped Afro-Cuba can be seen by comparing it with Afro-North America.

When, How Many, Where, and Who?

"Why do the Latinos get to play all the cool drums?" was the first question I asked my teacher when he *finally* let me study congas. As a college student, I was stuck in a practice room learning xylophone etudes while the Puerto Ricans were out in the park, jamming on congas. I knew there was a strong African influence in Latin percussion, but we had blacks in the United States, too. Why weren't hand drums historically part of our tradition as well? Or to put it more accurately, how could the slaves of Latin America conserve so much more of their culture and religion than those in the North?

Of course, North American music has been profoundly influenced by the contributions of African Americans: gospel, blues and jazz characterize our music as much as any European form. As Samuel Floyd says:

> The emerging African-American genres were not formed by the insertion of African performance practices into the formal structures of European music, as the conventional wisdom would have it, but were molded in a process that superimposed European forms on the rich and simmering foundation of African religious beliefs and practices. The foundation of the new syncretized music was African, not European (85).

This could be true (being a white jazz musician I would prefer to see it as an even split), but in Cuba they still retain musical traditions that can be traced directly back to specific African ethnicities. They still have knowledge of various African languages, and they still worship gods who, although altered, are clear representations of deities in specific African religious traditions. The question is, Why there and not here?

1) The time factor

As I stated in Chapter One, the United States abolished direct slave trade from Africa in 1807. While there was undoubtedly some smuggling, the African American population base was pretty much set at this time. Once separated from Africa, North American slaves would begin to lose their cultural heritage. This process, as we shall see, was hastened both by social factors and by the actions of the slave owners.

Cuba formally banned the slave trade in 1820 but was still smuggling them as late as the 1870s. In fact, Cuba was importing slaves at its fastest rate during the nineteenth century. This influx reenforced the African presence on the island, strengthening its connections to the old continent and maintaining a more directly African presence in Cuba.

I have talked to a number of Cubans whose grandparents were slaves and to two older people whose parents were born as slaves. To them, the connections to Africa are not seen as statistics but are felt as part of family memory, still fresh in the hearts of at least some older Cubans.

2) Relative number of slaves

Reliable statistics are hard to find on the numbers of slaves imported into the New World. Because there was so much smuggling, no one knows exactly how many slaves were brought to Cuba so estimates vary widely. Most are between 520,000 and 700,000, but Gaunche cites Pérez de la Riva's estimate that some 1,247,900 Africans were brought to the island between 1774 and 1873 (1996: 50). However, the well-informed Isabel and Jorge Castellanos believe that around 850,000 Africans were brought to the island during the trade (1988: 25), and that seems to be closer to what the historical records indicate (Gaunche, 1996: 50).

We do know that both the size of the general population and the percentage of blacks within it continually fluxed. Gaunche cites Cuban census figures to show the increase and decrease in the numbers of Africans living in Cuba, starting at 50,000 in 1774, peaking at 450,000 in 1841, then declining sharply to a few thousand by 1899 (1996: 45). He does not indicate the size the general population during this time, but we can assume it fluctuated as well.

By comparison, the United States imported approximately 500,000 Africans during the slave trade (Thomas, 1997: 804). This number is less surprising when you consider how early the trade was curtailed here. Again, because populations continually fluctuate, it is difficult to find exact numbers, but consider that approximately half as many Africans were brought to a country at least twenty-five times as large as Cuba. In 1841 there were almost as many Africans living in Cuba than were brought to the United States during the entirety of the slave trade, so there were fewer Africans within a much larger population. While the African-American contribution is fundamental to North-American culture, the United States as a whole retains fewer specific African traits than does Cuba. This is partially because of the numbers.

3) The different societies of Cuba and the United States

At first glance, the existence of Voodoo cults of New Orleans would seem to refute the idea that North America retained less of its African heritage than Cuba. Voodoo is an African-derived religion that has survived to the present day, but Louisiana was a very un-American place. Claimed first by the French, then the Spanish, then the French again, New Orleans did not become part of The United States until the Louisiana Purchase of 1803. It did not see itself as American. The waves of northerners coming to New Orleans after the purchase were viewed as foreigners. Louisiana had evolved linguistically and culturally separate from its neighbors. Most importantly, it was the only Catholic area in the American south. Floyd says that:

> For those slaves introduced to Roman Catholicism, "Catholic notions about the role of Christ, Mary, guardian angels, and patron saints as intercessors with the Father in heaven for men on earth proved quite compatible with African ideas about the intervention of lesser gods in the day-to-day affairs of human life, while the supreme god remained benevolent and providential but distant" (Raboteau, 1978: 23). This African-Catholic syncretism made the transition for Africans to Western culture easier in Latin America and in some parts of the United States, particularly New Orleans, and served as support for the continuation of African traditions in the New World (39).

We will examine syncretism more closely in the next chapter, but for now a consideration of New Orleans seems to support the idea that the music and religion of the Cuban slaves evolved along a different path than those in the United States partially because of the different treatment they received in the Catholic South.

Another consideration is the difference in English and Spanish legal traditions. Slavery had died out in England at an early date, but in Spain and Portugal it was still a fact of life. Consequently the Spanish had a code of laws dealing with the rights and treatment of slaves. England did not, so the various colonies were left to adopt their own legislation. As Hugh Thomas says:

> These laws were formulated with the immediate interest of North American planters as the deciding factor; slaves could not therefore marry; they had no legal right to possessions; they could not sue; they could not buy their freedom; they had in short no legal being and were chattels. Slaves in Cuba, as in all Spanish colonies, had the benefit of hispanic, and hence Roman law (with, of course, its modifications and subsequent changes); the Church knew them; they could have and exchange property; they could marry; they were legal personalities, even if their rights were often only theoretically guaranteed by law. Time, custom, humanity and interest might mitigate Anglo-Saxon severity, and the practice of law under Spain often deny utterly the formal theory of codes. But the law did have a number of precise consequences which coloured Spanish slave life (1998: 34,35).

This familiarity and identification with the African was evident in the church as well:

> The North American church and white master class, by denying to the slave real rights as Christians, were often found proclaiming that Negroes were accursed of God, being descended either from Cain or from the serpent who tempted Eve—and who was supposed to be the Negro incarnate. Of this odd theological attitude there is no trace in Spanish slave society (35).

While no one is claiming that the Spanish treated their slaves humanely, it is clear that their traditions of both law and theology contributed to a better general situation than in the North. And peoples who have more help and support facing the hardships of deculturation would be able to retain a greater share of their own identities.

4) The differing ethnic backgrounds of the slaves

Ned Sublette cites slave-trade history to put forward the theory that the slave populations of Cuba and the United States came largely from different ethnic backgrounds, and then examines the differences in our musics to identify those influences.

According to Sublette, there was some overlap but a larger percentage of North American slaves came from Senegambia, whereas the foundation of Cuban slave society is Bantu. The Senegambians had ties to the Maghreb and to Islam. Their music has quarter tones in the scales (like the blues) and a strong 12/8 feel that can be characterized as swinging. The Bantus, thousands of miles to the south, had little connection to the Saharan world or to Islam (which is one reason why the Spanish sought them as slaves), and no sense of blues or swing in their music. Their music is very polyrhythmic and structured around the concept of the temporal line (see Chapter Seven).

Most Afro-Cuban music is also structured around the temporal-line clave, and also lacks both the swing and the quarter-tone melodies of the blues. African American music swings and has the blues but lacks the intricate polymetrics and temporal lines found in Cuban music. (Clave was, and is, found in the second-line bands of traditional New Orleans jazz but has been mostly lost in the music as a whole.) That Cuban music does not swing in the way jazz does, and that Cubans really do not have the blues is obvious to any North American who has ever heard them try to play it, but we are just as awkward trying to phrase a solo over the clave. Of course, we can learn and so can they, but we all play with an accent because there are fundamental differences between our traditions. If one listens with an honest ear, it becomes obvious that what Sublette says is true. While there is some overlap, the musics of the two countries come, at least in part, from different roots.

So the time factor, the societies of Cuba and the United States, the relative numbers of slaves in the populations, and the ethnic backgrounds of the slaves themselves all contributed to fundamentally different situations which produced fundamentally different cultures in the two countries. Perhaps the African experience in the United States is more of deculturation than transculturation. While African influence is strong here, it is stronger in Cuba. The confluence of forces which shaped the island left its transformed African traditions melded into the fabric of its people, yet still recognizable, still distinct.

The various Afro-Cuban languages, musics, and religions found on the island today are the result of this transculturative process. While they still have connections to specific African peoples, they have been fundamentally transformed in ways that could not have happened in Africa. And since religion is the spiritual foundation of most Afro-Cuban drumming, we must consider it first before exploring the music itself.

Chapter Five

Afro-Cuban Religion and Drumming

African styles of worship, forms of ritual, systems of belief, and fundamental perspectives have remained vital on this side of the Atlantic, not because they were preserved in a "pure" orthodoxy but because they were transformed. Adaptability, based upon respect for spiritual power wherever it originated, accounted for the openness of African religions to syncretism with other traditions and for the continuity of a distinctive African religious consciousness.

Albert J. Raboteau
Slave Religion

I sat with my students on a bench in a courtyard, along one wall of a low, cinderblock building. From within we could hear the deep roar of a friction drum and the irregular rise and fall of chanting through the closed door. We were at a *planta*, an *Abakuá* initiation, at Alejandro's invitation. He told us that we were very lucky to be there because this ceremony, normally held every two years, was the first in over five. As the musicians practiced on the far side of the courtyard, we could tell that Alejandro was not happy with them. He told me later that they had forgotten the rhythms, needing coaching before the ceremony could begin.

The initiation had begun days ago and we were there only for the final act. The twenty-two new members were easy to spot—bare-chested and bare-footed—with symbols carved into their backs that would, in time, heal into permanent scars. As a man emerged from the building with a goatskin still dripping blood, I couldn't help smiling at the looks on my students' faces, but they relaxed a little as the smell of cooking filled the air.

I was excited. I had practiced the rhythms and studied the books, but I had never been at an actual Abakuá ceremony—something few foreigners get to see. This was obvious from the looks the neighbors gave us. One old man came up and shook my hand, but the others avoided us. We were in Paragua, a poor area on the outskirts of Havana, and Americans were not common there.

Another man began to draw intricate designs on the cement in the courtyard. These were Abakuá *firmas*, holographic magic whose complicated patterns seemed familiar but which I could not identify. Once he finished the drawings, the man spat streams of liquid from three bottles, covering each pattern with a different fluid. Then he set fire to a pile of herbs which smoldered on their wooden tray, surrounded by the half-empty bottles.

The chanting had stopped and the crowd sat quietly along the courtyard wall, under the tall trees and out of the noonday sun. We relaxed on the bench in the herb-scented peace, but just as my eyes were getting heavy a man sprang from the *fambá*, the temple building, with a shout. We all jumped as he ran, first towards us then into the center of the yard, singing and shaking some very rustic sounding bells. He was the *morua*, the interpreter and guide for the ancestral spirits about to make their entrance.

The morua returned to the fambá door. Pleading and coaxing in a singsong voice, he lured a timid *íreme* out of the dark doorway. There are many iremes, incarnate symbols of ancestors and natural forces, in the pantheon of the Abakuá. Their diverse costumes, the most distinctive of all the Afro-Cuban raiments, are difficult to describe. This one wore a light-green coverall with goldish-yellow and red borders, and his head was covered with a conical mask. Alejandro had asked us not to take pictures, and I thought longingly of the camera, unused on my belt, as I tried to describe him into my tape recorder. As I listen to the tape now, I'm transported back to the scene: the ireme moves in turn to each corner of the courtyard followed by the morua and surrounded by initiates. The drums play, the ireme dances, and they all sing responses to the words of the morua.

Then quickly the initiates and deities disappeared back into the fambá, and from inside we could hear chanting and the growl of the *ekue*, the friction drum that is the voice of a god. While the chanting got louder, an older man brought out a large clay pot and set it in the middle of the firmas just before the morua led the ireme, followed by the initiates, back into the courtyard. The initiates formed a circle around the costumed deity and the pot, and one of them knelt before the ireme to receive what looked like a blessing. As he stood up, the initiates locked arms and began to rotate slowly, circling the firmas, the ireme, the morua, and the pot. The crowd moved in to watch, shouting encouragement as the circle spun faster. I looked at my students all frozen at attention except for one who was screaming incoherently into his tape recorder. The tension grew as the initiates sped up, straining and sweating, concentrating on keeping the circle intact as they ran faster. They were now going at top speed, and the crowd was roaring when one lost his hold and the circle dissolved. They charged the pot and it vanished beneath them. We heard a loud crack, and a cheer rose from the men as they piled on, tearing at whatever was within.

In a minute or so they began to pull away one by one, and the other Abakuá moved in toward the broken pot to pick up the few remaining pieces of what we now realized was goat meat. Alejandro came over to us, licking his fingers and laughing. After things calmed down, I asked him the significance of what we had seen and he said they had come together, sacrificed together, and been reborn together, and the goat was the symbol of their being together forever as one.

After a short rest, the first ireme was joined by another who led the initiates out to the street where they paraded up the block, stopping at times to bow and sing, announcing their ascendancy to Abakuá membership. Alejandro led the musicians and I could see him, still teaching the rhythms to a younger player as they walked. He was trying to demonstrate the traditional low-drum patterns but seemed frustrated by the young man's inability to grasp the significance of the rhythms. As I followed them I saw two of my students in the throng, but the others were on the sidewalk, buying beers for pretty girls and practicing their sign language on the neighbors. Eventually, Alejandro came to take us back to town.

I am not the first to point out that the role of science is to manifest knowledge, or that the role of religion is to manifest wisdom. In a way, they are different maps of the same terrain. The purpose of each is to derive meaning from existence, and each provides specific insights that the other cannot.

When studying science it is important to understand that it is a human construct based on observable fact, but that other viable constructs can be created from the same facts. When studying the stories of human belief it is better to see them all as a tapestry of interwoven meaning. The goal is not to pinpoint the right one among the false, but to see where each fits in the larger weaving as a way of understanding its contribution to a larger significance.

It still surprises me how many people see their religion as divine truth while all others are, of course, superstition. The realm of myth tells us about ourselves transcendently beyond any single viewpoint. "Truth is one, the sages speak of it by many names," the Vedas tell us. And scientists (a relatively atheistic bunch) study myth as a key to understanding the human mind. So when considering myth it is possible to read the deeper meanings sympathetically without accepting it as the only divine truth—and without dismissing it as primitive superstition. Seek the middle ground.

In writing a book like this I must thread my way between these two perspectives. Presenting a myth from a scientific viewpoint can seem condescending, while telling it from the believer's viewpoint seems partisan. Either approach will offend someone, and that cannot be helped, but it is important to understand a story from both perspectives, balancing the original message—looking out—against its scientific context—looking in.

So far, we have looked at why and how slaves were brought to Cuba, who they were, and how they adapted to, and influenced, Cuban society. Next, we need to examine the religious beliefs they brought to the island and explore how these beliefs were altered in Cuba, so we can consider the effect they had on Cuban music. As Samuel Floyd says:

> In traditional African culture, there is no formal distinction between the sacred and profane realms of life, or between the material and the spiritual; thus there was in traditional Africa no word for "religion" because the Africans' religion permeated and was the basis for all aspects of life, including education, politics, harvesting, hunting, homemaking, and community welfare (15).

What were these ideas and practices? Castellanos and Castellanos list five common traits in West African religion:

1) Belief in a unique and primordial being, a supreme God, creator and owner of the universe.

2) Belief in a pantheon of divinities who act as intermediaries between human beings and the creator.

3) Ancestor worship or veneration of ancestors who, after death, act as spiritual supervisors to the living.

4) Belief in other spirits, beyond the ancestors and divinities: the dead with whom the living can communicate and who exercise a positive or negative influence in the living world.

5) The practice of magic and magical medicine (1988: 55).

Beyond these traits are other considerations which, while not universal, are important to examine.

Trance and Possession

My most vivid memory of my first Santeria ceremony, as I described in the Introduction, was of the physical power of the drum and song, and of the music's direct connection to people possessed by the gods. While I understood possession as a concept, I was completely unprepared to cope with it manifesting itself directly in front of me. In the years since my first ceremony, I have studied trance and possession in general and seen it practiced many times. But while I have read a fair amount of the literature, both by skeptical scientists and credulous adherents, and despite a lot of firsthand observation, I still find the subject complicated and intellectually dangerous. It is also of supreme importance in that it touches the heart of religion in general and Santeria in particular as a demonstration of the very real presence of the divine at the ceremony and in the lives of the believers.

The question, "Do the gods actually possess people?" is more theological than scientific. This distinction should be obvious, yet both scholars and scientists have been relatively unsuccessful in keeping their biases out of their work. Scholars who are also believers often view their belief systems as self-evident truth, so their work seems uncritical or unconcerned with presenting both sides of the issue (see Gonzalez-Whippler: 1994, 196, or 1982, 124, or Murphy: 96). This is fine as long as the reader understands that the authors are describing their experience, presenting a viewpoint. Scientists, on the other hand, often go to extreme lengths to appear rigidly methodical, so objective that the question of belief and its importance to the believer is negated (see Rouget and just about everyone he quotes in his book). This is fine as long as the reader understands that the author is not seeking the meaning of, or meaning in, those belief systems. So how can we approach this minefield of a subject? By looking at it from both viewpoints. Alberto Cutié was the first author I have read who uses the concepts of *exoteric* and *esoteric* (23) to describe these perspectives. Exoteric refers to knowledge or understanding as viewed by an outsider. Esoteric is knowledge or understanding as conceived by the initiated, the insider. By considering it from both viewpoints one can understand its significance without having to take sides.

Trance and possession are related, sometimes the same and sometimes as separate phenomena. There are different types of trance, some not associated with possession, found on every inhabited continent in the world. Researchers refer to it as an altered or dissociative state. Possession is an altered state of consciousness in which a person believes himself or herself taken over, or "mounted" by a deity who talks and acts through the person possessed. Trance and possession are central to any understanding of both West African and diaspora religions. And since much of the music of the Afro-Cuban traditions is religious, the relationship between possession and music is at the heart Cuba's African-derived drumming traditions.

Believers esoterically view possession as a direct connection to the divine. It is a privilege bestowed on those who have earned it. Scientists sometimes view it exoterically as a form of mental disease. Both agree that is is also a social behavior. That is the important point: it is socially sanctioned. The Castellanos say:

> At the same time it is important to insist that trance and possession are *social* constructions that form an essential part of the religious system. It is true that for

every Afro-Cuban believer trance constitutes a mode of communication with supernatural forces characterized by changes in personality that the western world interprets as erratic and neurotic forms of conduct. But, while in our society neurotic or psychotic comportment is found at the margins of social reality, in the Afro-Cuban cults possession forms an inherent part.

And later:

> We believe that it is important to insist on the fundamental role social conventions play in the religious trance process. In Regla de Ocha, for example, a believer possessed by Changó, or any other orisha, does not exhibit anarchical forms of conduct. From our cultural perspective we characterize such actions as strange, but a detailed examination reveals that it is neither erratic or casual. On the contrary, the conduct of the possessed is strictly regulated by a system of social rules based in the characteristics traditionally associated with the orishas: a son of Changó, for example, will become someone viral, fiery, violent: a daughter of Ochún, for her part, will show herself as feminine and coquettish . . . but never vice versa. Moreover, if someone manifests modes of conduct during trance that are not associated with pre-established and ritual behaviors, those present would conclude that the trance has been faked, or that the person has a psychological disturbance and should go to a psychiatrist or counselor (Castellanos, 1992: 166, 167).

To make this a little clearer, in Santeria a possessed initiate would generally be mounted by his or her guardian angel, assuming the personality and behaviors of that orisha (but both Spiro and Ringquist say that an initiate may be mounted by more than one ancestor). This is different in the Congo religions, however, where any person may be mounted by a god, an ancestor, a force of nature, or the spirits of animals or sacred trees (Castellanos quoting Calleja Leal: 168). But in each religion possession has its own cultural forms which are sanctioned by the group, and its own religious functions which connect that group to their deities.

While there are many kinds of trance, in Afro-Cuban religions trance and possession function as spiritual mediumship. The god speaks through the person it has possessed. Believers seek its counsel to solve personal problems, to resolve disputes, or to improve relations within the community, for example. The deity advises people on the underlying causes of their problems and gives them solutions. I have seen this in Santeria ceremonies: a man possessed, dressed as an orisha, dispensing wisdom in the Lucumí language through an interpreter, helping people, keeping the peace, passing judgment. On several occasions I have been on the receiving end of their attentions, once being called back from the street so that the god, Ogún, could tell me of dangers to my family that he thought I should know. In the Congo religions a believer may also seek the help of a god or spirit to control a situation or person by magic as well. But though the form and function may vary, it is this direct connection with supernatural power that puts possession at the center, at the heart, of Afro-Cuban religion.

And here is where the problem lies. A thoughtful consideration of the relationship between possession and music only muddies the waters. For believers, the connection is obvious: music opens the door to the divine world and opens the minds of the faithful to be mounted by the gods. This does not need esoteric verification since it can be seen at every ceremony. For those who view it exoterically and study its manifestations in different cultures, the variety of divergent practices make forming any coherent understanding almost impossible. For example, in Santeria it is through music that possession is manifested, but that is not always the case in other religions (Métraux: 131). In his book, *Music and Trance*, Gilbert Rouget examines trance and possession in such a wide range of contexts—everything from the ancient Greeks to native Shamanism, among the Arabs and Italians, and through the African diaspora. He casts his net so wide, describing such a disparate panorama of beliefs and practices that in the end, in my opinion, he can come to no other conclusion than that there is no direct relationship. That is an historical-cultural approach, but in the empirical sciences very little research has been done either. Rouget destroys Neher's neurophysiological theory that drumming provokes trance (172-176), but with no really creditable research having been done in the field it seems premature to dismiss the whole concept without redefining the problem in light of the more recent breakthroughs achieved in neurological science. There is not enough evidence to make any kind of conclusions one way or the other because the basic research is just not there. It should be possible to understand the process in specific cases without having to create a unified theory which would account for every geographical and historical manifestation of possession known to man. And it should be possible to understand the actual mechanism without doing damage to the sensibilities of those who consider it sacred.

Rouget's position is that music has no direct power to trigger trance. "Music does nothing more than socialize it, and enable it to attain its full development"(326). This is understandable. He is defending science against those who believe music has magical or mystical powers, but by taking too strong a stance he has missed something important. The psycho-neurological effects of music trigger trance only in those who are initiated—those who have been properly prepared to become possessed. And it is only through music and dance that they can achieve this state, at least in Santeria. It never happens to the uninitiated, and it never happens to the initiated unless the music is playing in a ceremony. So music does not "socialize" or "enable" the initiate. Music is essential because the initiate has been trained specifically to respond to it. In Santeria there would be no trance or possession without the prayers of the songs and the calls of the drums. For those who believe, are willing, and are prepared to be possessed, it is music that calls the orishas down to earth. And in a batá ceremony, it is the drums that open the doors between the world of the believers and that of their gods. The drums speak both to and for the gods, and without them the gods could not manifest themselves among their followers. Whether you believe or not is beside the point as long as you grasp this fundamental concept, because without it no understanding of the religion or the role of its drums would be possible. (John Amira's viewpoint is different. He says, "I totally disagree with Rouget. Music has tremendous power to trigger possession, but contrary to what you are saying, I have personally known non-initiates to be fully possessed in front of the drums, and I have also seen initiates possessed outside of ceremonies without drums. I also feel that trance and possession are two different things. Trance is an altered state of consciousness while possession is a displacement of consciousness.")

Animism

The dictionary defines animism in this context as "the belief that natural phenomena and objects, as rocks, trees, the wind, etc., are alive and have souls" (Webster's). When it is written like this, the western reader cannot help but to understand it as a primitive superstition. There is no scientific evidence that rocks, trees, and wind have souls. But, again, this definition is exoteric, written by outsiders and containing no hint of how believers might understand it.

I once heard a story, I can't remember where, about a Native American who laughed at the white soldier who was telling him that there was no rain god when the rain god was drenching them both at that very moment. The misunderstanding was not about the facts but in the interpretation. It was no less logical for the native, whose life had always been affected by the power of the rain, to see it as a forceful being with a volition of its own, than it was for the soldier, who was taught in school that rain was a natural phenomenon, to view it as the result of a scientific process.

The powers of nature are there for all to see, so putting names and faces to them, personifying them with the characteristics that are so obviously theirs, is not really such a stretch of the imagination, if one is willing to make that stretch. When the western mind views a painting of Yemayá, the Lucumí goddess of the sea, it jumps to the conclusion that the Lucumí conceive her in the same way: as a woman swimming around in the ocean. But when Alejandro dips his hand into the Caribbean and says a prayer to Yemayá, he is paying homage to the sea itself, that powerful, mythical, natural miracle whose presence defines the lives of all those who live near her, and he is acknowledging the power she has exerted over his life and over the fates of his ancestors who once traveled, safely if miserably, across her to this island when so many others disappeared beneath her waves. It is not hard to see why he thanks her for his life. When seen this way, the western mind may still not believe that the sea itself is alive, but it no longer has reason to scorn those who do.

Syncretization

So what happened to these African beliefs and traditions in Cuba? The transculturation that so strongly altered the various ethnic identities of all Cubans also affected their religions:

> Religious syncretism is the process by which a certain deity is identified by its believers with the powers, tributes, attributes and ceremonies of another or other deities. In the case of Cuba this process can be simple or extremely complex. As an example of simple syncretism we have the case of Saint Francis of Assisi, syncretized with Orula or Ifá in the cults of Santería. As an example of complex syncretism we have the Virgin of Regla; syncretized with Yemayá of the santeros and who is jointly syncretized with Baluande of the Paleros and with Okandé of the Abakuá. Syncretism constitutes one rule in the development of all the religions and is characterized by the incorporation of doctrinal principles or of ritual procedures (Gaunche, 1983: 353).

The syncretic nature of Catholic evangelism is an important factor in the history of the church's global expansion. Northern Europeans, Native Americans, Asians, and Africans have all blended their beliefs and traditions with those of the Catholic Church. The clergy certainly encouraged the blending of African and Christian beliefs and practices that led to the syncretized nature of some religions in Cuba. Indeed, Hugh Thomas says that:

> From the sixteenth century onwards, priests had in this spirit encouraged Negroes, slaves and freed men, to seek some blend between Catholic and African religious practices, so that Christian saints could, in processions and ritual, receive the enthusiastic adoration which Africans in their native land lavished on their own gods. Perhaps the idolatrous nature of much of Catholic practice, the beards on the figures of the painted Christs, the baroque and golden saints, the dragons and the marvelous animals, the incense and the gloom, was more sympathetic to Africans, themselves dominated by mysterious signs and omens, than was the clean, sparer Christianity of the Anglo-Saxon north. These matters are difficult to resolve: the slave-ships carried not only men but gods and beliefs. Some Africans, even some slaves, may have been genuinely Christians: but most of those who seemed to be or said they were continued to worship African deities (1998:39).

At first glance, the practice of deliberately syncretizing Christian theology with the beliefs of various conquered peoples seems cynical at best. But Octavio Paz, writing about the process in Mexico, sheds some light on their reasoning. Paz believed that the discovery of millions of people in Asia and the Americas who had never encountered the Christian Gospel created a crisis for European theologians. How could the universal word of God be unknown to so many? Various scholars created different responses to the problem. For example:

> The majority of Jesuits believed that the ancient beliefs of the Indians were a glimpse of the true faith, which by natural grace or because the Gospel had been preached in America before the arrival of the Spanish, the Indians still conserved confused memories of the doctrine (58).

Seen in this light, the syncretic process was an honest, if pragmatic, attempt to rectify rather than negate their beliefs by bringing them back to the true religion. Whatever their reasoning, by syncretizing their theology with that of the slaves the Catholic clergy helped to preserve more than it realized. "One of the reasons for syncretizing African deities with the Catholic saints was to hide their African religious practices from the Spanish" (Gaunche, 1983: 367). Those practices were not fully revealed until long after abolition. And while scholars often note the incorporation of Christian beliefs into slave religions, they sometimes miss the fact that the flow was two-way. Whites have adopted African beliefs into Christianity as well. In Cuba it is not uncommon for a Christian to go to a palero for a spell or a *babalawo* for a consultation. So the absorption of African beliefs into Cuban Catholicism altered it as well.

There is also another intriguing theory—and I stress that this is only a speculation—underlying the syncretization of European and African deities. Fernando Ortiz points out that there are many similarities between West African mythology and those of Greece, Rome, and the Old Testament (1991: 79). The personalities and traits of some deities can be identified in other traditions. For instance, Ochún, who is syncretized in Cuba with *La Virgin de la Caridad de Cobre*, is, like Venus, the goddess of the waters, and of love. Yemayá is perhaps a variation of Aphrodite, with many of the same traits and attributes.

We know that many of the stories of Christianity were passed down from the Greco-Romans and that many of their myths came from Egypt. So, if this canon of myths traveled from Egypt north through Greece to Rome, to be absorbed into Christianity, it is conceivable that it could have also traveled south into sub-Saharan Africa, as well. Ortiz goes on to make similar speculations about the origins of the Abakuá societies, and Métraux draws similar, but more generalized conclusions (359). Basil Davidson writes:

> Here in the forest belt of Guinea there were powerful states and societies of which much is known and recorded... These forest states had seldom or never lost touch with the trading empires of the Sudanese grasslands and, through them, with the peoples of the Nile and North Africa. Many elements of their broad and varied culture, whether in the symbols of religion, the manners of government or the techniques of art and industry, reveal an ancient and creative interweaving of ideas that were both native to the forest and assumed from northern neighbors.

It was from these forest states that Europe, by way of Arab and Berber intermediaries, drew the bulk of its supply of gold after medieval times. It was to them that grassland caravans took the copper of Darfur and Saharan Teguidda so that the master artists of Ife might cast their fine sculpture. For many centuries before European arrival on the coast, these countries were profoundly involved with the world to the north (227).

So Ortiz' theory speculates that there may be a common basis for some of the deities and myths of both the West Africans and medieval Christianity. If this is true then the syncretization of at least some Afro-Cuban deities with those of the Catholics was an act of reunion, not creation. Of course, this is only speculation as there are few written traditions in West Africa. These kinds of things are easier to say than they are to prove. In fact, Dr. Alén strongly insists that there is no direct connection between the two, only similarities that have developed out of shared need: a goddess of the sea, for instance (2000 b). So I include it here as an intriguing speculation, not as a statement of fact.

At one time there were many African-derived religions in Cuba. While their influence is still felt, many, but not all, have been lost or absorbed into the four main syncretized, transculturated religions still found on the island today. Those remaining should not be confused with the original African traditions. They have been separated in both time and space, and the social forces acting upon them have set their New World manifestations on a different path from those of the mother continent. Some core beliefs have been altered or conjoined with those of different ethnicities. Others are rooted in a different time and show marked differences from the way the religions have evolved and are practiced in Africa today. Another factor (first suggested by Moreno Fraginals but quoted here from Maria Vinueza) which limited Cuban slave groups in the reconstruction of their ethnic identities was that the slaves brought to Cuba would have been young, generally between the ages of fifteen and twenty, since the sugar plantations needed strong laborers to work the fields and mills. Vinueza says, "In African communities, history and culture are generally transmitted by oral tradition, so the level of knowledge is directly located in the oldest, the wise men" (1988:29). These were left behind. But despite, or perhaps because of, the many forces working on and against them, the slaves fought hard to retain what they could of the traditions they had brought with them. Because of this, the connections between the various Afro-Cuban religions and their African antecedents are still broadly discernible today.

Afro-Cuban Religions and Drumming Groups

For our purposes, the most important of the four Afro-Cuban meta-ethnic heritages is that of the Lucumí. Their religion, Santeria, is the most influential of them all and, because it is the spiritual foundation of batá drumming and central to our studies, we will deal with it in a separate chapter. Here are brief synopses of the other three. I include them so you can get a sense of how they relate to each other and to Santeria.

Reglas de Congo

Slaves of Bantu/Congolese origin, their descendants, and their cultural heritage in Cuba are referred to as *congo*, after the ancient kingdom from which they were sold. Those brought to Cuba were from the *bacongo, ambundu, bambala, bangui, kuba,* and *mongo* peoples of today's Zaire, Congo, Uganda, Gabon, Angola, and Zambia, (CIDMUC: 20, 21) among others. The Bantus are one of the most important linguistic groups in Africa and are found across large areas of the continent. As such they are a heterogeneous group with regional differences in language, culture, and religion which commingled in Cuba in ways that would never have occurred in Africa. So cultural traits from different bantu groups were absorbed into the Congo heritage in Cuba.

The Congos formed many cabildos in Cuba, mostly in the central part of the island (Vinueza and Sáenz: 76). Each cabildo had a Catholic facade, often Saint Anthony of Padua or Saint Francis of Assisi. Perhaps the reason so many cabildos were dedicated to Saint Anthony is that he is the patron saint of Portugal, and the Congo region of Africa was under Portuguese influence during the sixteenth and seventeenth centuries. It was in these cabildos that the range of religious practices known as *las reglas de congo* was conserved and reshaped.

The best known is *regla de palomonte* (*mayombe*), and it is common practice to refer to all the interrelated Congo religions by this name, but in fact it is one of several. The others are *regla kimbisa, musunde,* and *brillumba* (Castellanos, 1992: 130). This is not a major dispute. Miguel Barnet voices the majority opinion when he acknowledges the various branches of Congo religion but also states that the concept, Regla de Palomonte, "is a definition that can include the other tendencies of the Congo sects of Cuba, and that it has in fact absorbed almost all of the witchcraft rites of the others" (1995: 99).

Nevertheless, they are differentiated by the way they understand good and evil, by the manner they do or do not accept Christianity, and by many other variations in beliefs and practices (Vinueza: 1996a). Almost every casa templo has its own rites and traditions, and because Congo religions are widespread in Cuba there are regional differences as well. Las Reglas de Congo have also syncretized their deities with those of the other Afro-Cuban religions, most notably with the Lucumí (Castellanos, 1992: 138-140) and also with spiritualism.

Las Reglas de Congo are magical, animist religions whose practitioners seek to control the forces of nature, other people, and the spirits of the dead. They believe that if you have part of a thing you can control it. If you have water from a river you can regulate its flow. If you have soil from the earth you can increase its crops. One part represents the total. If you can control that one part you can control all.

The main focus of the religion is to pay homage to the *nganga* (or *prenda*), the principal cult object of the Congos. It is a large pot, made of metal or clay, that contains various natural elements, objects of magical power (CIDMUC: 53) and sometimes symbolic representations of persons whom the paleros wish to control or dominate. The prenda also often contains the bones of a dead person whose spirit has formed a pact with the Congo priest. So it is often through the powers of the dead that the magic of the Congos is manifested.

Congo music and dance are very influential in Cuba. Some instruments, songs, and dances have been lost, most notably the *garabatos*, or *lungowa*, from which the paleros may derive their name. These were hooked sticks (*palos*) with which they struck the ground, awakening and notifying the powers of the earth. They were associated with death and were often used in funeral ceremonies (León, 1984: 71). Maria Vinueza, writing in CIDMUC, says that this tradition is practically extinct (53) although I have seen it reenacted by various professional groups, and ritual palos are still used in religious ceremonies (199). It is interesting to note that, although the Congos use a variety of drums, none of their instrumental accompaniments are associated with a specific deity, as they are in Santeria, but the different chants are sung over the same rhythms (León, 1984: 73). This is also true for their dances (Vélez: 16). While there are still players of rarer Congo-tradition drums, the three most important Congo drumming groups in Cuba today are *makuta, yuka,* and *palo*.

Makuta Drums

The term *makuta* has several meanings, among them "something of medical or magical power" or "something that brings together or unites" (CIDMUC: 199). While it is impossible to pinpoint exactly when Makuta drums were recreated in Cuba, they are one of the earliest and most traditional of the Congo drumming groups. Their shape and type are very similar to drums still used in West Africa (211) and Lydia Cabrera's informants referred to Makuta as "the father of the Yuka drum" (1986: 76). Unfortunately, they are falling into disuse. No new sanctified drums are being made, and they are played now in only five towns: two in Villa Clara, two in Cienfuegos, and one in Sancti Spiritus (CIDMUC: 212).

The Makuta instrumental ensemble generally consists of two or three drums, a hoe blade (*guataca*) or other metal instrument, and a stick played on the side of one of the drums (Ortiz, 1996: 59). In the transcriptions I collected from Roberto Vizcaino, he uses a *katá* (a small, hollowed out log) to play this part, but in Robert Fernandez's transcriptions it is omitted (20, 21). There are two or three large, single-headed drums in the ensemble. The largest is generally called *nsumbi* or *ngoma*. The term "ngoma" means "drum" in Bantu, and in Cuba it has come to refer imprecisely to all Congo drums in general or the largest drum in any group (CIDMUC: 199). The smaller, or middle in the three-drum ensemble, is called *kimbanso, kimbandu, llamador, abridor,* or *bombo*. The smallest, played only in the three-drum ensemble, is called *tumbador* or *marcador* (200). From largest to smallest, these drums are also referred to as *caja, mula,* and *cachimbo,* generic terms used to denominate drums when the original names are no longer in use.

Makuta drums use differing tuning systems: nailed heads, rope systems, or tunable lugs, but they are large, tall instruments so the performers straddle them, one leg on each side, while supporting the drum with a strap that holds it at an angle off the ground.

They are used to accompany the various songs and dances of Congo religious ceremonies. One of the best known, *baile de bandera,* signifies reverence for the gods and religious objects of each cabildo, but today much of the original dance is lost. The same is true for its songs. The deaths of many of the elders have greatly reduced the repertoire of texts (Vinueza and Sáenz: 76). The music and song of baile de bandera can be heard on the Official Retrospective of Cuba Music, and there are transcription examples of Makuta in Fernandez (20, 21).

Yuka Drums

The Congo tradition of Yuka includes the drums, songs, dances, and secular festivals of that name. The term "yuka" is Bantu, meaning to hit or strike (Orovio: 512). Unlike Makuta, Yuka is secular, performed at parties or before more sacred ceremonies, during Congo festivals, and at birthday celebrations. Yuka comes from rural areas and interior communities and was once very common in the central part of Cuba, but today there are only a few groups still practicing this tradition.

Yuka dance was very influential in the development of rumba. One type is danced by a couple where the man courts the woman, trying to gain possession of her with a symbolic pelvic thrust called a *vacunao* (Vinueza and Sáenz: 78) that is still recognizable in rumba *guaguancó*. And Yuka drums also accompanied the *baile de maní* (peanut dance), a boxing dance similar to the capoeira of Brazil, now lost (León, 1984: 67), that was one of the precursors of rumba columbia (Moore: 276).

There are three Yuka drums most commonly called *caja, mula,* and *cachimbo* (León, 1984: 66) accompanied by a katá, and in CIDMUC's transcriptions, a guataca or other metal bell. Vélez also refers to a guataca-like metal instrument called a *muela* (66), while Alén and Casanova say that today there is only one group which preserves the original instruments and that those drummers use the three drums and a guataca. Alén and Casanova do not mention the katá, but that could just be an oversight. Neither my transcriptions or Fernandez' include a guataca part.

The drums are long and thin, usually with the single drumhead nailed to one end. They are played with the musician standing over and astride the drum, tilting it at an angle to the ground. The drum is held in place by a strap around the drummer's body. The mula and cachimbo are played with a stick in one hand while the caja is played with the hands alone.

The rhythms in Fernandez's transcriptions (26, 27) more closely resemble those I copied out in my lessons with Vizcaino. The transcriptions in CIDMUC: 195 are very different, reflecting, I think, the fact that there is, or was, much more repertoire for these instruments than has been recorded by scholars.

Palo Drums

Palo drums are played to accompany the songs and dances for festivals and ceremonies of the various Reglas de Congo known collectively as Palomonte. This may seem obvious but it is important to understand that, because the various numbers of drums, their range of shapes and constructions, and their different instrumental configurations, it is difficult to identify any specific set of traits which would define this ensemble. While they are Congo in origin, they are, in fact, a good example of the transculturation of African traits that affected all of the Afro-Cuban musical traditions.

They are relatively new drums. CIDMUC quotes an older informant, referring to the drums (not the religion) saying "In the decade of the 1920s Palo was unknown, only Yuka and Makuta were danced in the cabildos. They only knew two small Ngoma drums that were played while the sorcerer worked. The festivals of Palo with drums began in the 1940s in San Juan y Martínez by the descendants of Congo Loango" (375). This would explain why Ortiz does not mention them by name when he was writing in the 1950s (although a careful reading of his works reveal hints which are recognizable in hindsight). It is also interesting to note that Palo drums began to appear as the Makuta and Yuka traditions began to decline. Yet despite their range of constructions, different ensemble groupings, and surprisingly late appearance, Palo drums are well within the Congo tradition and are the most common instrumental ensemble used for Palomonte ceremonies in Cuba today.

Bearing in mind that there is considerable variation, we can still describe a prototypical Palo ensemble. The drums generally have large cylindrical or barrel-shaped wooden shells with a drumhead nailed across one opening. There are two to four drums in a group (CIDMUC: 371), and they are sometimes referred to as Ngoma, but this term is used more often by scholars than by the paleros themselves. The standard prototypical ensemble also includes a katá and a guataca as well, although CIDMUC mentions that some groups also use a shaker (371). There are no African names for the individual drums, but there are a variety of Spanish terms, the most common being, from largest to smallest, caja, mula, and cachimbo, in keeping with the generic terminology for drums that have lost, or never had, an African language denomination.

Palo drums are not sanctified and are used both in religious ceremonies and secular festivals, often in combination with other drums and instruments. The repertoire of songs and rhythms for the Palo ensemble is considerable, and it is obvious just from the transcriptions I have gathered from Vizcaino, from those included by Fernandez (23, 24), and from the field transcriptions found in CIDMUC (372-374) that there are more rhythms and variations than have been systematically collected by scholars up to this point.

Regla Arará

One of the great slave-trade centers was the African kingdom of Dahomey. At the time of the trade, this area was called the Slave Coast for obvious reasons. It extended from the River Volta to the mouth of the Niger River. Dahomey consolidated at the beginning of the eighteenth century, extending its power down to the coast by 1727 (Vinueza, 1988: 18). The Dahomeyans had strong relationships with the French who were responsible for bringing many Dahomeyan slaves to their New World colonies, Louisiana and Haiti. But large numbers were also brought to Brazil, Cuba, Santo Domingo, Trinidad, and the United States, so Dahomeyan cultural traits can be found today in these countries as well. While the Dahomeyanos did sell slaves from neighboring and related groups (the Yorubas and Ashanti, for example), many were from their own ethnicity, the Ewe and Fon peoples.

In Cuba, these slaves, their descendants, and their traditions are referred to as Arará. According to María Vinueza, the most likely explanation for the term, Arará, is that it derives from the port city of *Alladá*, from where many Dahomeyan slaves departed for the Americas (23). Since slaves were often identified by the ports they came from, this is a reasonable assumption. Because they were comprised of different African ethnic groups, they differentiated between themselves by calling themselves *arará mahino, arará savalú,* or *arará dahome*, among others, depending on the ethnicity with which they identified (29). The Arará established themselves first in Havana in the seventeenth century and later expanded to Matanzas and Santiago where their cabildos flourished until the end of the nineteenth century when they began to decline. Today there are only a few temples left in Matanzas (CIDMUC: 245).

The Arará had much contact with the Yorubas both in Africa and Cuba. To some extent they were related, so their interactions were a process of mutual exchange, and there are now elements in each culture which originally came from the other. Because of this, Arará deities (called *vodú, vodún,* or *foddun*) are often identified by their Lucumí orisha or Catholic saint name. For example, the Lucumí orisha, Babalú Ayé, called *Asohano* by the Arará, was originally Dahomeyan. The Arará have syncretized their beliefs with those of the Catholic church as well, so Babalú Ayé is also called San Lazaro. Because Arará music and dance have been closely tied to those of the Lucumí, and sometimes performed in the same ceremonies (Vinueza, 1988: 48), there has been an artistic interchange as well, but the Arará still retain their own drums, songs, and dances.

The Arará musical ensemble consists of a lead singer, chorus, drums, a metal bell, and shakers. The bell is generally called *ogán* or *oggán* (71) and the shakers are generally called *atcheré* or *cheré* (87). The number and names of the drums differ depending on the locality and group. Since the Arará tradition was conserved by people in different places and times, the various cabildos developed their own instruments and playing styles. Originally there were a larger number of drums and drum names, but as the practice of Arará declines, the instruments and their music are becoming simplified. (For a more complete listing of drums and drum names, see CIDMUC: 239.)

The drums are sometimes referred to collectively as *hun*. They are cylindrical and the heads are fastened to the shell with a system of ropes tied to pegs. They are played either with two sticks or with hand and stick depending on the drum. Two naming systems seem most common today. The first refers to them individually, from smallest to largest as *hun, hunguedde, huncito,* and *hunga* (Vinueza: 70, 71). The transcriptions in Vinueza's book include parts for as many as four drums (135). This same author, writing in CIDMUC, indicates that at least one cabildo used five drums (239), but generally three or four are found in today's groups. The second is more commonly a three-drum ensemble called from smallest to largest: *güegüe, aplití* (or *aplintí*) and *yonofó* (Fernandez, 32. Vélez, 63). But again, these are not definitive.

In my studies with Roberto Vizcaino and Laurentino Galán, I have transcribed four separate rhythms for Arará, but there may well be others. The four I have are Afrekete, Jervioso, Masé, and Tiñosa. Roberto Fernandez names the first two as "Sabalú for Afrekete" and "Sabalú for Asoyi"(32,33). The transcriptions in Maria Vinueza's book are identified by song, not rhythm, but despite the name confusion and various manifestations of the patterns from different sources, there is an obvious familial relationship between them.

While all the Dahomeyan traditions on the island have Ewe-Fon roots, it is important to distinguish between those which arrived directly from Africa and those which were transplanted from Haiti. The French brought many Ewe-Fon slaves to Haiti where they developed traditions different from those of Cuba. In successive waves of immigration, those slaves and their descendants brought a variety of beliefs and practices to Cuba which differ from each other as much as they do from those of the Arará who came to Cuba from Africa. The first wave of immigration (1789 to 1804) brought *tumba francesa,* a nonreligious music and dance tradition which combines French and African influences. The second wave (1910 to 1930) brought Vodú to Cuba. Cuban Vodú has evolved along different lines than its Haitian counterpart. It can be divided into the *radá* and *petró* branches, each with their own ceremonies and drums. The last wave (1980s) brought today's Haitian Vodú to the island as well. Franco-Haitian immigrants imported a variety of songs, instruments, and rhythms to Cuba, but these Dahomeyan traditions, while related, should not be confused with those of the Arará.

Abakuá

The slaves brought to Cuba from the area between the mouths of the Niger and Calabar rivers were known as the *carabalí*. They were of diverse but related peoples, the *ibo, iyo, ekoi, hausa,* and the *ibibios* (CIDMUC: 20), among others. The Carabalí formed many cabildos and cofradías to conserve their traditions and support their people. Among the most important and interesting are the Abakuá societies or *potencias abakuá,* found only in Havana, Regla, and Guanabacoa, and in the sea ports of Matanzas and Cárdenas (Ortiz, 1991: 123). Abakuá was historically Cuban, but political events and population shifts have now helped to establish societies in several cities in the United States, most notably Miami and New York.

Abakuá, from the African word, *abakpa* (Brown: 13), is an interconnected system of men's lodges whose members are also called *ñáñigos*. It is not a religion. Abakuá has its roots in the *ekpe*, or leopard societies, of Old Calabar but has evolved along its own lines in Cuba. Although the Abakuá tradition is Carabalí, it is important to understand that its members were drawn from different ethnic groups, including many whites, whose beliefs and practices were further modified by the historical and social dynamics of Cuban society and syncretized with those of the Catholic church. Because of these factors, Abakuá should be seen as a Cuban entity with strong African roots, not as a purely African tradition preserved in the New World.

Having said that, it is obvious that these African roots, at least those of the Ibibios, are still strong. In his book on Ibibio music, Samuel Ekpe Akpabot lists a number of Ibibio cultural traits that, to me, still bear a strong resemblance to those of the Carabalí. He describes several different secret societies among the Ibibios, including the Ekpe societies, which were still active as of 1975 (25-37), mentions a legend similar to that of the Abakuá (30), and refers to the supreme being named *Abasi* (73) as do the Carabalí. He also includes several photographs of drums which have obvious similarities to those of Abakuá (20, 34), and a photograph of an "Ekpe masquerader in ceremonial dress" (33) which bears a distinct resemblance to an Abakuá *íreme*. There are, of course, many differences as well, but while a more detailed study would be required to identify exactly how these Ibibio traits were transculturated in Cuba, it is apparent that some still survive among the Abakuá.

The purpose of the Abakuá society is to aid its members, protect its secrets, and guard its traditions, and their reenactments of its myths are religious theater which manifest those beliefs. Lydia Cabrera says:

> In the society of our Náñigos, that spirituality continues breathing in the atmosphere of the first mornings of time, the object they fundamentally pursue is to protect themselves from adverse and mysterious forces, to achieve this power by means of them, and the desire a thousand times and unbreakably, to triumph over death, with the means that assure the immortality of the soul (1958: 22).

The Abakuá recreated their belief systems in Cuba drawing on influences from the leopard society traditions of various peoples. These were "compacted" (Brown quoting Thompson: 13) into two branches, the *efí* and *efó*, which represent tribes from the two sides of the *oddán* river. The Efó possess the secret of the voice of *Tanze*, but the Efí are the keepers of the drums, and some of the legends of the sect recreate the fight between the two to control the voice of Tanze (Leon, 1984: 84, and Ortiz, 1993a: 218, and 1996: 76). This division is fundamental to Abakuá as an expression of the "geography of sacred memory" (Cabrera, 1958: 63). That is, as an essential understanding of the place, the people, and the dynamic of the myths and beliefs of the Abakuá. However, Cabrera deliberately pointed out that she drew on Cuban sources for her information about the

Calabar (63) because it becomes obvious very quickly that the historical and anthropological evidence from that place and time is much more complicated (Sosa, 1982:45-73) than is represented in Abakuá cultural memory. The tribes of Calabar were interrelated, forming larger groupings which were re-conceived and recreated by the Carabalí in Cuba. The concepts Efí and Efó were "redistilled in Cuba as local institutional denominations, which the Abakuá diasporic imagination, not to mention the scholarly imagination, projected back across the Atlantic and mapped onto the African continent" (Brown paraphrasing Palmié: 14).

Abakuá is based on and structured around a myth and a sacred drum called the *ekue* which represents the voice of God. Its ceremonies reenact this complicated legend which has many variations and alternate versions. Here is a simplified description.

The Legend of Tanze

Abasí was the greatest of gods. He chose to communicate with his people through a sacred fish called Tanze that lived in the river. The voice of the fish was the voice of God and could only be interpreted by the warlock *Nasakó*. One day a young princess named *Sikanekua* went to the river to collect water. When she returned, she discovered that she had caught Tanze as well. She went to her father, *Iyamba*, who was chief of the tribe, and showed him what she caught, but before they could return him, Tanze died and the tribe lost the voice of God. So Nasakó decided to make a drum that would be the voice of Abasí, and he sacrificed Sikanekua so that the drum would have a head. They put her skin on the drum but it would not speak. So Nasakó underwent many labors and tried many different animal skins on the drum, but none would speak except the skin of a goat. With this drum, the *ekue*, he restored the voice of Abasí.

The body of Abakuá myth, the ceremonies based on it, and the social structures of the people who recreate it are much more sophisticated and rich in meaning than I have related here. This is just a synopsis. Those who wish to understand the intricacies of the Abakuá should read the works of Cabrera, Sosa, and especially Brown, listed in the Bibliography.

In order to join the Abakuá, a man must go through an arduous initiation process. He must prove that he is good and honorable. He must be a good husband, son, father, friend, and person, and he must prove that he is ready to kill or die to protect the society. The ethical code of the Abakuá, historically at least, is very severe. Once initiated, a member can rise through a hierarchy of various ranks called *plazas* (Cabrera 1958: 20, Brown: 64, 65). The most important plazas embody the characters in the myth, and each has specific ritual duties to perform. They are manifested in the ceremonies as iremes, Abakuá members costumed to masquerade as the various entities of the myth. It is for these ceremonies that the drums are played.

In the Ibibio language the generic word for drum is *ekomo* (Ekpe Akpabot: 20). Among the Abakuá drums are generically referred to as *enkomo* (CIDMUC: 213). Besides the ekue there are two other sets of drums in Abakuá. The first, the "altar" or "symbolic" drums (Brown: 94), represent the various personalities of the myth and are used ritually in the ceremonies rather than to make music. The second is a set of four drums called *conjunto biankomeko* which are played to accompany the songs and dances during the ceremonies. They are, from smallest to largest: *biankomé, kuchi yeremá, obi apá,* and *bonkó enchemiyá*. (There are many spellings and pronunciations for these names. I listed those of CIDMUC: 213.) This ensemble also includes a metal bell called *el ekón*, basket shakers called *las erikundi,* and two sticks played on the sides of the bonkó enchimiyá called *los itones* (218).

There are two interrelated rhythmic styles for conjunto biankomeko which loosely correlate to the Efí and Efó denominations in the mythology. Roberto Vizcaino says that the Efó style comes from Matanzas while the Efí style comes from Havana (1999), but Justo Pelladito says that, while each province has its own style, the Efí and Efó designations are differentiated as much by the songs as by the rhythms (CIDMUC: 217). Alejandro says that both Havana and Matanzas have their own versions of the Efí and Efó styles. But all agree that the Efí style is played faster and the Efó is slower. (For good transcriptions of these rhythms, see Fernandez: 54, 55.)

Photos of all the drums discussed in this chapter can be found in the section starting on page 81.

The religions of Afro-Cuba are diverse but interconnected, and they are tied as well to the Catholic church, as it is to them. Each has evolved along its own trajectory, absorbing traits from other religions while retaining essential beliefs of the distinct African cultures from which they were born. Some are lost to us, known only through historical records and in the memories of those old enough to recall an earlier time. Others, as we shall see in the next chapter, have developed into sophisticated spiritual philosophies which perhaps surpass the original African belief systems on which they are based. But to understand any one of them, all must be seen in relation to the others. Placed within the larger tapestry of the European, Asian, American, and African peoples and traditions which comprise, even today, the national character of Cuba, each can be understood for the specific contributions they make and by the influence they have on each other. It is a complicated, ever-changing dynamic—one that no one grasps completely—which is essential to any understanding of the subject of this book. That is why I started with such generalities: a history of the slave trade, slave life in Cuba, the forces which acted on the slaves and their descendants, and the religious beliefs and drumming traditions which evolved from these powerful processes. Bearing this in mind, we can now consider our main objective: the religion of Santeria and the drums which connect its gods to their followers.

Chapter Six

Santeria

> What may have once begun as a subterfuge, an attempt to fool Catholic observers while preserving the ways of the *orishas*, became a genuine universal religious vision in which a Catholic saint and a Lucumi *orisha* were seen as different manifestations of the same spiritual entity. As the Yoruba had become the Lucumi in Cuba, so the Yoruba religious vision had become santería, an attempt to honor the gods of Africa in the land of the Catholic saints.
>
> Joseph M. Murphy
> *Santería*

My relationship with Alejandro has changed over the years. Originally, I was one of many foreigners who studied with him to learn something of the drums. Most satisfy their curiosity and move on, but some continue their studies, deepening their understanding of the music and the religion over time. As I moved from the former to the latter, I became his friend and he became my mentor.

Alejandro stopped charging me for lessons long before this book became a real project. I am not special in this, he does it with other students once they prove their commitment. He has said many times that he is not concerned with money but is required by his beliefs to teach the knowledge that was given to him by his father, and I have seen him work for hours with young drummers who had no money but who paid him with loyalty and effort. So as I kept returning to Cuba for more instruction, demonstrating my commitment, he began to take more responsibility for my training. In return he made it clear that he expected me to take the journey seriously.

Through the course of our discussions, I began to understand that Alejandro believes different people bring different dynamics, different needs to their apprenticeship. I believe he sees himself as a facilitator helping each along his or her own path. In my case, I started as a skeptical observer, not playing the drums but transcribing the rhythms for my students. I began to play them because it is easier to write out a rhythm once you have it in your hands. As I started to grasp the size of the repertoire, I only hesitantly made a commitment to transcribe the music in a more systematic form. Making the commitment to actually learn all these rhythms took much longer. Throughout this transition, he has patiently kept doors open for me while I decided whether or not to walk through them.

This apprenticeship has been difficult for me. As a secular foreigner studying the beliefs of others, I could take refuge in the concept of objectivity. By keeping my distance I could respect the tradition without becoming part of it. But no matter how much I pretended that my presence was as a guest, I knew that I was becoming recognizable to the community, a part of it even as an outsider. The drummers knew me. I spent evenings sitting on porches with the santeros, the musicians, and their families, drinking their rum and eating their food. I was developing a relationship with the religion.

My world view is secular, but with a Protestant upbringing. Both Catholicism and African religion are foreign to my spiritual understanding. So my involvement with Santeria still challenges me to evaluate myself in an ongoing, uncomfortable struggle. This evaluation became a crisis when Alejandro told me that to truly understand the batá I would need to play them for Santeria ceremonies. The essence of this music is religious and the drums speak only as part of the living religion. They are only alive when they speak in the voices of the gods during the ceremonies, so to experience these voices I would have to make some commitment to Santeria, or be left outside. In order to do this, I had to earn the right to play the sanctified drums. I explained to him that my spiritual conception was very different from his and that I would have a hard time participating at that level in a religion in which I was not a believer. He answered that spiritual belief is a journey and that it did not matter where I started from as long as I undertook it seriously. I was hesitant to cast off my objectivity and step across that line, but in the end I realized it was cowardice to ignore my teacher's advice. If I was to continue my journey into the music, I would have to take this particular plunge.

What had started as an intellectual exercise had turned into a painful struggle. My journal from that time is filled with doubts worried from every perspective, and with various rationalizations, justifications which sought to find a way to understand this struggle, a way to accept it. I never resolved it, but I overcame my fear and agreed to undertake the ceremonies. My dilemma had no guideposts in my experience and no references in my reading. How was I to commit myself to something I didn't believe in? And how was I to remain honest with my mentors while remaining honest with myself? Just going through the motions would be a thin hypocrisy, making me a liar in my own eyes and an obvious fraud to them. My only solution was to explain my predicament to my soon-to-be *padrinos*, Alejandro and Mayito Angarica. Neither saw it as a problem. Mayito told me that I think too much, that I make things more difficult than they need to be. Alejandro told me that I would understand my problem better in time, but only if I faced it.

So I decided that if I was to undergo the ceremonies, I would do them as honestly as I could and try to abide by the results. In the end, I underwent four ceremonies: *una consulta*, a checkup of my spiritual health, *la mano orula*, which introduced me to the god of divination, *jurar el tambor*, which gave me the right, if not the knowledge, to play the sanctified drums, and *itá*, which seeks the advice of the orishas and reveals which of them is my personal guardian.

Alejandro has asked me not to write about the details of the ceremonies, saying that each person should experience them personally. I can say that they were a physical and psychological ordeal—a series of tests which I did pass. I emerged shaken but not shattered, changed by having confronted challenges not usually faced by fifty-year-old, postmodern secularists who think too much.

My results were a little odd, I think. I was found to have strong spiritual power, but my lack of belief would be a hindrance to me. An unusual result, apparently, which seemed to have left some of the priests unsatisfied. Alejandro, who knows me better, told me that in the end the only one I need to prove myself to is myself, and that this would be my journey.

During the ceremonies I had time to consider what it means to be challenged and judged by others, and what it would mean to fail. I was made aware that life can hold very real, very painful realities, and that in order to face them I must work to be physically and mentally strong. And to overcome them I must strive to be a man who is responsible for himself and honest with those he encounters. These revelations may sound like platitudes to you, but after facing their expectations and my own limitations these lessons are now very real to me.

As part of the ceremonial process I had been taken to a nearby Catholic church where I was to honor my mother, who had recently died and who they felt was particularly close to me in spirit. While we attended a mass for the souls of the dead, I was struck by the number of santeros in the congregation. They were the descendants of the black slaves who had sat in these pews so many years ago, looking up to the same images of these very white saints, and finding in them a spirituality in common with that which they had brought with them from Africa. The Catholic conception was that I was to pray for my mother. The *santero* conception was that I was to pray *to* her. Despite my background, and hers, I couldn't help thinking that to be in communion with someone I had loved was not the worst way I could spend that morning. Growth, intellectual or spiritual, is both serendipitous and continual.

So, having stepped across that line, even in my own complicated way, I will never again view the religion or its drums in the same light. But that understanding is subjective and, while it can be used as a guide for judging the depth and accuracy of others' contributions, it cannot replace an objective study of Santeria's belief systems or the specific information which they contain.

Olodumare

Any survey of Santeria should begin with *Olodumare*, the Supreme Being who created the universe. As is often the way with incarnations of the infinite, Olodumare is a paradox. After having made the world, he retired from it, removing himself from direct interaction with humans. Yet he is often depicted in the stories of Santeria as having relations with both men and gods. He is regarded as all powerful, yet was persuaded to give up his powers because he was too sick to be their reliable protector. There are many aspects to his personality, and so he has different names which reflect his different roles: *Olorún, Olofi,* and *Olofín* also refer to Olodumare's incarnations.

Having chosen to remove himself from the world, Olodumare entrusted his creations, a pantheon of gods called *orishas*, to mediate between himself and humankind. Because of this, there is no cult which prays directly to Olodumare. Instead, believers direct their supplications to the orishas who still involve themselves in the affairs of men.

There are several debates over the nature of Olodumare and the gods he created to serve him. When considering the hierarchical structure of Cuban Santeria's deities, the direct influence of the Catholic church is impossible to miss, as are parallels to the pantheons of the Egyptians, Greeks, Romans, and the Norse. And the syncretization process (the direct identification of the Catholic saints with the Yoruban orishas) is only one of the processes that has altered their powers and personas from the original Yoruba conception. This syncretization is dismissed by some as a simple mask which protected the religion from Spanish interference. Some people still believe that by shedding the Catholic aspects of Santeria its truths can be more fully revealed, but a careful examination reveals that not only do Catholic beliefs pervade many core aspects of Santeria but that it has absorbed beliefs from other Afro-Cuban religions as well. So Santeria faces criticism from both practitioners of the African version of the religion, some of whom see it as a devolution of their beliefs, and from Yoruba revisionists who do not understand that even if its Catholic traits were completely purged, the orishas of Santeria have evolved along their own trajectory since their separation from the mother continent. There is no consensus on these issues, and well-meaning people will take confrontational positions when they are raised.

The other question is, if a religion has one omnipotent God who rules over a pantheon of lesser beings (including saints, angels, the spirits of ancestors, and the personified powers of nature), is that religion monotheistic or polytheistic? This has been a point of dispute between Catholics and Protestants and an issue for scholars of Egyptian religion as well. This hierarchy, referred to by the Castellanos as "implicit monotheism" (1992:16), does not have to be viewed as an either/or conception. Seen from one viewpoint, Santeria can be considered polytheistic. Seen from another it can be monotheistic. Or it can be understood as being both. The orishas, like the saints, can be viewed as aspects of a divine unity or as individual beings with unique characteristics and histories. In fact, it is important to keep both concepts in mind when exploring these beliefs, and in so doing, the paradox—the one and the many—should cease to be an issue.

The Orishas

Orisha religion was brought to the New World by Yoruba slaves, and various traditions based on these belief systems can be found in many Latin American countries, the islands of the Caribbean, and the United States. Even in Cuba there is a range of practices, so the religion is better understood as a system of interrelated beliefs that vary by region and temple tradition rather than as a unified whole. But, however diverse the details, the larger religious principles are consistent and universally understood.

While Santeria is the popular name for this religion in Cuba, its proper name is *regla de ocha*, a term which translates most simply as "rule of the orishas," or more exactly as "the fundamental religious precepts of the orishas." For believers, the orishas are humanity's connection to the spiritual world, so they are central to any understanding of the religion.

The Cuban orishas are fewer in number than their African counterparts and have evolved relationships and identities which have followed a different trajectory than those of the old continent. They have become amplified. Deities who were once city gods have become embodiments of universal truths, and their personas have accommodated themselves to their new home by redefining themselves and their powers in answer to the challenges imposed on them by Cuban society. The Castellanos cite sources which estimate that there are between four hundred and seventeen hundred Yoruban orishas in Africa (1992:22). While there are no definitive estimates of the number in Cuba, Ned Sublette says that *La Sociedad Yoruba* in Havana has statues and dioramas for thirty-three orishas (213). Of these, only twenty-two are acknowledged in the *oru seco*. Unquestionably, there are fewer orishas in Cuba than in Africa, and two processes help explain this fact.

While the most powerful, well-known, and universally recognized orishas are still found in both Africa and Cuba, others were regional or village gods, or were venerated by small cults within the population. So if few slaves were transported from that village, region, or cult, those orishas would never have been able to establish themselves in the

New World. (It is also possible that some orishas were known in Cuba in the past but have been lost or forgotten over time. I state this only as a speculation, but George Brandon [76] does theorize that the earth cults, the *onile* and *ogboni*, were transported to Cuba but later died out.)

Some orishas still exist but have lost their individual identities to a greater or lesser extent and have become avatars or aspects (called *caminos*) of other gods. Thus, the Yoruban orisha, *Olufon*, has become a camino, the Cuban incarnation of Obatalá (Castellanos, 1992: 23). This is a complicated process. In another example, the African orisha, Olókun, has become strongly associated with Yemayá in Cuba and can only speak through her. So, while some santeros believe that Olókun is a distinct deity, others believe he is an incarnation of Yemayá (55). In either case, he is strongly associated with this goddess.

In these ways the number of orishas and their relationships to each other have changed over time. Some orishas never made it to Cuba. Others, perhaps, have been forgotten. And others have had their identities absorbed into the aspects of more powerful deities.

There are also strong similarities between the gods of different Afro-Cuban religions. A person can be a member of more than one—in Alejandro's case, a santero and an abakuá. While he certainly knows the difference between them, he cannot help but notice the similarities as well. Santeros call the omnipotent god Olodumare, while the paleros call him *Sambia, Nsambi,* or *Sambi* (Vélez: 13). Since there can be only one omnipotent god, these must be different names for the same being. Changó of Santeria is very similar to *Ebioso* (*Jervioso*) of the Arará, and Ogún is similar to *Sarabanda* of the paleros. The identification of one with another is both logical and inevitable. (For a surprising discussion of the relationship between Santeria and Palo in Matanzas, see the interviews in the DVD, *La Fuerza del Tambor*.) So while I am not aware of any comprehensive study of the subject, it is obvious that there are relationships between the various religions and perhaps some interchange of attributes between their deities as well.

All belief systems change over time. Christianity and Islam have certainly evolved from their historical roots without losing their spiritual potency. So the examination of this evolution in Santeria is not an attempt to undermine these beliefs, but rather as an explanation of the forces that have acted on them. You can study the history of the Bible or the Koran as texts and still find spiritual truth within them, if you so choose, just as you can consider the forces which have influenced Santeria and still maintain belief in the spiritual power of the gods themselves. Santeria is a powerful, sophisticated, and complete conception of the universe. As the Castellanos say:

> Contemplated in all its details, this pantheon and its accompanying myths integrate all in a system of interpretation of nature and of society: and constitute a corpus that is a philosophical, "scientific," and teleological world view of the Cuban yorubas. For each natural or social phenomenon there is always one or more orishas and one or more *patakíes* (or sacred legends) that explain all. And the same occurs with every one of the innumerable avatars of human existence (1992:25).

Each deity has its own nature, powers, and concerns. Some are cosmogonic, responsible for the creation of the universe and the earth. Others influence the weather, the rivers, or the oceans. Some are gods of metal or plants, of sickness or medicine, of the hunt or agriculture, and one of them can divine our spiritual dynamics and, in so doing, can affect our futures.

Each orisha has its own representative color(s), day of the week, number(s), plant (s), precious stone(s), animal(s), and principal festival day. Some are associated with certain metals. Each is identified with one or more Catholic saints. (Or, in the case of Obatalá, with Jesus as well.) In my researches it quickly became apparent that there are discrepancies in the literature about the specific characteristics of certain orishas. This is possibly due to variations in the beliefs of the informants or resources consulted, or just bad scholarship by certain authors. In any case, these discrepancies muddy the waters sufficiently to make a precise study of these characteristics difficult, so I will include only those that I know to be generally accepted, and will leave a more thorough study of the subject to those who are in a position to identify the origins of these discrepancies more exactly.

Since the natures, attributes, histories, powers, and stories of the orishas are complicated and extensive, the descriptions given below are only sketches designed to introduce the reader to the various gods. I must note that there is a surprising number of disagreements about the identities, attributes, relations among, and even the names of the orishas. I cannot resolve them here. I can only present them as Alejandro gave them to me. Those interested in exploring these issues further should refer to the bibliography at the back of the book.

The orishas represented in Alejandro's Oru Seco are:

Eleguá is the god of destiny. He is the guardian of the spiritual pathways, the *caminos*, that men and gods must travel. He is the first to be called for all ceremonies because only he can open and close the doors to the spiritual world. He is both messenger and spy for the gods. Eleguá is powerful and capricious, a trickster who plays malevolent pranks on those who displease him but who is capable of great largesse with those he chooses to help. He is deceptive rather than evil, a warrior who can appear in the guise of a child or an old man. His colors are red and black. Eleguá is syncretized with The Child of Atocha, Saint Anthony, and Saint Roque, among others.

Ogún is the god of war, of metal, and of the work that is done with metal tools. He can be both violent and rebellious. Like Eleguá, he is the son of Obatalá and Yemayá, but he was banished from his father's house for having an affair with his mother. Ogún is the keeper of secrets and the force behind the realization of human potential. His various incarnations have different colors, but those most commonly associated with him are green and black. Ogún is syncretized with Saint Peter, Saint John the Baptist, Saint Michael the Archangel, and Saint Paul.

Ochosi is the god of the hunt and of justice. He is strongly associated with Ogún. In one well-known story, Ogún could cut his way through the forest with his machete but could not kill any game to eat. Ochosi could kill with his bow but could not get through the forest to where the game was. So, with the help of Orula, they teamed up to hunt and were successful. Because of this they are always together. (Mikael Ringquist disagrees. " In my own experience this is not necessarily the case. My own padrino ["Puntilla"] did receive Ochosi separately from Ogún at a later time. I cannot remember if he had "two" Ochosis or not. There was also a priest of Ochosi in the Boston area named Luis who had a similar situation. The Ochosi was in the form of antlers, possibly from a deer.") As god of justice, Ochosi is responsible for the law, prisons, and lawyers, as well. His color is violet. Ochosi is syncretized with Saint Norbert.

(A brief aside here: The toque, Imbaloke or Obaloke, played at this point in the Oru Seco, is sometimes identified as a minor orisha, but for both Alejandro and my other teacher, Laurentino Galán, it is another toque for Ochosi, not a distinct god.)

Inle is a god of medicine and healing. Surprisingly, he is less venerated than in the past. He is believed to be very strict, difficult to follow. He is a river god and strongly associated with Yemayá and Olókun. His colors are blue and green. Inle is syncretized with Saint Raphael.

Babalú Ayé (Chopono) is the god of sickness and infirmity. As such, he is represented as an old man, lame and covered with sores. Because his origin is in Dahomey (Castellanos, 1992:57), he has close ties to the Arará in Cuba (Cabrera, 1996:104), so some of whose beliefs were absorbed into the Lucumí tradition. His identification with Saint Lazarus stems from a story in which Babalú Ayé was brought back to life by Olodumare just as Christ resuscitated Lazarus. As god of sickness, he is especially associated with smallpox, leprosy, and, now, HIV. His color is purple. Babalú

Ayé is syncretized with Saint Lazarus.

Osain is the god of spiritual herbs (*ewe*), and is a healer. He is very important since most ceremonies cannot be performed without his herbs. So *osainistas*, the priests of his cult, must have a profound knowledge of plants and their religious properties. He is represented as having one arm, one leg, one big ear (which is deaf) and one small ear (which hears all). According to Cabrera (98), he is venerated by santeros, arará, and paleros. Osain is syncretized with Saint Sylvester and Saint Joseph.

Ósun is the lookout for the warriors (*los guerreros*), Eleguá, Ogún, and Ochosi. When initiates undergo the ceremony to receive the warriors, they also receive Ósun who will advise them of approaching danger. He is depicted as a rooster.

Obatalá is the greatest and oldest of the orishas, and the father or mother of a generation of gods (by most accounts, Eleguá, Ogún, Ochosi, Ósun, Dadá, Orula, and Changó). He is the creator of mankind and the god of purity and peace. Obatalá is wise, closely associated with Olodumare, and can be male or female in various incarnations. His color is white. Obatalá is syncretized with Our Lady of Mercy, Jesus, Saint Joseph, and Saint Manuel.

Dadá is the guardian of newborn children. She is the sister of Changó. Dadá is syncretized with Saint Ramon Nonnato.

Óke is the god of the mountains and guardian of the orishas. He lives with Obatalá. Óke is syncretized with Santiago Apóstol.

Agayú is the god of the sun. Like Yemayá (the sea) and Babalú Ayé (sickness), he was born at the same time as the earth. His colors are red and green. Agayú is syncretized with Saint Christopher.

Changó is the god of fire, passion, thunder, music, and dance. He is courageous but impetuous. Because of this, he is closely associated with his father, Obatalá, who helps keep him under control. He is passionate and a great lover of women, music, and dance. He is brave and cunning, and has been known to take what he wants. He is a sworn enemy of Ogún. As the god of music, he is also the owner of the batá drums. Changó dresses in red and white with a castle-shaped crown, and he carries a two-headed ax. His colors are red and white. Changó is syncretized with Saint Barbara.

Orisha Oko is the god of agriculture. Much revered in Africa, he is considered a secondary orisha in Cuba. As the Castellanos say, the slaves "forced to produce for the benefit of an owner, had no reason to ask protection for harvests that were not theirs"(1992: 62). Orisha Oko is syncretized with *San Isidro el Labrador*.

The Ibeyi are twins, the protectors of children. (Mikael Ringquist says their names are *Taiwo*, "first one out," and *Kehinde*, "last to come.") Depending on the informant, they are the sons of Changó and Oyá or Changó and Ochún. They are generous and friendly, loved by both gods and men. They are syncretized with Saint Cosme and Saint Damian.

Yeguá is a virgin. Daughter of Obatalá, she asked her father to send her somewhere safe, so he sent her to the cemetery, where she now receives the spirits of the dead. She renounced men and sex. Yeguá is syncretized with Saint Clare.

Oyá is the goddess protector of the dead and of cemeteries. She can control lightning, whirlwinds, and tempests. In Africa she was a river goddess but may have lost this characteristic in Cuba (Castellanos,1992: 45). She is known in Cuba as Changó's second wife, stolen from his enemy, Ogún. She is a powerful orisha who fights with Changó against Ogún. She is very jealous and dangerous to her rivals in love. Her colors are dark red (*vino*) and white. Oyá is syncretized with the Virgin of Candlemas, Saint Teresa of Avila, and the Virgin of Montserrat.

Yemayá is the goddess of maternity, of the seas and rivers, and the patron of sailors. She is the eternal mother: beautiful, good (though potentially dangerous), and ample. Her relationships with the other orishas vary considerably, depending on the informant, but she is closely tied to Orula and divination, and to the spirits of the dead. Her color is light blue. Yemayá is syncretized with the Virgin of Regla.

Ochún is the goddess of love. Sometimes called the African Venus, she is much loved and venerated in Cuba and is the patron orisha of the island. She is beautiful, intelligent, and caring. In some incarnations she is a river goddess. In others she lives with her husband, Orula, or with one of her many lovers, Changó. In Africa, Ochún was a goddess of the *iyesá* tribe, neighbors of the Yorubas, but in Cuba she was incorporated into the Lucumí pantheon, although she still retains her own cult and drums as well. Her color is yellow or gold. Ochún is syncretized with the patron saint of Cuba, *La Virgen de la Caridad del Cobre*.

Obba is the goddess of marital sacrifice or abnegation, and of the home. She is Changó's principal wife who was so worried about her marriage that the jealous Oyá convinced her to cut off her ear and feed it to Changó as a way of binding him to her. When Changó discovered the trick he was so shocked he moved out of her house. Although perhaps somewhat gullible, she is also beautiful and knowledgeable, and is a teacher and writer as well. Her color is rose. Obba is syncretized with Saint Catalina of Siena and Saint Rita of Casia.

Orula (Orunmilla or Orunla) is the god of divination. He is the keeper of knowledge and can discern a person's spiritual dynamic, conveying solutions for problems and foretelling the future. Orula never assumes the role of guardian orisha and must be petitioned through the Oracle of Ifá and its priests, the *babalawos* (see below). Orula's colors are yellow and green. He is syncretized with Saint Francis of Assisi.

Oduwa (Odudua) is the orisha of both solitude and androgyny. Seen as the mother/father of the Yorubas, he/she is closely associated with both Obatalá and Olodumare, and with the creation of the earth. Oduwa is syncretized with Jesus Christ, among others, and is closely associated with the Eucharist (Bolívar: 165).

Sacred Stories

The sacred stories, called *patakíes*, are the ethical heart of Santeria. These are myths which convey the religious teachings, moral parables, and creation stories of the religion. In them are the tales of the gods, descriptions of their powers and personalities, the mythical past, and the histories of their interactions with each other and with mankind.

The word "myth" has developed bad connotations, and many people believe it to be synonymous with a lie or an untruth. This is not the meaning I intend when I use the word here. Myths are the universal stories which permeate the fabric of culture. The truth found there is not in the fact of the event but in its meaning. The stories of Genesis are some of the oldest in western civilization. Some of them can be found in the writings of people who predate Christianity by thousands of years. These myths are valuable clues as to where we come from and why we are who we are. The question is not "are these stories true?" but "what do they tell us about ourselves?" It is in this light that we need to understand the patakíes of Santeria.

There are hundreds, if not thousands, of patakíes, preserved orally, written down by initiates, and collected by scholars. Some come directly from Africa, others show some Cuban influence, while others are of Cuban origin. There are variant versions of some, and different stories told in different places. The Castellanos state that some of the patakíes are drawn from the *odus* of the Oracle of Ifá (see below), a logical idea, but one that I would not suggest without their testimony to give it credence (1992: 45). To sort all this out would be a difficult and somewhat unrewarding project, which I will leave to scholars who have the time and resources to focus on the subject, but a working knowledge of the sacred stories is essential for anyone who wishes to understand the people who tell them.

While a comprehensive study of Lucumí myth is beyond the scope of this book, I include three here to give you a sense of their place in the religion. Whether one believes them to be historically accurate or not, it is important to hear or read these stories for the insights they give into the world of the santero.

> Eleguá was the son of King Okú Boró and Añaguí. One day, when he was a young man, he was walking with his entourage when he saw a brilliant light with three eyes, on the ground. When he approached it he realized it was a dried coconut. Eleguá returned to the palace, told his parents what he had seen, and put the coconut behind a door. All were amazed to see the light that came from the coconut.
>
> Three days later, Eleguá died. Everyone had much respect for the coconut, but in time, the people forgot about it. It was in this way that the people found themselves in a desperate situation and when the old ones met, they came to the conclusion that the cause was the abandonment of the coconut. They found it empty and eaten by insects. The old ones agreed to do something solid and lasting, and they decided to put a sacred stone (otá) in the place of the coconut, behind the door. This was the birth of Eleguá as an orisha.
>
> (Bolívar, 28)

> A white lily had given birth to Inle, and everybody says he was a lovely looking young man. One day he met Yemayá [the sea goddess], who fell so much in love with him that she took him to the bottom of the sea to have her fill of the lovely youth.
>
> Time passed and the goddess got bored of her lover—she wanted to take him back to where they'd first met. But Inle now knew the mysteries of the sea, having searched out its deepest secrets. So Yemayá cut out his tongue to prevent him from revealing anything.
>
> Since then, those who want to talk to this orisha must do it via the owner of the sea.
>
> (Arce, 232)

> Ochosi is the best of the hunters and his arrows never miss. Nevertheless, at one time, he was never able to get to his prey because the luxuriant growth on the mountain impeded him. Desperate, he went to see Orula who advised him to make an offering. Ochosi and Ogún were enemies because Echu had sown discord between

them, but Ogún had a similar problem. Although nobody could make paths in the mountain as fast as he, never was he able to kill his quarry and they escaped. He also went to Orula and received instructions to make an offering. It was in this way that both rivals went to the mountain to carry out the ceremony with his own offering. Without warning, Ochosi dropped his offering on Ogún who was leaning against a tree trunk. They had a heated discussion, but Ochosi apologized and they sat down to talk and resolve their problems. While they talked, far away passed a deer. Fast as light, Ochosi notched and shot an arrow that went through it's neck, leaving it dead. "You see," breathed Ochosi, "I am not able to reach it." Then Ogún took his machete and in less than the call of a rooster, had opened a path to the deer. Very happy, they arrived at the animal and shared it. From that moment they agreed that they were necessary, one for the other, and would never be separated, because they had made a pact in the house of Orula. It is because of this that Ochosi, the hunter, always walks with Ogún, the owner of metal.

(Bolívar, 71)

The sacred stories are fundamental to Santeria. They include the creation of the universe, the gods, the earth, and man; the precepts of ethical and moral understanding; its religious values and their instruction; explanations of the natural world and of human society (for more on this see Castellanos, 1992: 63-80). And in their study you will discover an understanding of the Lucumí that you will not find in books like this one.

Beliefs and Practices

For santeros, the dynamic of the universe, the force which moves everything, is called *aché*, which can be loosely defined as spiritual power, grace, or energy. Olodumare, the god of all, is aché, and his children, the orishas, are its ways. Joseph Murphy says:

> As one enters more deeply into santería, one sees this vision of *ashe* with increasing clarity. All things that we are accustomed to call beings are, in reality, *caminos*, ways of *ashe* that can be liberated and channeled by those who understand them. The person of wisdom, the true *santero*, learns to work with these forces. By words and actions, *ashe* can be awakened in what seem to be objects and people to bring about the fulfillment of their destinies. Stones, leaves, animals, and people are vibrations brought into harmony by *santeros* to further them on their road in the way of Olodumare.
>
> *Ashe* is the current or flow, a "groove" that initiates can channel so that it carries them along their road in life. The prayers, rhythms, offerings, tabus of santería tune initiates into this flow. They are lifted out of the self-absorption and frustration of ordinary life into the world of power where everything is easy because all is *ashe*, all is destiny (130).

The various orishas manifest and represent the force that moves the universe, the earth, and all the beings on it, and all are incarnations of various energies—good and evil, hot and cold, strong and weak—which must be kept in balance for one to be physically and spiritually healthy. It is the maintenance or recovery of this balance that is at the heart of Santeria ritual and practice, and it is around this dynamic that its institutions are structured.

The Santeria community revolves around a network of organizations called *casas de ocha* (orisha houses) in Spanish and *ilé* in Lucumí. They are the basic unit—at once religious, familial, and social—of the religion. There are many of them scattered throughout the neighborhoods of Havana and in various places around the island. Some of them are quite old, having been handed down through generations within families and among believers.

An orisha house is usually governed by a *padrino* (godfather) and a *madrina* (godmother). Rituals and festivals are held there to initiate new members, to commemorate the anniversaries of initiations, and to celebrate the annual festivals of the various orishas, among others. Many of the ceremonies are private, attended only by members, but there are public festivals as well.

Within each orisha house is an altar or shrine comprised of various containers, called *recipientes* or *soperas*, often kept in a vertical cabinet called a *canastillero*. Each orisha has its own recipiente (except for Ochosi and Ogún who, as we have seen, always travel together). Recipientes can be of clay, porcelain, metal, or other materials and in each are the *otá* (small stones) or other objects that contain power from the orisha. The room in which the shrine is kept is called an *igbodú*. Smaller versions of these shrines can often be found in believers' private homes as well.

Santeria is a mystical, participatory religion whose followers are required to fulfill certain obligations and sacrifices to achieve various levels of spiritual empowerment. Many believers undergo ceremonies like those I experienced, but others undertake a more arduous initiation process, generally referred to as *hacer santo* (to make saint), to become a priest (*babaloche*) or priestess (*iyaloche*). The newly initiated are called *iyawó*. They serve an apprenticeship period, learning the ways of priesthood before attaining full status within the community.

Santeros believe that each person has a guardian orisha (*el ángel de la guardia*) who can be revealed to them through ceremony. A person reflects his or her guardian's personality and character, is expected to fulfill that orisha's expectations, and should be an honorable representative of his or her guardian on earth. In the case of an iyaloche or babaloche, a person devotes his or her life to the veneration of that guardian orisha. And there is another type of priest who has a guardian like everyone else, but who undertakes further responsibilities in the *oraculo de ifá*.

The Oracle of Ifá

Contrary to popular belief, Santeria divination is less about predictions of the future and more, as the Castellanos say, "to clarify our mission in this world and to help us fulfill it completely" (1992: 63-80). Santeros believe that each person has a destiny, a fate, a role to play in his or her life, which has been given to them by the orishas. Since people are not automatically aware of this destiny, they can become lost or entangled in problems that hinder their ability to fulfill their fate. Divination enables believers to become aware of their life's purpose and of the hindrances that are complicating its achievement.

While several orishas have some power to divine our spiritual dynamics, it is Orula who is the keeper of the most powerful divination, the Oracle of Ifá. A priest initiated into Ifá is called a *babalawo*, literally, "father of the secrets." Babalawos are the most respected of all Santeria priests for their wisdom, knowledge, and spiritual power. However, as with batá drummers, some are better regarded than others, depending on their reputation and performance. Most santero priests practice divination to some extent, but it is to the babalawo that people go when they have major problems or questions to ask of the orishas. Philip John Neimark says:

> The babalawos of the Ifa tradition predict events by focusing on individuals and their idiosyncratic harmony or disharmony with the energies of the world. The process of forecasting future events is intimately related to the specific energy balance and behavior of the client *now*. Harmonious energy, for instance, will always be the precursor of favorable future events, while disparate, negative, or dissociative energy will always be the root cause for negative future occurrences. The diviner alters the probabilities of future events by restoring harmonious balance in the individual through ritual, sacrifice, and prayer. In a pragmatic sense, the diviner sees what is likely to happen if clients remain in their current state and understands that restoring harmonious energy enables them to alter unpleasant future events. The focus is on individuals, not problems (Epega: viii).

There are four divination methods in Santeria: coconut shells (*obi*), cauri shells (*dilogún*), the board of Ifá (*tablero de Ifá*), and the chain (*ekuele*). The first two are accessible to all initiates, but the latter two are used only by babalawos. A detailed study of these methods would be outside the scope of this book, so for a closer look at each see Castellanos: 1992, 113. But a brief examination of one method will help make the general concept clearer.

The *tablero de Ifá* is used when a very precise answer is needed. The tablero itself is a small wooden tray on which the babalawo spreads a special powder (*yefá*) that is used to record the results. The babalawo makes the actual divination by holding sixteen palm nuts (*ikines*) in his left hand then attempting to pick them up with his right. If one nut stays in his left he makes a double mark (1 1) on the tablero. If two remain he makes a single mark (1). If none, three, or more remain he recasts the nuts. He continues until he has two vertical columns of four figures. This is an *odu*. There are sixteen principal odus from which two hundred and forty more are possible. So in all there are 256 odus in the Ifá Oracles. Each is a description of a spiritual dynamic, told as a parable. For example:

3. Ìwòrìméjì

11 11
1   1
1   1
11 11

Odù Ìwòrìméjì speaks of people gifted with the ability to see things in their true perspective. They dream often, have clear vision, and grow up to become diviners or spiritualists. Clients for whom this odù is divined should be advised to worship Ifá. This will bring them good prospects: long life, wealth, a wife, and children (Epega: 10).

The babalawo can repeat this process many times, building an understanding of the client's spiritual dynamic and interpreting the odus in relation to that person's needs. The next step is to learn what must be done by asking questions of the orishas. To do this the client is given a shell and a stone which are shaken together then separated at random between the left and right hands. The babalawo casts one or more odus then checks one hand. The stone indicates "yes" and the shell "no." By repeating this process they uncover the course of action to be undertaken by that person.

It is through divination, with the help and guidance of a priest, that believers come to understand their spiritual dynamic and make changes which will lead them to the health and happiness, and balance, to fulfill their purpose in life.

The Égun

Another important aspect of Santeria is ancestor veneration, which was discussed in general terms in Chapter Five. The Lucumí call the spirits of the dead *égun*. For the santero, they play a role in everyday life: influencing events, causing trouble, and giving advice, depending on the spirit and the situation. For the postmodern Euro-American, the logic of an active presence of dead relatives and ancestors may be difficult to grasp.

The existence of spirits is a matter of belief or disbelief, and obviously outside the scope of this book, but the égun are fundamental to Santeria in that they identify the santero in time, lineage, and place. Without them, he would not exist because he would have no history to prove his identity.

Ethnicity and tribal affiliation are very important in African society. Who you are depends on who you are with, and group affiliations provide community interaction, physical protection, and the means to survive. To be separated from one's tribal support system is more than a death sentence, it is nonexistence. For the millions of African slaves brought to the New World, the separation from their societies meant that they had vanished from history. But history had not vanished from them. Even though they were physically separated from their communities, many were able to preserve their family stories, so some Afro-Cubans today know their lineages all the way back to Africa. This inheritance is the gift of existence. So it is through the égun that the Lucumí know who they are. It is through the égun that they know their place in history and in geography. And it is through the égun that they maintain their direct connection to the African spiritual world that is the legacy of their ancestors.

But even égun veneration has had interactions with Euro-Cuban beliefs and has been influenced to some extent by the nineteenth-century cult of spiritism (*espiritismo*), systematized by Allan Kardec. The effect of this influence is debatable and perhaps variable, so I mention it here because it is a contentious issue in Santeria scholarship, and one needs to know where the land mines lie to avoid stepping on one. I have not seen anything which I could identify as being influenced by Spiritism, but that does not mean it does not exist within the religion. For a more thorough (if somewhat socialist) exploration of the relationship between Santeria and Spiritism see Argüelles: 172.

Joseph Murphy says, "Santería recognizes four principal ritual ways of approach to the world of the *orishas*: divination, sacrifice, trance, and initiation" (134). I see them as the forces impelling an upward spiral. Believers are drawn to the religion by divination, a chance to improve their spiritual and physical health, and to understand better their path through life. It is through sacrifice that they strengthen their resolve and empower the orishas to help them on their journey. The initiation process deepens this connection and eventually allows them, through trance, to connect directly with the divine.

The batá drums are at the center of this process. It is through the god of the drum, *añá*, that the other orishas are called to the ceremony. It is through the rhythms of batá that the orishas can be present in the possessed bodies of their priests. And it is through their physical presence that the power of Olodumare is manifested on earth. In the end, the drums speak both to the gods and for them. For the santero, batá are a swinging door between the world of man and the realm of the gods.

Carvajal teaching near the ENA

Carvajal teaching in Havana Vieja

Women's batá group performing at the ENA

Bata drummers at a ceremony in Matanzas

Drums in the Museo de la Música, Havana

Batá drums

Iyesá drums

Arará drums

Makuta drums

Palo drums

Yuka drums

Abakuá drums

Batá drummers performing near the ENA

Students dancing the orishas at the ENA

Eleguá

Ochún

Professional dancers representing the orishas

Changó

Yemayá

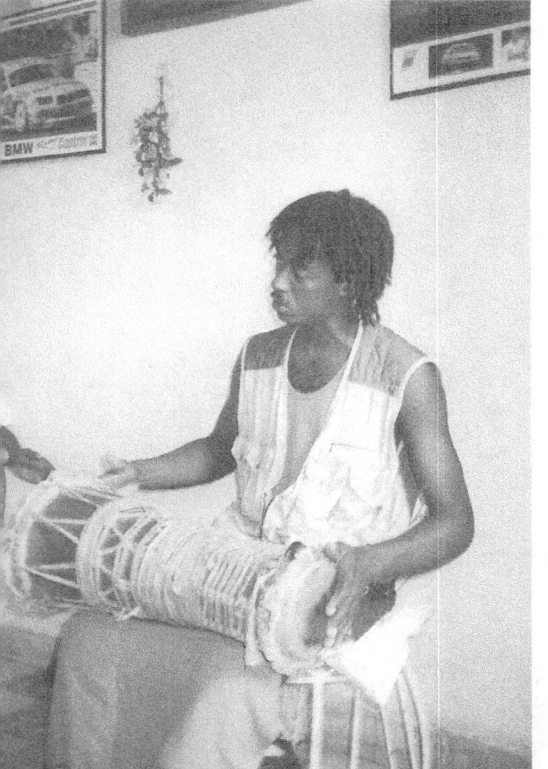

Batá drummers at a ceremony in Havana

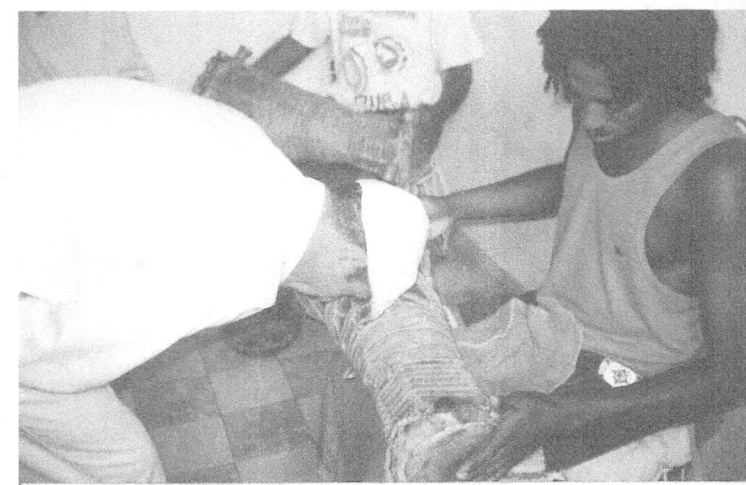

Paying homage to the drums

Teacher and students

Student and teacher (the authors)

Section Two

The Music

Chapter Seven

The Batá Drums

> The drum is sorcerer. It is the call of the blood, the spirit of Ancestors that passes the most hidden secrets on to the children. Under its influence, men rediscover the time when Heaven and Earth lived together in the same calabash—before they quarreled and separated. It was the time of Celebration, the time of Orú, which neither began nor ended and delivered all.
>
> Liner notes to
> Cuba: Merceditas Valdez y los tambores de Jesús Pérez

Afro-Cuba retains a number of interrelated religious and musical traditions in different languages and from different roots. Evolving over a four-hundred-year period, these traditions continue to change today, redefining themselves in relation to each other and as part of the island's people as a whole. It is a complicated heritage that even the Cubans are still sorting out, yet there are good reasons to make the effort.

The components of African-derived art—the dance, song, and drum—while divisible, are aspects of a unity. One that, unlike Western music which can be considered distinct from both the time when it was written and the audience who listens to it, cannot be separated from the lives of the people who make it. Ortiz says:

> In modern white society, music is socially segmented and occasional, it is of one sector and of one moment, while that of African communities is social sonority, like the word, constant in the life of all (1993b: 29).

This music and dance is essential to life and woven into the fabric of a universe in which all things have spirit. Music is not something you do, it is who you are. The worshippers at a Santeria ceremony are not divided into congregation and clergy. Everyone participates. To them, it is not a performance to be judged but an act of worship with roots in the life of the spirit. In this sense, all music is inextricably religious, as is life itself. Of course, it is a matter of degree. The chants and batá drums of Santeria are sacred, yet *bembé* is less so, even though it often uses the same songs. *Comparsa* and *rumba* are not sacred yet they speak from an African world view where the divine is part of daily life, and where the sound of the drum is the voice of God.

Music serves many purposes in the various religions: to call or drive away spirits or as sonic representations of the sacred animals of myth. A god resides inside the drum. Music intensifies the power of the words. The psychological effects of drumming are mystical, hypnotic, and help the believer to make contact with the divine. Ortiz says:

> In every way, in those simple instruments of mystical invocation their musical value is little or none; they are not played for their esthetic effect but for their transcendental magic, yet when their sonorities, combined with song as exclamations of exaltation, cooperate in the emotional effusion produced by the rite in the complexity of its elements they produce by "conditioned response" the mystical phenomenon of possession (1993a: 261).

While I disagree as to its musical value, Ortiz has put his finger on the essence of the religious music of Afro-Cuba. The drums speak to the believer from the divine world.

Drums That Talk

It is important to have a clear understanding of the role of speech in African and, to a lesser extent, Cuban music. John Miller Chernoff said it concisely, "African music is derived from language."

> When the earliest European travelers described drum-signaling between villages, they assumed that the beating was a kind of code. In reality, the drums actually speak the language of the tribe. During my first day practicing with Gideon [Alorwoyie], I was following him well until he suddenly performed a rather complicated series of rhythms and then went back to the basic rhythm he was showing me. A few minutes later a man who had passed at that moment returned with two bottles of beer. (75)

While not everyone agrees, most scholars believe that the drums of Cuba are losing their ability to talk in the strict sense. In 1952 Ortiz wrote that:

> In earlier times there predominated in the orthodox drummer the influence of his ancestral liturgical tradition and the batá would "speak" with the tonal language of the Yorubas and with the archaic phrases intelligible to the gods: today the language of Africa is transformed, its semantic tonality is forgotten and the musical tastes of Cuban society are imposing themselves (1996 v2: 206).

Inevitably, this trend continues. CIDMUC writes:

> Today, among groups of players a smaller knowledge of the various toques for each orisha can be observed, with them using the same toque or rhythm to accompany songs dedicated to various gods, thus the exclusivity and rigorousness of yesterday has been lost (331).

While I cannot disagree with either of these statements, I do feel that they identify only one of the processes acting upon the drums today. It may well be that there are fewer toques now than in the past, but the body of knowledge still needed to play the drums in their ritual context is absolutely vast, as anyone who has ever tried to master these rhythms can tell you. And while patterns may have been lost, new ones are being created. José Eladio Amat says that some older toques are no longer played, but that other, newer rhythms, most notably Chachalukafú and Ñongo, were created in Cuba, not Africa. Some things die when others are born.

Eladio Terry (2000) states the same about the Lucumí language. Some years ago, I had a young Yoruban from Nigeria in one of my classes. Although our song texts were taken from Lázaro Pedroso, compared against other sources, and then checked with several Cuban musicians, he said the pronunciation was strange and difficult, and that he only understood an occasional word. It is reasonable to assume that, cut off from Yoruban society, the Cuban use of the language would begin to evolve in a different direction.

However, the role of speech in the formation of the traditional sets of rhythms cannot be underestimated. The drum that speaks, the *tambor parlante*, in its many incarnations, is an integral part of Afro-Cuban music, and a drummer that can reproduce those traditional rhythms, one that can "speak the drum" (Vinueza and Casanova: 67), is honored and respected. So while the drums may no longer talk in a fluid, conversational sense, many drummers still have a clear sense of the meanings of the rhythms and their musical function in each specific piece. Although the connections between the various talking drums of different ethnic traditions and the original African languages from which they come vary considerably, and some have been lost, the sense of speech is still there in the music. So it is important for anyone wishing to perform them accurately to understand the nature of the talking drum within these traditional rhythmic sets.

History of the Batá Drums

It is no longer possible to identify the first set of batá drums in Cuba. There are many theories and little proof. Compounding the problem is the fact that the drummers of Havana and Matanzas disagree where and when the drums were first made, so attempts to trace their lineage through the musicians has proven to be a complicated task. As Victoria Rodríguez says, "History and legend march hand in hand, and many times lead to confusion" (339).

According to Ortiz, the first batá in Cuba were played around 1830 in Havana in a Lucumí cabildo called *Alakisá* (1996, V. 2: 221). The story goes that a slave named Añabí, also known as Ño Juan the Cripple, was working at a sugar mill when a cart load of cane broke his leg. He was taken to a slave hospital in Regla where he heard Lucumí drumming for the first time in Cuba. There he also met another slave, Atandá, a drummer whom he had known in Africa. They knew that the drums being played were not consecrated, so they constructed a set with all the appropriate rituals and baptized them as *Añabí*, meaning born of the Añá, the first consecrated batá in Cuba. Even if this story is true, it indicates that batá drums, however unsanctified, were being played before this time. CIDMUC doubts the accuracy, or at least the verifiability, of the 1830 date, pointing out that Ortiz does not cite a reference. But they go on to say that the Lucumí cabildo, located next to The Church of the Virgin of Regla, was founded in 1866, inferring that it was around this time that the first drums in Havana might have been built (339).

However, the drummers of Matanzas say that the first batá in Cuba were constructed in that province. Amado Díaz, a well respected *batalero*, believed that the drums were linked to his family, saying that the first known set was built by his great-grandfather, Clemente Alfonzo, in 1874 in the town of Cidra (339).

These accounts conflict, although both may be true, but since neither the written or oral evidence points to a definitive source, it seems impossible to state accurately when and where the batá were first recreated in Cuba. Both Havana and Matanzas, however, have their own batá drumming styles.

While consecrated batá were never numerous—Ortiz estimated that in the 1950s there were only eleven sets usable for ceremonies (1996, Vol. 2: 224)—both the drums and the religion have steadily migrated from these two centers to all parts of the island and beyond. There is a New York style which grew out of the Havana tradition (see Amira and Cornelius for more), and batá drumming can be found in many places in the United States (including Puerto Rico), Latin America, and Europe. However, while CIDMUC states that there are not many sets of consecrated drums on the island today (343), Alejandro says that there has been a construction boom in the last few years, due in part to *santurismo* (Santeria tourism), and there are now too many consecrated sets to keep an accurate count.

General Information

Batá, also called *ilú*, are the most sacred of the Lucumí drums in Cuba. While strongly associated with the orisha, Changó, they are played in ceremonies for all the orishas. A set of batá consists of three double-headed, hourglass-shaped drums that are laid horizontally across the player's lap and struck with both hands. The three drums in a set are called, from largest to smallest, *iyá*, *itótele*, and *okónkolo*.

The term *iyá* means mother in the Yoruban language. It is the lead drum that plays complicated variations from sets of traditional rhythms, which represent words in Lucumí, the Cuban dialect, separated in time and space from Africa, that is evolving away from the original Yoruban. The iyá fulfills the role of tambor parlante, speaking the words of the orishas in the modified tongue of their new land. And it is helped in this by the Añá, a sacred token within each consecrated iyá that enables it to speak. The Añá is made of various natural materials that are kept within a small bag attached to the interior of the shell.

The drumheads of the iyá are often encircled by many small bells called *chaworó* attached to the drum at either end. CIDMUC says that the word, which has a number of different spellings, means jingle bells in Yoruban (320). Their purpose is to call the orishas and to provoke possession trance states among the initiates.

The iyá sometimes has a resinous circle, called a *fardela*, attached to the larger head. It is made of various ingredients that might include tree resin, blood, honey, wax, vegetable or fish oil, and soap, as well as other substances which are kept secret. The fardela's purpose is to deaden the drum's ring and modulate its sound to the proper pitch and tone color.

The middle drum, the itótele, plays various repeated patterns in relation to the iyá, answering its calls. The term, itótele, could be translated loosely as "the one who follows," meaning it follows or answers the iyá.

The smallest, the okónkolo, is also called *omelé*. The term, okónkolo, derives from the Yoruban word *konkó,* meaning small. Omelé means child or youth, referring to the drum's size in comparison to the other two. It generally plays one repeated pattern that may vary slightly from one section to another.

Batá drums can be either consecrated, called Añá (or *de fundamento*), or unconsecrated, called *aberikulá*. Añá drums, which have been ritually constructed and sanctified for use in ceremonies, are always strap tensioned, but aberikulá drums, which are used for public demonstrations, concerts, or teaching, can be either strap or lug tuned. Only añá batá are used in the initiations, funerals, remembrances of ancestors, and other ceremonies that need sanctified drums. Their function is to invoke the orishas, inviting them to attend, to accompany the songs and dances, and to speak in the voices of the gods themselves. The owner of a set of sanctified drums is referred to as an *olubatá*.

The preferred wood for batá drums is cedar, but they can also be made of mahogany, oak, avocado, or almond wood. Traditionally, each drum was carved out of one piece of wood, and all three drums of a set were made from the same tree, but this is often impossible now. Today, unconsecrated drums are often constructed from slats, like a barrel, but añá drums are always carved from one piece of wood.

Cuban batá drums have retained the hourglass shape of their African antecedents but have evolved on the island, achieving a larger differentiation in the sizes of the various drumheads. Each drum has two heads of differing sizes. The large head is called *enú*, or mouth (*boca*), and the small one is called *chachá*, or butt (*culata*). Traditionally, the drumheads were made of he-goat, deer skin, or more rarely, calfskin. But today, most are made of cowhide.

Batá can be tensioned by either the traditional wrap or more modern lug systems. On the wrapped drums, the straps were traditionally made of bull or ox skin, but today are more likely to be cowhide. The lug system is easier to use, since the head tension can be adjusted with a wrench or key. Although these drums are not used in Santeria ceremonies, they are often used for teaching and for public performances.

There is no single tuning system for batá. The drums are made in various sizes and different sets are tuned for different purposes, but they all retain the relative pitch levels of low, medium, and high. They can be tuned in fourths or fifths. One method is to tune the smaller head of each drum to the same pitch as the larger head of the next smallest drum For example, the chachá of the itótele and the enú of the okónkolo can be the same pitch (Vinueza, 1996a).

The Acheré

A gourd rattle, called an acheré, is a shaker very similar to a maraca, the main difference being that it is larger and only one is used while maracas are played in pairs. The shell is generally made of a calabash or other gourd which is filled with seeds or peas and then attached to a handle. It is often decorated with designs and painted in colors that have religious significance. The term, acheré, is of Yoruban origin, and Ortiz says that the word is a combination of two Yoruban terms: aché, meaning spiritual power, and *eré*, a prayer or imprecation (1996, Vol.1: 200). Called *achiddí* by the Arará and *nsansi* by the Congos, this type of shaker is used in various musical groups including arará, batá, bembé, conga, dundún, gangá, kinfuiti, palo, radá, and tanbourin.

The acheré is used in batá and other Lucumí musical groups. Often played by the *akpuón* (lead vocalist), it has both a musical and religious function. Musically, it serves to mark the metric pulse and to enrich the group's sound. Its religious function is to call the orishas and to facilitate trance/possession among the believers. In fact, the acheré is not played during the Oru Seco specifically to prevent the possibility of possession. The acheré is generally used during the Oru Cantado to mark the pulse or play a temporal line pattern.

The Temporal Line and Clave

The *clave* is a Cuban manifestation of a concept called the temporal line, a repeated pattern that defines both the length and internal structure of the meter. It is a rhythmic anchor around which the other parts revolve. While there are many different temporal line patterns, there are only three basic claves: son, rumba, and six-eight. The term, clave, refers to the function, but *claves* refers to the two wooden sticks used to play the clave pattern. The clave is the reference point and rhythmic guide for the dancers and musicians.

While clave is a fundamental concept in most Cuban music, it can create problems when studying batá. While some toques can be, and are, played in-clave, others are too complicated to fit within its structure. Those who attempt to transcribe all batá patterns in-clave have to simplify the rhythms or alter the clave pattern to make them fit. The reason is that temporal line patterns were not part of the original music. They were added later in Cuba. So while you may hear people clapping clave during some toques at a Santeria ceremony, it stops when the drumming becomes more intricate.

My attempts to learn these toques in-clave created confusion at times during lessons with Alejandro. While sometimes the clave position was obvious and easy to find, in others it would inexplicably reverse itself when moving from one section to the next. We would finally work it out, then the next time the reversal did not happen. This was even more frustrating because Alejandro did not seem to understand why we were having a problem. It was only later I realized that Alejandro did not always perceive the entire toque as being in-clave. He was merely giving us a pattern to help us get started.

My efforts to include clave in every transcription created some pretty interesting but bizarrely flawed results. When I explained my problem to Alejandro, he burst out laughing, telling me to take it out. As usual, he was right. Once I removed it, the transcriptions began to flow more smoothly.

I mention this because my insistence on relying on the clave was a crutch. Many foreigners are trained to believe that clave is universal, almost a law, but Cuban musicians know that it is used only at certain times in some styles of music. They include it only when appropriate. People may clap clave at times in a ceremony, the acheré may play it, and you can find it even in Cuban transcriptions of the patterns, but it is not always essential. Alejandro only sometimes uses it when he is teaching. It was I who insisted on mandating it in the learning process, but it was he who told me to get past it and expand my understanding of the music.

So, yes, clave is important. Most batá rhythms, and the songs they accompany, are in clave. But some are not. Others are basically in clave but have transitions that are not. You can usually spot these in the transcriptions when you see a meter change at the beginning or ending of a section.

Adapting to Cuban Teaching Styles

For many foreign students, understanding and adjusting to Cuban teaching practices is as challenging as the music itself. Cuban teachers employ a range of approaches—some innovative, some traditional—which vary from extremely formal to shockingly relaxed depending on their personality, education, and background. Having some understanding of their traditional teaching methods (and the cultural attitudes which underlie them) will help you learn more effectively and, perhaps, deal with some of the uncomfortable issues that may surface during lessons.

Traditionally, aspiring batá drummers are trained within the temple community by teachers whose purpose is to pass on the religious beliefs and musical practices of Santeria to a new generation. This is a serious obligation for the teacher requiring a serious commitment from the student as the goal is the preservation and continuance of the religion itself. Each apprentice must first be accepted by a master teacher. Foreigners who can pay in dollars may have less trouble finding a teacher than Cuban apprentices, but they are often considered less serious and may have a longer journey to acceptance than their Cuban counterparts whose linguistic advantages and cultural ties give them a better head start. Both foreigners and Cubans also have opportunities to study outside the temple in various programs which teach folkloric music in classroom settings that acknowledge the religious component of the tradition without being part of the religion itself. These programs are often a good place to start, since the teachers are trained to work with students who may not have religious aspirations. Today, there is often a good deal of overlap between the traditional religious and the classroom folkloric approaches and a number of options for students who may start in one and end up in the other as their musical skill and personal commitment deepens.

An apprentice traditionally begins his study on the okónkolo, playing only that drum until the teacher is satisfied that he knows those patterns. Lessons evolve into rehearsals which may become limited opportunities to play in ceremonies. Then he repeats the process, learning the same toques on the itótele. Eventually, once the supporting patterns are mastered, he will be allowed to play iyá—maybe. Some apprentices do not complete this rigorous training. I have seen young drummers playing in ceremonies being aggressively corrected by both the older drummers and by the community in attendance. It is not an easy apprenticeship.

I have studied within this system with another teacher, and I found that it was very difficult to come away with useable transcriptions which I could take home to practice. He would complain about my poor technique while making me play a basic okónkolo pattern for three hours. When I tried to write out the other parts he told me to concentrate on what I was doing because I was not ready to move on yet. In the end, I came away with one okónkolo rhythm but nothing I could use after I returned to the United States. While the experience was unforgettable, it was not very productive, so after a few lessons I stopped studying with him.

With Alejandro, I started by transcribing the rhythms while others played, but he soon moved me to the iyá because by being at the center it is easier to write that part in relation to the others. This allowed me to comprehend the music in a different way. The iyá player controls the group so, while I was still unqualified to lead knowledgeable players, I did get a sense of how to direct the performance of my fellow students. However, once each set of transcriptions was finished, he would move me back to the okónkolo (where I belonged) to memorize the parts so I could play them without the sheet music. When teaching a new toque, Alejandro often requires his students to switch drums, learning all three parts during one lesson. He sometimes has the students sing songs that go with the toque, and occasionally makes them all dance as well. And he allows them to write out the rhythms.

This hybrid approach is more useful to those foreign students who have ambitious objectives but limited time and money. Initially, Alejandro did not emphasize the transcriptions, especially as writing slows down the lesson, but as my paper pile grew— and more importantly, became more accurate—he realized their value and began to facilitate the process. But it is important to understand that while Alejandro adapts to the situation for foreign and non-santero students, as his apprentices become proficient he reverts to more traditional methods. While they are more labor intensive, these methods are also very effective for those apprentices who are ready.

Since batá drumming is an oral tradition, the rhythmic patterns are remembered and taught using various systems of onomatopoeic syllables. (I think of them as teaching sounds.) Argeliers León lists them as *jin*, *ka*, and *kan* (1984: 43). CIDMUC lists them as *jin-ka*, *kin-kan*, *kin-ta*, *kin-ki-ta*, and *ki-la* (330). Both León and CIDMUC mention the syllabic systems as an introduction to the concept without going too deeply into specifics.

In fact, there are a large number of teaching sounds which vary from teacher to teacher. Alejandro uses them informally and in different ways. Some are traditional and indicate a specific rhythmic pattern:

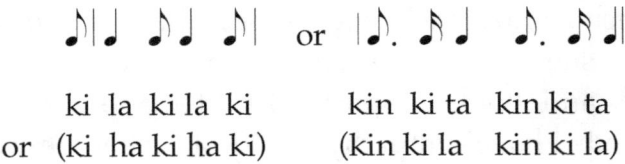

    ki la ki la ki   kin ki ta kin ki ta
or (ki ha ki ha ki)   (kin ki la kin ki la)

Often, he will sing the composite melody (the open-tone combinations of the larger heads of each drum) of the toque, using different teaching sounds depending on the pattern. At other times, he will sing the Lucumí words that the composite melody represents.

Since different teachers use their own variations of the syllabic system, there is no standard set of teaching sounds. Whatever syllables your teacher uses will work well as long as he is consistent and clear in his approach, but be sure to listen to and be able to repeat the sounds your teacher uses. They are a great help in learning the rhythms.

Batá Drumming, Gender, and Sexual Orientation

Traditionally, women were prohibited from playing batá, but this has changed in recent years. I have seen a number of performances by women's batá groups in Cuba. However, they are not allowed to play sanctified drums or during religious ceremonies. (For an insightful discussion of the reasoning behind the prohibition, see Hagedorn: 91.)

The Cuban teachers I know have no concerns about teaching batá to women—an attitude that contrasts sharply with many North American bataleros—and are happy to help women musicians get practical experience on the drums. Alejandro, for instance, says the rhythms are not secret, and are not sacred unless played on sanctified drums. They can be accessed by anyone with a CD player. So it is in the best interest of the music and the players that everyone gets good instruction regardless of gender. I believe his attitude is the result of the Cuban education system's division between folklore and religion. As a professional teacher, he is able to separate the music itself from its spiritual function. The rationale for prohibiting women drummers is irrelevant in a nonreligious context. He is, however, opposed to women drumming in Santeria ceremonies.

In the United States, the division between folklore and religion is less well defined, and women are showing a marked determination to play for Santeria ceremonies. This might explain why North American batá teachers can be less welcoming toward women students. (Carolyn Brandy also thinks that North American bataleros are more constrained by tradition than their Cuban counterparts. "The further away you get from the source of the tradition, the more people are rigid about 'doing it right.' So North American men have always lived with this pressure of 'doing it the right way' . . . even though the men in Cuba were already teaching us—the peer pressure here was too great for *any* of the bataleros to teach women back before—probably the mid 90's.")

To me, the underlying issue is less about equality and more about perceptions of the differing natures of men's and women's spirituality. Men and women have different roles within the religion. While I have sympathy for the heartfelt desires of those who wish to participate more fully, it seems disrespectful for outsiders to ask for acceptance within a community, then to seek to change that community for their own purposes—especially over the objections of the mentors who welcomed them in the first place. My concern is not about the spiritual validity of women playing for ceremonies, but rather is about the perceived lack of respect some show towards the beliefs and wishes of the inheritors and guardians of the spiritual tradition. Any woman who wishes to play for ceremonies must understand that her teachers will be offended, and that the Cuban Santeria community is unlikely to sanction or respect her desire to participate as a drummer. But in time this may change.

Gays and lesbians face similar issues. Traditionally, they were not accepted into the religion or its musical traditions. I state this simply as a fact which must be understood in its context. But while this attitude still predominates in theory, the gay community, in Havana at least, is out and certainly participates at all levels in the Santeria community. (Carolyn Brandy calls it "one of those don't ask, don't tell things.") Alejandro knowingly teaches gay and lesbian students, but within the folkloric, educational context, not as preparation for playing ceremonies. It simply is not an important issue for him. When I mentioned a gay Santeria temple I had heard of in the United States, he seemed slightly amused but was neither surprised nor dismissive. My impression was that he considered it as outside his tradition and, as such, something he could accept.

This is not true for all batá teachers, especially those in the United States. Some will refuse to teach gay students, and while I certainly do not agree with this attitude, I do understand it for what it is and would defend another person's right to act in accordance with his beliefs. In the same way, I would defend your right to view this information as you choose. It is simply better to be forewarned and to understand that these attitudes are cultural, not personal.

Abuse

While many progressive Cuban teachers are adapting their approach both to changes within Cuban society and to the influx of foreigners, among some bataleros there is still a tradition of teaching through abuse. Alejandro's father would hit him from behind when he made a mistake. He would move tables to his left and right, close to the drum so that if he lifted his hand too far off the head it would hit the table edge. I have heard stories from other students of being locked in practice rooms, being physically intimidated, yelled at, or forced to buy rum for the teacher and his friends.

While these kinds of abuses are relatively rare, they still occur, and it is important to state that they are not normal, they are not good teaching practices, and you do not have to subject yourself to them. In the same way that abused children can grow up to be child abusers, abused students sometimes become abusing teachers, passing on the misery to their students because that is the way they were taught. While I sympathize with their pain, I refuse to let them take it out on me. And neither should you.

In the course of your career it will be almost impossible not to encounter at least one aggressive, confrontational teacher. I have been on the receiving end of more than one, both in Cuba and in the United States, and have made a conscious choice not to allow anyone to damage my confidence in myself or my love for the art of music. If studying with a certain teacher is making you feel bad about yourself, find another teacher.

This chapter has been just a brief overview of the drums, their history, the practices surrounding them, and the issues related to their study. There is much more to learn and everyone's experience will be different. Batá drumming is rhythmically and melodically complicated. Its relationship to the many songs and dances of Santeria is intricate and challenging. Its role in the ceremony is fundamental to manifesting the physical presence of the gods whose worshippers call to them. It is the power that draws the orishas to earth, bringing to life the stories of the gods which their believers use to guide their lives to health and happiness.

As with any religion, one does not have to join to appreciate what it has to teach us. Some drummers enjoy the musical challenge while discounting its spiritual aspect. Others balance the music against the religion, respecting both as a friend to the tradition. Still others join the fold, choosing to embrace the spirit of the drums as a gateway to a direct experience of the divine. Whichever you choose is valid as long as you do not denigrate the choices of others. Each of us brings our own dynamic to the music, and each of us has a viewpoint worthy of the respect of others. Drum the way your head and heart tell you, and allow others to do the same.

Chapter Eight

Musical Form and Structure

> For the negro all orality is like a word that has no syllable, all sonority can be as music that has no note; for him all sound is the voice and tone of life, and his art seeks to comprehend, to represent all life, all his colloquy with the cosmos, and with its ineffable mystery.
>
> Fernando Ortiz
> *La Africanía de la Música Folklorica de Cuba*

I have attended many Santeria ceremonies since beginning my studies with Alejandro. They are always different and a real adventure.

On one trip, I had just arrived in Havana, still holding my suitcases, when Alejandro pulled up in a car. "Get in," he said, "we're late." An hour later, we were in an area called *Los Pinos* at a lavish party where the entire neighborhood was celebrating. I spent the evening leaning in through a window, watching the ceremony as the sun set. The people around me sang the songs and poured rum for us all as the celebration stretched into the night. I got home very late—hungry, thirsty, and happy—lucky to have spent my first night there, with the people drumming, singing, and dancing at the edge of the city.

Another time, Alejandro told me he would pick us up at one o'clock in the afternoon. By three o'clock the last of my companions had given up, but I was still there at four when he arrived asking where everyone had gone. An hour later, I was in the neighborhood called *Cerro*, behind the stadium where the *Industriales* play baseball. When we arrived I was surprised to see two sets of batá drums and even more surprised to be shaking hands with the legendary batalero, Papo Angarica. That night, Alejandro and Papo's groups played together (Alejandro told me the client thought more sound would draw more attention from the orishas). The two leaders took turns at the calls and variations followed closely by both groups. It was a master class on how great drummers create music together. Of course, that was the night I forgot my tape recorder.

Some ceremonies can be dark and portentous, like the one for Obatalá where the orisha himself dragged me into a back room to tell me of dangers to myself and my family. Others are happy, like the one for Eleguá, a children's party, where Alejandro caught me outside, swamped in kids, teaching them English when I should have been inside studying the music.

The structure of the ceremony depends on the orisha and the occasion, but the character of the ceremony depends on the client, the neighborhood, and the drummers. And, oh yes, the number of foreigners. I was at a ceremony in Matanzas where the client, wishing to show off, invited herds of tourists who ruined the sacred intent of the ceremony by pushing themselves forward to take pictures and sticking microphones in front of the drummers. Disgusted, most of the neighbors left early.

So while many factors can influence the character of the ceremony, its structure is set by the religious requirements of the occasion and by the nature of the orisha to whom it is dedicated. But whatever its purpose, there is an underlying format which most ceremonies follow.

What is a toque?

The word *toque* has at least two different meanings. The more general definition refers to the ceremony as a whole. Also called a *tambor* (literally, drum or drumming), a toque is a "musical/rhythmic performance" (Moore, 2006:197). There are different types of Santeria toques which use various songs and dances, and different percussion groups, including bembé, chequeré, cajón, iyesá, and most commonly, batá, depending on the orisha to whom it is dedicated and the purpose of the ceremony.

Alejandro calls the batá toque "Ceremony of the Sanctified Drum" (*la ceremonia del tambor de fundamento*). The normal instrumentation is the three drums, an acheré, a lead singer called the *akpuón*, and a chorus, called the *ankorí*, which usually consists of everybody at the ceremony who knows the songs. Since a ceremony can last as long as five hours, some groups bring four or more drummers and an extra akpuón as well, so the drummers and singers can rotate out of the group and rest.

Toques are held for a variety of reasons: to initiate new members, to celebrate the anniversary of one's initiation, and to honor an orisha on its Saints' day, among others. They are held throughout the year, but some months, December in particular, are busier than others.

The more specific definition of toque is as a percussive set-piece or salute to an orisha. Its underlying concept is not easily defined. It is not just a rhythm. In even the simplest toque there are at least three rhythms (one for each drum), and in the more complicated ones there are many sections with different basic rhythms and many variations. To call it a rhythm would be an oversimplification.

A toque is not quite a song, either, yet the patterns are melodies that may call the orisha's name and extol its spiritual paths. Sometimes, the iyá repeatedly speaks the words of the toque (Olumbanshé, for example) while the akpuón sings a separate but related song (Barasuayu) over it. The akpuón tells the story and the ankorí sings the refrain while the iyá's variations comment from underneath.

The different rhythms have their own meanings—words that can be seen as sentences or, in the case of the longer toques, as paragraphs. Some are prayers, some are calls. Others, Ñongo and Chachalukafú for example, are utility patterns used with different songs and toques. I point this out because some students become confused thinking that each orisha has only one toque. While some toques are dedicated exclusively to one orisha, there is more than one toque for each. Various toques accompany different songs, and some patterns are used in songs to different orishas. Remembering what toque goes with which of the many orisha songs is one of the biggest challenges for any batá drummer.

Each toque has a name, some as simple as that of the orisha to whom it is dedicated. Some are prayers, called *rezos*. In others, the iyá pattern repeats a ritual phrase, the drum speaking the words by which it is known.

Toques vary considerably in structure, length, and technical difficulty. Some are short and simple, others are long and complicated, and can become extremely fast. They are structured in sections (Alejandro calls them sequences), each representing a *camino*, or spiritual path, for that orisha.

So a toque is a specific group of related rhythms, structured in sections. These toques are then grouped in sets called *orus*. In each oru the toques are arranged in a specific order which can be altered depending on the occasion. There are three orus in the Ceremony of the Sanctified Drum. Having said that, it is important to understand that there is a great deal of variation within this structure. Ceremonies to different orishas and on different occasions will vary considerably in length and character, so the following should be viewed as a very general outline.

The Oru Seco

The first part of the Ceremony of the Sanctified Drum is called the Oru Seco. The word *seco*, "dry" in Spanish, means that the batá drummers play alone with no song or dance. (It is also sometimes referred to in the literature as the *oru de igbodú* but I have never heard that term used in the Havana Santeria community, so I think it has fallen into disuse.) The Oru Seco opens the batá ceremonies as a supplication to the orishas to attend and participate.

The Oru Seco is performed only on batá. There are twenty-two toques in the Oru Seco, more or less, beginning with Eleguá, the gatekeeper and guardian of the spiritual pathways. The actual number of toques can vary, depending on the ceremony, and can sometimes be reduced.

The basic toque order for the Oru Seco (while there are others) in this book is:

1. La Topa   (Eleguá)
2. Ogundere   (Ogún)
3. Agueré Ochosi   (Ochosi)
4. Imbaloke   (also Ochosi)
5. Inle
6. Iyakotá   (Babalú Ayé)
7. San Lazaro   (also Babalú Ayé)
8. Osain
9. Ósun
10. Obatalá
11a. Dadá
11b. Óke
12. Agayú
13. Titilaro/Meta (Changó)
14. Orisha Oko
15. Ibeyi
16. Yeguá
17. Oyá
18. Aro   (Yemayá)
19. Rezo de Ochún (Ochún)
20. Obba
21. Orunla
22. Oduwa

The Oru Cantado

The second section of the Ceremony of the Sanctified Drum is the *oru cantado*, or sung oru. (In the literature, it is also called the *oru de eyá aranla*—— the term *eyá aranla* means living room, which is where this part of the ceremony is often held—but I have never heard this term used by the Santeria community in Havana.) This central part of the ceremony contains drumming, songs, and dances which honor the orishas. The order of the songs and toques is similar to the Oru Seco, but here the drums play toques to accompany songs whose order and number can vary widely depending on the situation. So the events and structure of the Oru Cantado can vary depending on the nature of the orisha to whom it is dedicated and on the purpose of the ceremony.

Alejandro gave me two basic forms of the Oru Cantado:

1. Eleguá
2. Ogún
3. Ochosi
4. Inle
5. Babalú Ayé
6. Orisha Oko
7. Dadá
8. Ogüe
9. Ibeyi
10. Osain
11. Agayú
12. Changó
13. Obatalá
14. Obba
15. Yeguá
16. Oyá
17. Yemayá
18. Ochún
19. Orula
20. Oduwa

Then the last song is sung to *el ángel de la guardia*. In some casa templos they do not sing to Oduwa.

Other form:

1. Eleguá
2. Ogún
3. Ochosi
4. Inle
5. Orisha Oko
6. Babalú Ayé
7. Osain
8. Dadá
9. Ogüe
10. Ibeyi
11. Agayú

12. Changó
13. Obatalá
14. Obba
15. Yeguá
16. Oyá
17. Yemayá
18. Ochún
19. Orula
20. Oduwa

After Oduwa, they sing to *el ángel de la guardia* or to the orisha for whom the ceremony is dedicated.

The next section, the *wemilere*, is thought to be separate by most people, but Alejandro seems to consider it as connected to the Oru Cantado. While orisha possession can occur anytime during the ceremony, this more loosely structured section of song, dance, and drumming facilitates possession, allowing more time for this essential connection between the believers and their gods.

The Oru Égun

The last section of the Ceremony of the Sanctified Drum is the *oru égun*. The égun (ancestors) are the spirits of the dead. Also called the *cierre*, or closing, this oru is a shorter set of batá toques which return the gods and spirits to the heavens.

1. Toque a Égun
2. Toque Alaro (one section of this toque)
3. Cancán de Égun
4. Oyá bi iku
5. Babalú Ayé (Iyakotá and Babalú Ayé)
6. Osain
7. Yeguá
8. Yemayá (Aro)

After the Oru Égun they sing two songs to close the ceremony:

Canto a Eleguá
Olókun

The role of the drums is to call to the orishas, to accompany their songs and dances, to facilitate trance/possession, to speak in the voices of the gods, and to send them back to the sky when the ceremony ends. So how the drums accomplish their responsibilities depends on the situation. The iyá plays variations which reproduce Lucumí speech while leading the itótele and okónkolo through the sections of a toque, and from one toque to the next, following the songs and dances of the ceremony. Form follows function in Santeria, creating an ever-shifting maze of spiritual expression, but within this complex range of choices there are specific mechanisms for moving the music through the ceremony.

Calls, Conversations, and Transitions

A call (*llamada*) is a rhythmic pattern that signals a change in the toque. Always made by the iyá player, a call can start the toque, ask for a response, signal a transition between sections, start a conversation, or indicate a transition to the next toque. A call can be a unique rhythm played only once, or the basic pattern for the next section, depending on the toque structure.

The most basic type is a simple call and response. The iyá drummer plays a call that is answered by the itótele or occasionally by the okónkolo. For example, the last section of Osain, called Obanlá, contains a broken-triplet call played on iyá that requires an eighth-note response pattern from the itótele. Alejandro often teaches Obanlá as the first pattern new students learn to give them a sense of call and response.

The most important call and response is the one I think of as ¡*Pare!* (Stop!). It is an open followed by a muff (see Chapter Nine for a description on the various tones). (Michael Spiro tells me that this is Lucumí, *di dé*, or "stand up," while Mikael Ringquist says, "I was taught that the phrase is *agó*, 'Excuse me, make way.' ") When the iyá player makes this call he is usually signaling the other drummers to stop (although it is also used during Meta to signal the end of a sequence). Used in performance to signal the end of a toque, it can also be played during rehearsal to stop the group during a toque. Alejandro often uses this call to stop us so he can explain a problem. I have included it at the end of the Oyá transcription as an example.

The movements into, within, and between sections are signaled by initial, transitional, and conversational calls. The initial call signals the beginning of the toque. Each call is distinct and only for that particular toque. One of the best known and most recognizable is the call into La Topa, the first toque of the Oru Seco. Its unique, out-of-sync pattern is often the very first heard by listeners who are new to batá. During the Oru Cantado, the akpuón calls the beginning of a song, followed by the iyá player calling in the drums, but in the Oru Seco the iyá always makes the initial call into a toque.

The transitional call signals the beginning of the next section. Depending on the toque, it can be either a one-time rhythm, the basic pattern for the next section, a call and response, or a combination of the above. The call from section four to section five of La Topa is a good example. By adding the triplet at the end of the pattern, the iyá is signaling the section change to the okónkolo and itótele.

A conversation (*lengua*) is an abrupt and sometimes prolonged exchange between the iyá and itótele. Their length and complexity vary, but conversations contrast sharply with the basic rhythm. The okónkolo usually, but not always, plays the same pattern during the conversation, although its rhythm may change from section to section. The conversational call signals the beginning of a conversation. For instance, there is conversation in section one of Yeguá. Called by the iyá, it is played three times before returning to the basic rhythm.

Transitions between toques can be signaled by a brief pause, by a direct call into the next toque, or by a transition called a *viro* (or *vuelta*). The most distinct viros are more conversation-like and a little longer than a normal call. Starting at the end of one toque, they transform themselves into the next. A good example is the viro from Orisha Oko to Ibeyi.

Each toque is unique and beautiful in its own way. Each reflects the character and spiritual power of the god it represents. Old orishas walk slowly, others wield iron or dance playfully. Their different natures are manifested in the tempos of their music, in the sections that follow their pathways, and in the rhythms that extol their powers. Each toque is a musical portrait, and the relationships between toques are like those between the orishas: similar or contrasting, close together or far apart. By learning the larger structures and the smaller calls that move the music, one can begin to grasp the world of the orishas and the people who love them, and one does not have to be a believer to appreciate the wisdom to be found there.

Every batá student starts by learning a rhythm, then another. With time and effort one begins to piece together the great jigsaw puzzle of how they fit together, how they flow from one to the next, and how they join with the songs and follow the dances that make up the ceremonies which manifest the spiritual world from which they come.

The religious beliefs and practices of Santeria are extensive and intricate. Its original form has been influenced by other religions, both African and European. While some knowledge has been lost, Santeria has drawn on new inspirations and created new meaning which continues to evolve through time and across distance. This process is ongoing and multilayered, so although Santeria's core belief systems are generally consistent, its rites and practices vary both regionally and from temple to temple.

So does its music. Just as the ceremonial structures can change depending on the necessities of the event and the practices of that temple, so does the role and repertoire of the songs and drumming. Some changes are small: if the ceremony is dedicated to Obatalá, the drummers may choose to add Rezo de Obatalá to the Oru Seco. Other changes are larger: the repertoire of songs in a ceremony depend on which orisha is being honored, altering the Oru Cantado. But it is important to understand that these different religious functions and attendant musical variations are accommodated within the larger structure of the ceremony itself.

The more one studies these issues the more complicated they seem. Beyond the daunting task of learning to play the batá toques—no small achievement in itself—looms the specific question of how to execute them in relation to the songs they accompany and the more general question of how those songs are ordered in the contexts of the various ceremonial alternatives. These questions are beyond the scope of this book (although I hope to address them in a later volume), but we can begin the task by looking at the specific structure and more limited range of variations found in the Oru Seco.

Chapter Nine

The Oru Seco

> The performance of an orú seco is a deep experience, as cerebral as the masterworks of your favorite Catholic contrapuntalist. Anyone who thinks African music is not intellectual will be silenced by this repertoire. This is head music. In this writer's opinion the orú, sung but especially dry, is the pinnacle of Cuban classical music.
>
> Ned Sublette

The toques of the Oru Seco are the central repertoire of batá drumming, and their mastery is the serious student's first major goal. They comprise approximately twenty-five percent of the toques played in Cuba, so there are many important patterns not found here, but because they contain all the fundamental structures of the music, they serve as a foundation for understanding the drumming, song, and dance of the larger ceremony of which it is only one part.

For those Cubans who grow up in a temple, there are traditional methods of learning these toques which pass the knowledge from one generation to the next. For those who learn them later, the teachers have adapted their methods to the requirements of Cuba's school system. For most of us who come from abroad, the process of learning the music demands that we modify and expand the process yet again if we hope to achieve any permanent gains.

The music of Santeria is an oral, or aural, tradition—written music is a foreign concept—and its inclusion requires adaptation from both student and teacher. Alejandro has many students, some far more advanced than I, but he tells me that I am the first to attempt the transcription of his Oru Seco in western notation (although others have done the same with their teachers). The transcription process has been an education (and a great source of amusement) for him, as well as for me. Writing the music down is essential for me (1) because I have a bad memory, (2) because I do not live in Cuba and do not have daily access to a teacher, and (3) so I can share the music with those who have not had the opportunity to travel there.

But while notation is useful, it also creates problems which must be transcended before the music can be mastered. These transcriptions are a rickety bridge which must be carefully crossed, a poor crutch that must be left behind before one can hear the music as it was conceived. It is only by memorizing the rhythms that one can leave the confining structures of the visual behind to experience the freedom of the living music itself. That having been said, it is even more important to understand the nature of the notational barrier in order to traverse it.

On Transcribing Music

There were no spelling standards in English until Samuel Johnson published *A Dictionary of the English Language* in 1755. The dictionary formalized the letter choices that were, until then, decided by the writer. Before the advent of the dictionary, there were many ways to spell the same word. It is similar with music. There is considerable variation within and between traditions. To transcribe folkloric music freezes it. No longer part of a breathing, evolving world of sound, but just little black dots on a page. You now have a static slice of a continuum. And, as with the written word, choice is lost by confining it to paper.

There are often errors or simplifications in transcriptions and many inflections that just cannot be written down. The transcriber also negates the influence of the performers themselves. Different players perform variations from different eras and places, or one performer may execute a rhythm differently depending on the ceremonial context. I have studied with different teachers who taught me the same rhythm, completely differently. Which is right? This kind of stuff can drive you crazy without a sense of humor and an understanding of the complexity of the subject. Given all this, it is impossible to publish some of these little black dots with any claim to definitiveness or accuracy.

Each transcription in this book is just one model among many, frozen and simplified. I have tried to present these patterns as Alejandro gave them to me, with some kind of context, and with a feeling for the history and character of the people who treasure them. But it is essential for anyone who wishes to play the batá knowledgeably to collect recordings of the music, to study the history of Cuba, to see the music performed, and to find a teacher. Do not rely on these little black dots. Journey to the people who make the music by using the transcriptions as a roadmap.

Imposing a written organizational structure on the Oru Seco is a subjective task. Simply naming the toques and numbering their order creates problems. Some people simply title each toque with the name of the orisha whom it salutes and, indeed, some toques (Oyá, for example) are named for their orisha, but some orishas have more than one toque in the Oru Seco (Iyakotá and San Lazaro are both dedicated to Babalú Aye). Other toques have names distinct from their orisha (Titilaro is dedicated to Changó). So, while using the orisha's name to identify the toque may be correct, it is imprecise and may leave a novice with the impression that there is only one toque for each orisha when in fact there are different toques that are used in differing contexts (La Topa and Olumbanshé are only two of the toques dedicated to Eleguá). Also, toques played for one orisha in the Oru Cantado may be used for another in the Oru Seco (Óke, for example). And some toques (Chachalukafú and Ñongo) are utility rhythms played in songs to many orishas. So while naming each toque and section may seem more complicated at the beginning, in the long run it should help the student place each pattern in its various roles in the larger context of the batá repertoire as a whole.

Alejandro says there are twenty-two toques in the Oru Seco, yet an objective analysis of the material produces a murkier scenario. Determining which should be numbered and which should be considered as part of the preceding toque based on their musical attributes puts one in conflict with the traditional numbering system.

For example, some toques (Rezo de Ochún) contain only one section. Others (Aro) contain as many as thirteen. Some toques borrow patterns from others (the second section of Aguéré Ochosi is similar to the second section of Iyesá, a toque not in the Oru Seco), or transition into others while still being considered as part of the same toque (Osain transitions into Obanlá, a toque usually associated with Obatalá), while Iyakotá and San Lazaro are both dedicated to Babalú Ayé and played together, but are counted separately. It would be more logical to number only those toques that have their own initial calls, or to number toques to each orisha separately, but within Alejandro's system that is not possible.

I have kept Alejandro's naming system and have added letters to the numbering system to differentiate between toques when clarification is needed. So they are titled and numbered more or less as he gave them to me. I have included the names of certain internal sections when Alejandro directed me to do so. Some are simply part of the toque, are direct or bridged transitions (see page 101), or are toques that can be played separately as well. A rhythm has a more precise identity if it has a name. Alejandro sees the toques as interrelated sentences that flow, one to the next, in various combinations. Since he does not write them down, their relationships are natural and obvious. But as I write them out I must make choices as to how they should be identified on paper. I have made these choices, as best I could, based on his system, but different arrangements can be, and are, made by others.

Adrian Coburg (2004) forgoes numbering altogether, and his toque order is different than the one given to me by Alejandro. This in itself is not surprising as different groups vary the order to some extent, but Coburg chose to separate patterns which Alejandro insists are part of the same toque. For example, Alejandro teaches La Topa as the first toque in the Oru Seco. He lists five sections ending with *apukenke*. Coburg lists "Elegba" as the first orisha in the Oru Seco but transcribes the patterns as *igbara ago/latopa*, then *agongo ago*, *bobo araye*, and *abukenke* as separate toques. This is not wrong, the patterns are very similar to those taught by Alejandro, it is just a different conceptual approach. Given the differences in order, spelling, conception, and the many divergent rhythmic variations between the two transcription sets, it becomes clear that flexibility and an acceptance of other player's versions are essential because there are many ways to conceptualize and perform this music.

The toques in this Oru Seco are my transcriptions of Alejandro's version of the patterns as he teaches them to his students, and should be understood as such. They are not, nor could they be, definitive. They are simplifications (1) because Alejandro chose what should be included from a larger repertoire of variations and (2) because I found it impossible to notate every touch in every pattern in every section of every toque. He also altered the touch combinations (but not the basic pattern) on certain toques as he played, leaving me wondering which to include. When I asked him, he said it was up to the player to choose for himself.

I have adopted, and adapted, this notational system for clarity, although performers accustomed to other systems probably will not agree. Two other notational systems in use now are box notation and customized note heads. Box notation is fine for teaching basic rhythms to people who do not read music, but it is too inflexible for notating complicated patterns and far too large on the page for long passages of improvisations. The two problems with customized note heads are that they require the performer to learn nonstandard symbols, and that different teachers creatively develop their own sets, forcing students to learn new symbols every time they go to a new teacher. I have tried to avoid these problems by making the notation in this book as clear and standardized as possible.

I cannot emphasize strongly enough that these transcriptions are not presented here as *the* way to play the rhythms, only a way (or one of the ways) that each rhythm is played, or transcribed, by a specific person. Many more and different ways can be found, and there are endless variations that have never been written down and that could never be fully notated.

Olavo Alén's book, *Pensamiento Musicológico*, pointed the way for me to understand more fully the limitations of musical notation. In the second essay he writes about the relative pitch relationships in Tumba Francesa and the difficulties of transcribing them into a standard tuning (2006: 98). This is also true in batá, and not only for the pitch. The rhythm, tempo, and meter, as well as the pitch, are all relative.

There is a lot of variation in the rhythms both in terms of note choice and feel. Different variations are executed depending on the context, for instance, which song is being sung with the toque. Different drummers know different variations. Some know more, some fewer. And the time-feel itself is an acquired skill, not learnable from reading the transcriptions.

Tempo varies depending on the context within which the toque is played. When a toque is played for different songs, the tempo will vary. The initial tempo also depends to some extent on what came before, and the ending tempo may vary slightly depending on what is coming next.

Pitch is very relative. While the akpuón and coro seek a certain sonic texture, the actual pitches, as well as the key of the tune, will shift within certain parameters during the performance. Also, the tuning of the drums varies from group to group, from night to night, and during a performance.

The meter may be in some ways the most subjective aspect of the music. If it is polymetric, the transcriber has to make a series of choices as to how to write it down. Often, one drum is in duple meter while another is in triple. The transcriber can choose to notate it either way. Both can be right but both can cause problems. Some rhythms can be transcribed differently but sound the same, or be written the same yet sound differently, and this is as much a metrical problem as a rhythmic one. For instance, an okónkolo drummer playing the ki la pattern may feel it in six-eight if he hears it in relation to the rhythm of the iyá, but he might also feel it as a dotted eighth and a sixteenth if he hears it in relation to the rhythm of the itótele. It is generally useless to ask Alejandro about problems like this because he is happy to hear it played either way.

This brings up two issues:

1. The fact that there is variation in the traditional musical architecture does not mean you can do anything you want with it. All the variables in the orisha song and drumming traditions are executed within a range of practical standards which are unmistakably obvious to people who know the music. To step beyond them, either through ignorance or hubris will not endear you to people who truly value the music.

2. The fact that it is written in standard notation does not mean that you can apply our euro-traditional pitch and rhythm standards to the music. If the akpuón were to sing *bel canto* and the coro in perfect, western harmony, the music would be ruined. One of the plagues computers have brought to music is the absolute quantization of both rhythm and pitch. People are so used to standard tunings and drum-machine pulses that any variation sounds wrong. This marginalizes a whole range of possibilities that would (and used to) make our music more interesting sounding.

The fine line one must walk between these poles is an artistic path, and not one that can be easily or definitively resolved. Only by truly knowing the music in the context of the people who play it can one hope to become part of the living tradition itself.

Playing Techniques

In Havana-style batá drumming, the group should be arranged with the iyá player in the middle, the okónkolo player stage right, and the itótele player stage left.

Lay the drum horizontally across your lap. Tie the external strap, if there is one, around your legs so the drum does not slip. Players will sometimes cross their feet to support the drum, but it is bad form to put one foot up on your knee. Keep them on the floor.

Right-handers should play the enú with the right hand and the chachá with the left. Left-handers should reverse the drum so they can play the enú with the left.

The playing spot depends on which drum you are playing and the size of your hand. Generally, the larger the drum the closer to the center you play. Alejandro plays the enú of the iyá with his hand in the lower middle of the drum. It may be a while before you can get a good sound that far in, but try to keep as much of your hand as possible on the drum. Play the enú of the itótele more or less where you would play on a conga drum, that is, with the base of your fingers on the rim on the drum. Play the enú of the okónkolo more or less where you would play on bongos, that is, the length of your fingers only. Playing the chachá is similar on all the drums. Try to keep as much of your hand as possible on the drumhead, resting your palm on the rim, but allow the head to ring when struck.

Remember, the batá group plays a compound melody. That is, the melody is created by the interplay between the drums—open tones generally land on different beats—so pay attention to their placement in relation to those of the other players. Each separate rhythm is only part of the melody, so knowing your pattern is not enough. You must hear it as part of the larger melody. Do not hit the open tones too hard as this distorts the sound, but strive instead to produce a clear, ringing pitch that matches those of the other players. This will result in smooth, even sounding melodies.

Body language and eye contact are very important when playing batá. Just as a violinist will convey his intentions to the pianist without speaking, so must the iyá player signal any impending changes to the rest of the group. This is especially important when making direct transitions from one section to another. Looking up and indicating a coming change with your body motion will go a long way toward helping the others make the change with you. Do not leave them guessing. Feed them the change so that there is no question of when it comes.

The tempos are very important. While there is some latitude and some toques speed up during the performance, be sure to start the toque at the tempo indicated in the score. The iyá player establishes the initial tempo with his call and controls the tempo throughout the toque. The others follow.

When learning a new toque, switch drums so each player can learn all the rhythms, but when preparing for a performance it is better to stay on one drum so you can memorize your part. Do not use the transcriptions when performing. Once memorized, the music will change character, become freer, and the drums will begin to sing.

One Last Warning About Time Feel

Let me emphasize, yet again, that these transcriptions are only an approximation of the living music. It is not only polymetric and polyrhythmic, but it is, as Michael Spiro puts it, "in fix."

> In western music, there is a clear distinction between various types of subdivisions. Specifically, divisions of the beat into two, three, or four subdivisions (eighths, triples, and sixteenths, respectively) are clearly labeled as different kinds of rhythms. But a major difficulty for those of us raised in Western cultures is that in Afro-centric musics the rhythmic distinction between three subdivisions per beat and four subdivisions per beat (triple vs. duple), is frequently blurred. In several cases, the difference does not exist at all—there is a completely "new" kind of subdivision at work. [ ] Instead of being evenly spaced, certain subdivisions are pushed closer together, which makes the time feel blurry. [ ] I call this "averaging" of rhythm between a four and six feel, "fix," (**Four** and **Six**), and it is an **essential** component of learning to swing in these styles (38).

Still not clear? While those notes played on the beat remain where they are, the notes played in between are shifted slightly closer to, or farther from, the pulse to flatten out the rhythm. Duples will hint at being triples and triples will hint at being duples. For example, in a broken triplet the second note can be played slightly early, in effect making the rhythm almost a duplet. The "fix" varies slightly from rhythm to rhythm, toque to toque, group to group, and city to city. It creates ambiguity. By sliding the rhythm slightly forward or back, the group can hint at being in a different meter. By shifting the rhythms more overtly, the group can actually change the meter of the toque, which is one reason why you will hear different versions of a toque that are literally the same rhythms but in different meters. For those of us who seek to know *the* way to play a rhythm, this can be very disconcerting. There is often more than one right way, so get used to it.

Even before I understood the concept of "fix" I was instinctively trying to account for it in the transcriptions. There are lots of duplets in the triple meter toques and triplets in the duple meter toques. These are my attempts to notate various ambiguities. In the cases of certain calls, I could not find a way to transcribe them in "fix" so you must listen to recordings and watch other players to get a sense of how to bend the patterns into "fix."

The limitations of western notation, combined with the "fix," create a lot of possibilities for executing the rhythms on the page. Some are more stylistically correct than others so listen to the music to get a sense of the feel, but understand also that there is no *one* definitive way to play these rhythms. There is only better and worse, more knowledgeable and less. That is why, in the end, it is art not science.

Notation Key

There are four types of strokes in this Oru Seco: open, muff, slap, and touch.

o   Open

The open (*abierto*) is played only on the enú. It is the first of the two melody strokes. A well-played open has a rich, ringing, fundamental pitch with little overtone. Some players produce it with a direct, straight-on stroke, others rotate their arm in a downward doorknob motion using the index finger as the axis. Rest your palm on the rim after hitting the drum but let the drumhead ring.

m   Muff

The muff, or half-open (*presionado*), is played only on the enú. The muff is not a dead stroke. The goal is to raise its pitch while retaining some of the tone. Think of it as a sharped note. It is produced by striking the drum then keeping your palm and fingers in contact with the drumhead, pressing slightly to bend the tone upwards. It is the combinations of open and muff tones that reproduce Lucumi speech, so strive to produce distinctive, consistent pitches that will "speak the drum."

s   Slap

The slap (*tapado*) is played only on the chachá, and every stroke on the chachá should be a slap or a touch. It is similar to a slap on congas in that the hand is slightly curled so that the tips of the fingers strike the drum first producing a high-pitched pop. All slaps on the chachá are open. Lift your fingers off the drumhead and let it ring. Whenever possible, press your other hand against the enú for support while striking the chachá.

t Touch.

The touch (*fantasma*) is played on both enú and chachá. Also called *una caida de dedos*, a drop of the fingers, it is a timekeeper, used to keep the hands in motion and the pattern even. Each player uses touches differently. Some use them more than others, and since they produce little sound, some transcribers omit them. I have included them in these transcriptions when they are an integral part of the pattern. They are indicated by a "t" and a smaller note head.

Note that there is also another type of stroke, called the *campaneo*. (Mikael Ringquist says that, "you hit the chachá with the fingers close to the edge, making a ringing sound as opposed to a slap sound.") Alejandro does not use this technique, so I have not included it in the notation key.

In the transcriptions, all notes on the enú are open unless otherwise indicated, and all notes on the chachá are slaps or touches.

I have tried to give a sense of the flexibility of the musical structures by notating many sections as open vamps within which the performers can play the variations and conversations ad lib until called into the next section. Many have more than one road map for going from one section to the next, and some of these choices are indicated in the transcription notes at the beginning of each toque or in the score itself, but it would be impossible to include every possible option and variation, so keep your mind open and expect the unexpected when playing with others.

Final Thoughts

These transcriptions by themselves are not sufficient to master the batá. They are rough, incomplete, and inaccurate approximations of a much more complex repertoire of rhythms. Think of them as lead sheets. Just knowing the basic chords and melody of a tune is not nearly sufficient to play it with professional musicians. Different musicians change the chords, the feel, and sometimes the form of a tune. They bring different concepts and contexts that must be mastered over and over until that tune is enriched with many things that cannot be found in the bare bones of a lead sheet. It is the same with batá. Bataleros play and feel and travel through the music as an ever-changing language, each following his own path. To travel with them you must have a strong grasp of the music as it flows like conversation. No two are ever the same.

Also, the relationship between the toques and the songs they accompany is fundamental to any approach to this music. If one does not know the songs and dances, one cannot play the toques correctly (as I can personally attest from my lessons with the master bataleros who have tried, as patiently as possible, to point me in the right direction). Connecting these rhythms to the songs is perhaps the hardest part of a student's training. But unfortunately, that is outside the scope of this book, so use these transcriptions as a starting point to enter a much larger world where the static dots on these pages will be left behind in the swirling eddies of music as a living language.

Chapter Ten

Musical Transcriptions of the Oru Seco

Some pages have been left blank to facilitate page turns.

1

La Topa

The first toque of the Oru Seco is dedicated to Eleguá. It has five sections and five calls. Call 2 is within Section 1 and is not a transition. It only requires a response from the itótele and may be played more than once. There is a direct transition into and out of Section 2, requiring only a slight change in the iyá pattern, that leads back to Section 1. Call 3 leads into Section 3. Call 4 leads into Section 4. Call 5 leads into Section 5, Apukenke. La Topa segues directly into Ogundere at the end of Section 5 when the iyá player makes the initial call at the new tempo into that toque.

La Topa, 2

Call 2 (ad lib. May be played more than once)

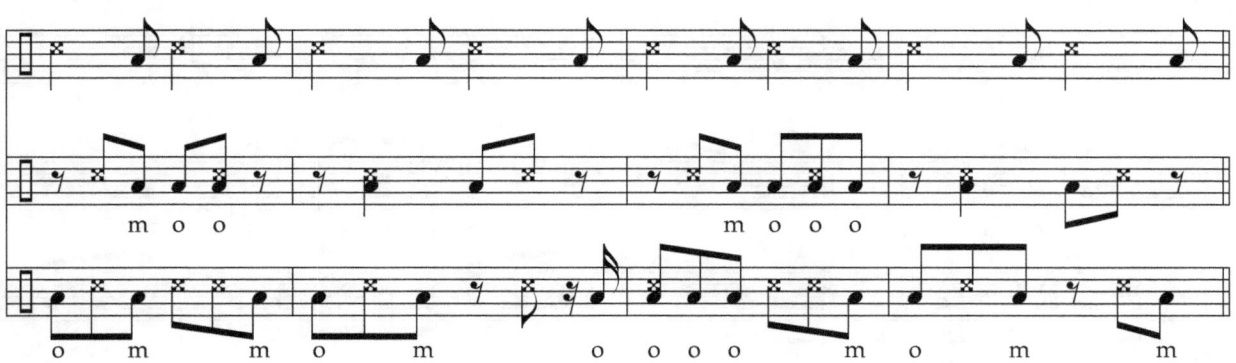

Section 1   Transition to Section 2

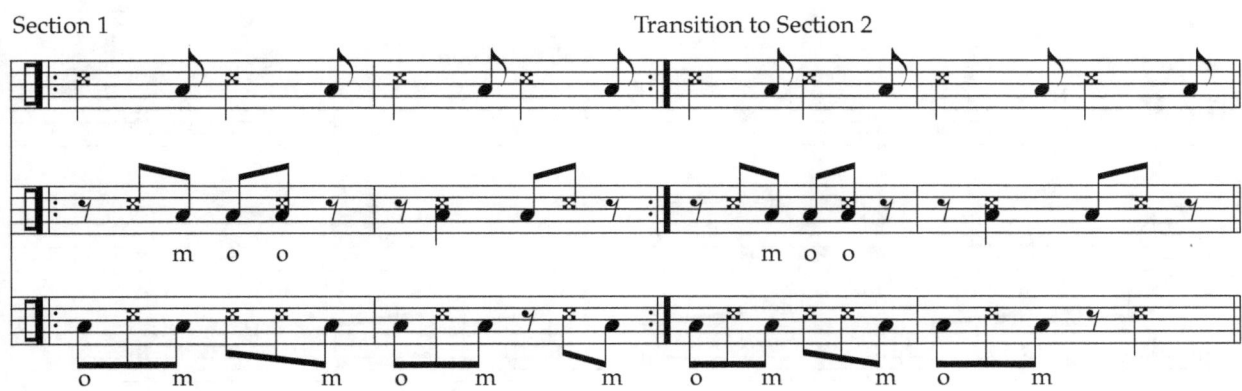

Section 2   Section 1

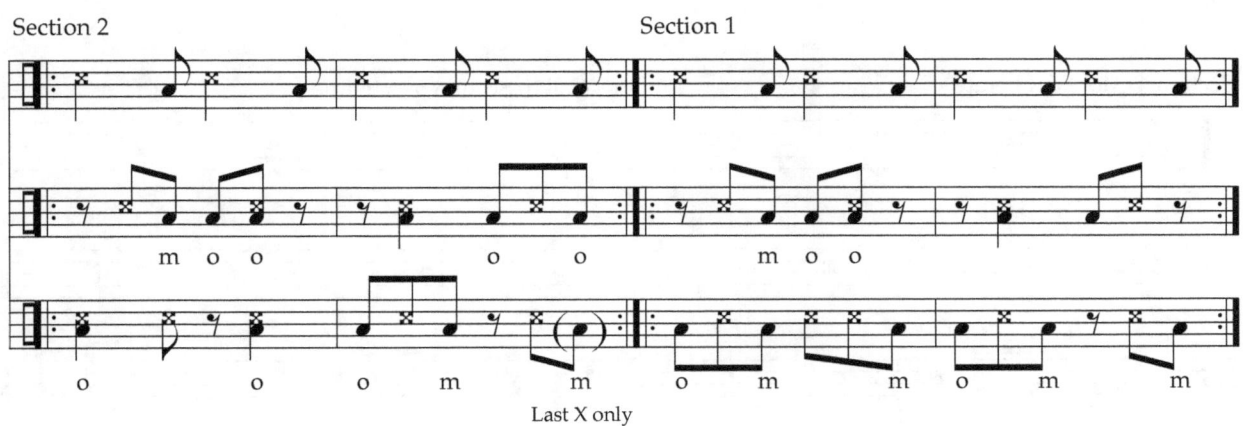

Last X only

La Topa, 3

Call to Section 3

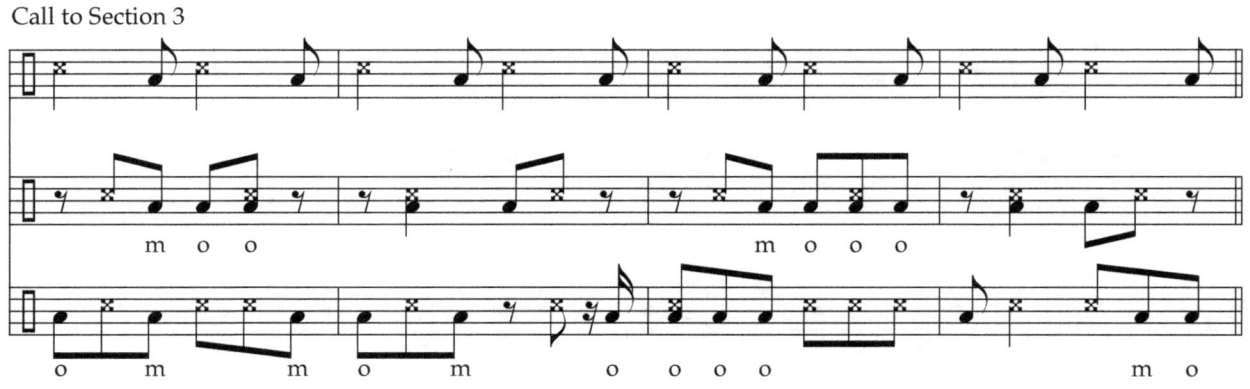

Section 3   Call to Section 4

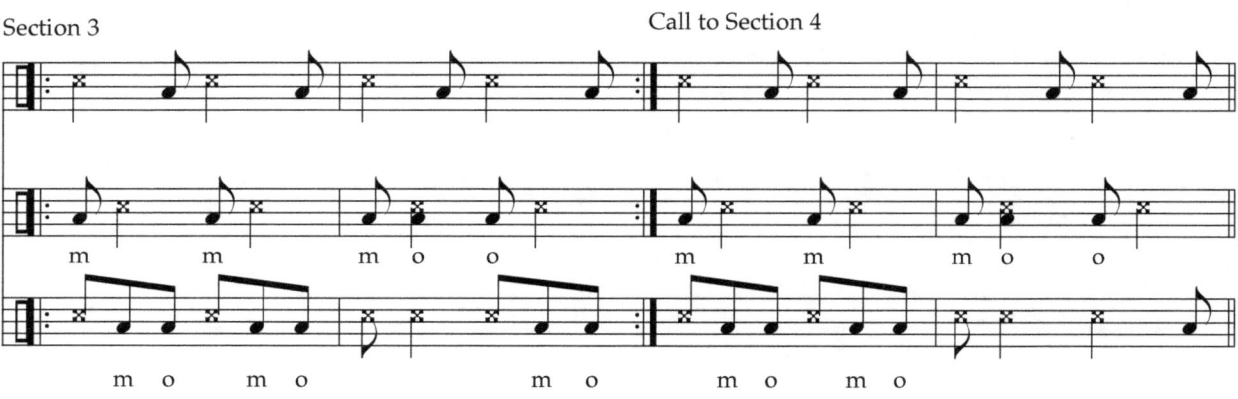

Section 4. More deliberate   Call to Section 5. A tempo

115

Section 5. Apukenke

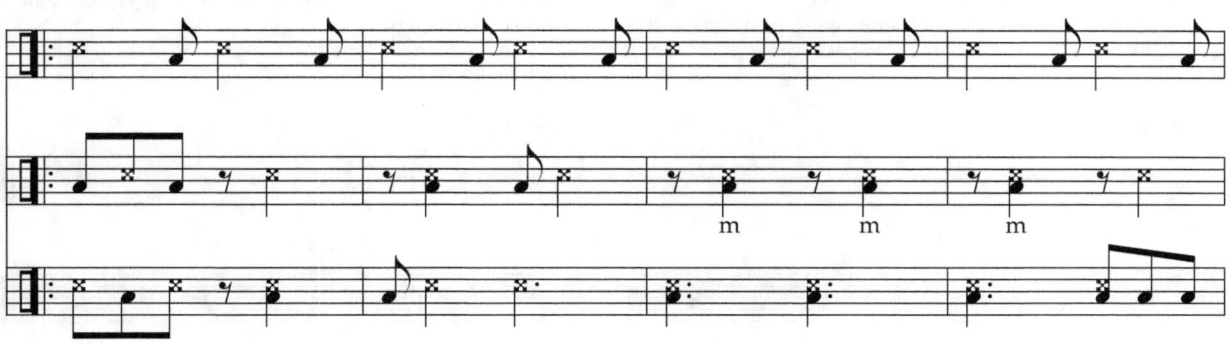

La Topa segues directly into Ogundere.

2 Ogundere

The second toque is dedicated to Ogún. It has two sections. After the initial call, the iyá performs two sets of variations listed and played in ascending order. When ready, the iyá signals the transition into Section 2 by changing to its basic pattern. The itótele changes to its Section 2 pattern immediately. There is one iyá variation included in Section 2. When ready, the iyá returns the group to Section 1 by reverting to its basic pattern. The toque ends when the iyá plays the initial call into Agueré Ochosi.

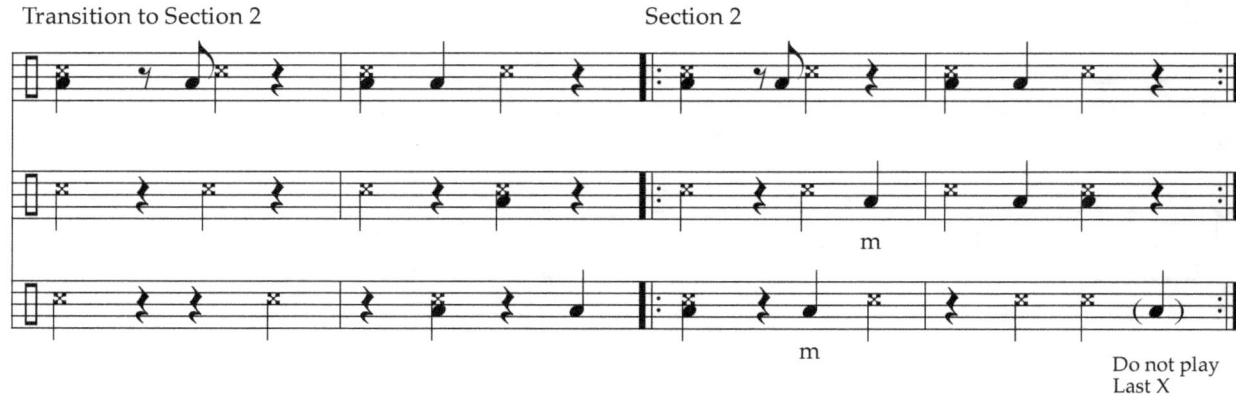

Ogundere, Iyá Variations

The variations in Section 1 can be repeated ad lib but must be played in ascending order. For instance, you can play Basic, V1, V2, Basic, V1 but not Basic, V2, V1.

Section 1 Variations

Set 1

Go back to Basic before playing Set 2. Return to Basic between variations by leaving out last note of fourth bar of each variation then call into next variation when ready. Variations must be played in ascending order.

Set 2

Section 2 Variation

Agueré Ochosi

The third toque is dedicated to Ochosi. It has eight sections and five calls. The initial call establishes the tempo. There is a direct transition into and out of Section 2. Section 3 is the same as Section 1. Call 2 leads to Section 4. Call 3 leads to Section 5, Call 4 to Section 6. Call 5 is not traditional, but Alejandro includes it to strengthen the transition into Section 7, whose tempo is a little faster. Section 7 is played three times then transitions directly into Section 8. Note that the Call in Section 7 is notated on the fourth time through the basic pattern. In fact, this can be played ad lib but after the third time you must transition into Section 8. Agueré Ochosi segues directly into Imbaloke at the end of Section 8 when the iyá player makes the initial call into that toque.

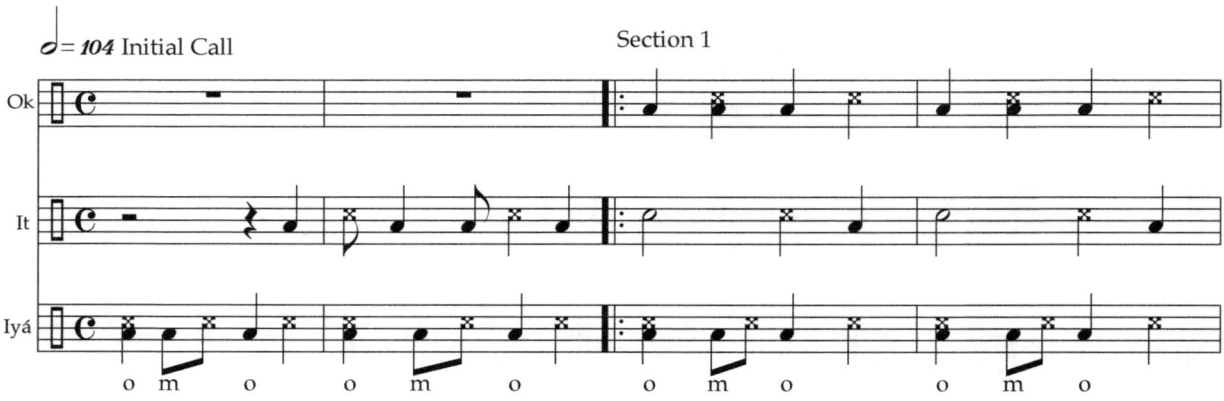

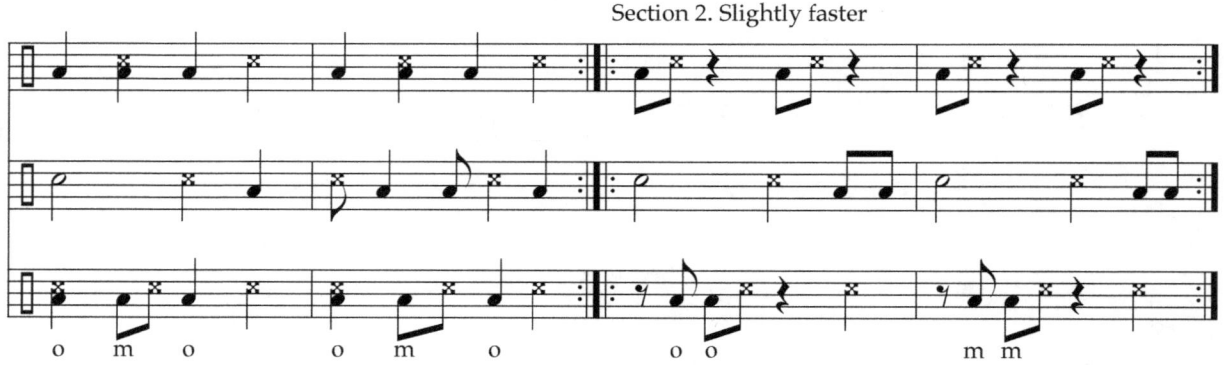

Aguaré Ochosi, 2

Section 3. Tempo 1

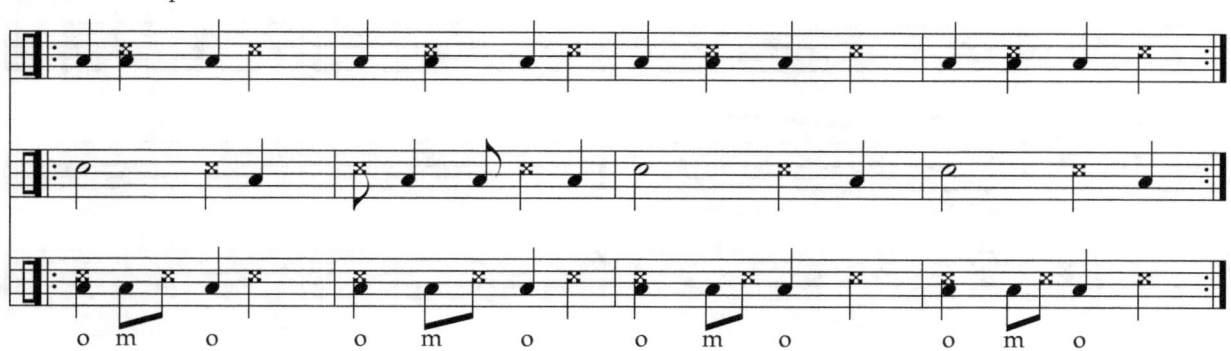

Call to Section 4

Section 4. Slightly faster   Variation

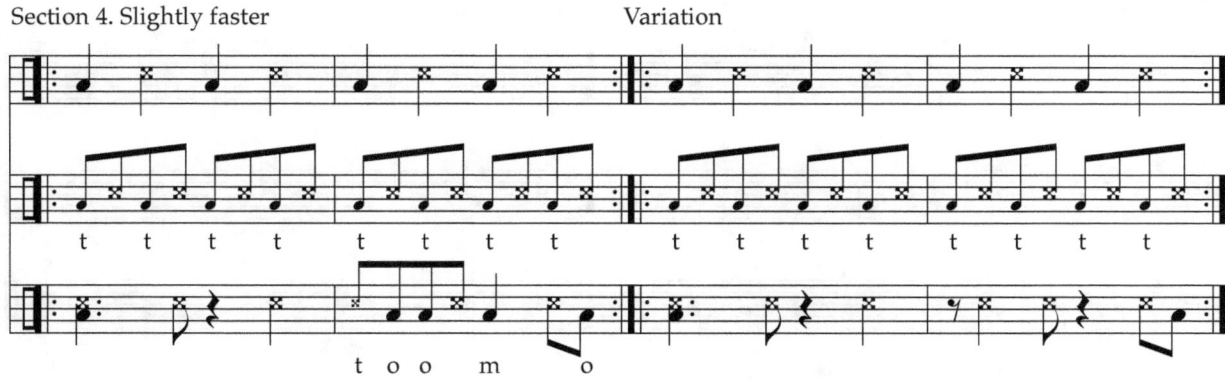

Agueré Ochosi, 3

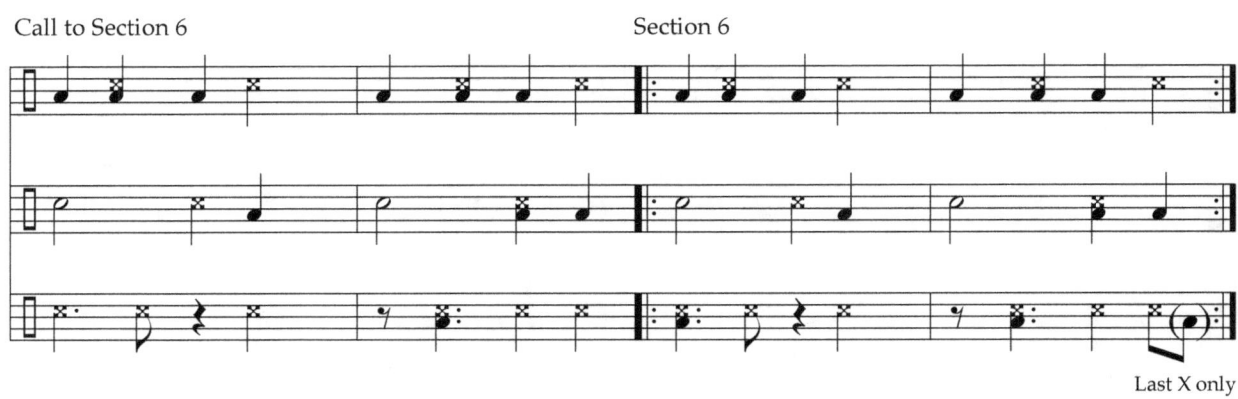

Last X only

* This call is not in the traditional version but can be added to make the transition stronger.

Agueré Ochosi, 4

Play 3X then go to Section 8

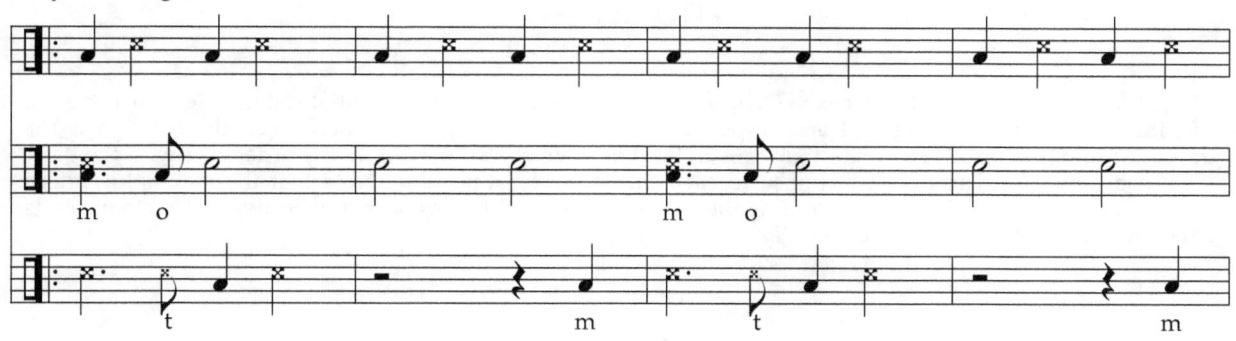

Call (ad lib, see intro notes)

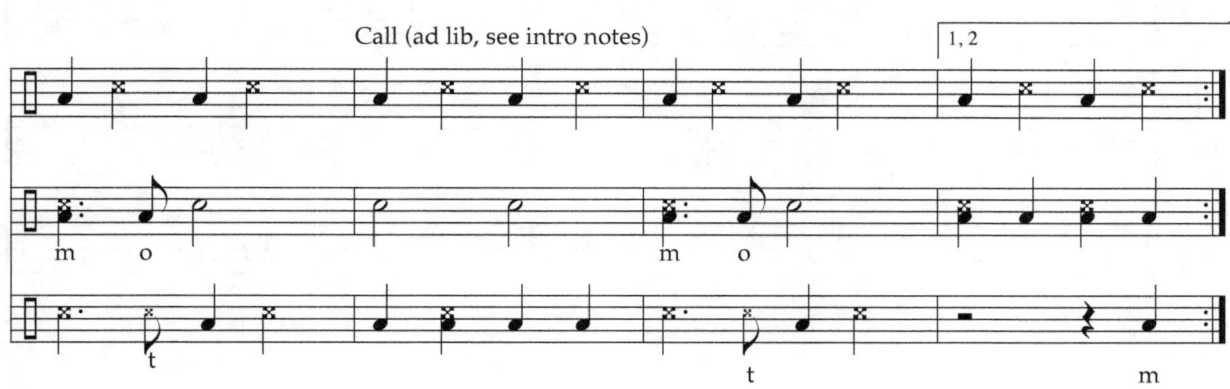

Section 8

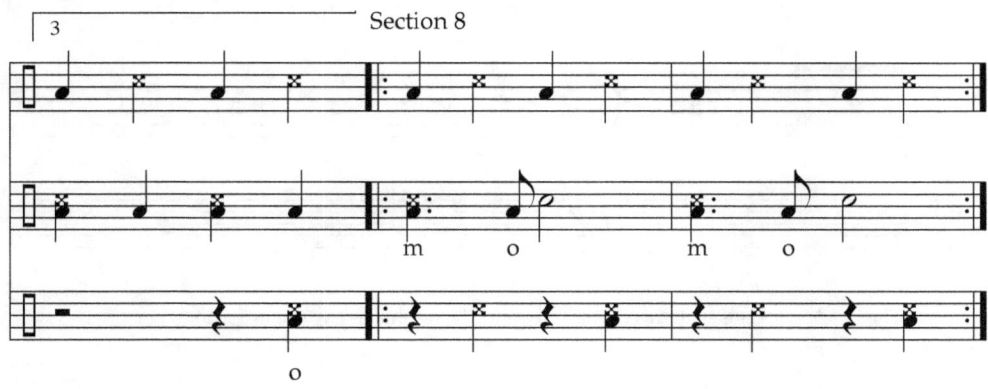

4

Imbaloke

The fourth toque is also dedicated to Ochosi. It has two sections. After the initial call into Section 1, the iyá and itótele perform an ad lib call and response several times during the section. Then the iyá signals the transition into Section 2. There are four calls in Section 2 which can played in any order and with the basic pattern in between. The itótele response to each call is always the same. Note that the okónkolo pattern changes during Section 2. After performing the call set, the iyá transitions back into Section 1. This toque ends when the iyá makes the initial call at a slower tempo into Inle.

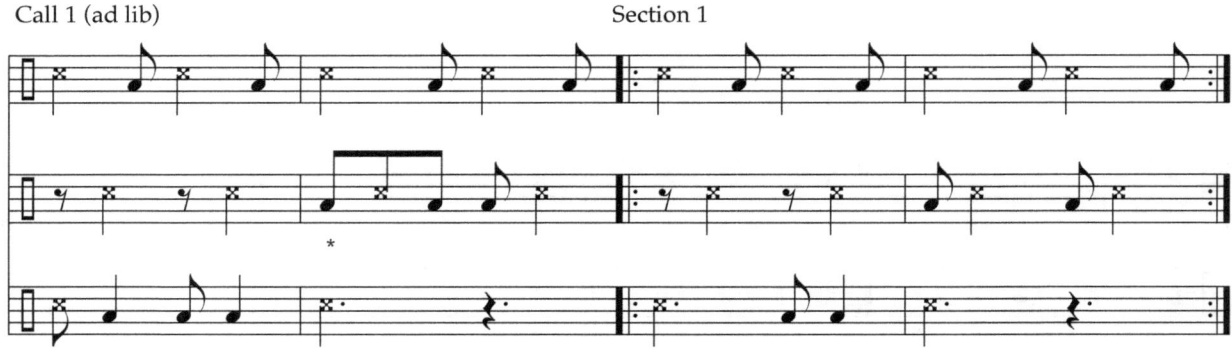

* The itotele responds with this rhythm any time the iyá makes any call in Sections 1 or 2.

Imbaloke, 2

Transition to Section 2   Section 2 (Basic)

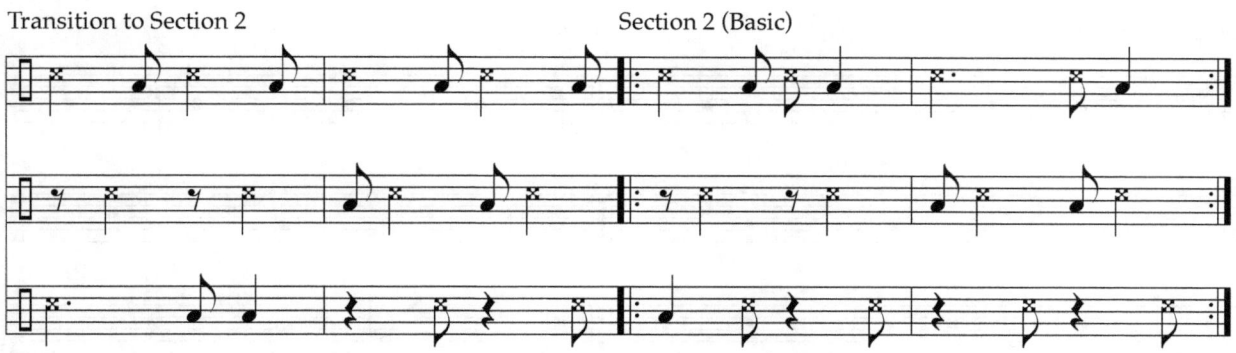

Call 2**   Call 3

** The iyá can play these calls in any order and with the Section 2 Basic in between. When the iyá calls, the itotele answers. When ready, play Section 2 Basic then return to Section 1.

Call 4   Call 5

Imbaloke, 3

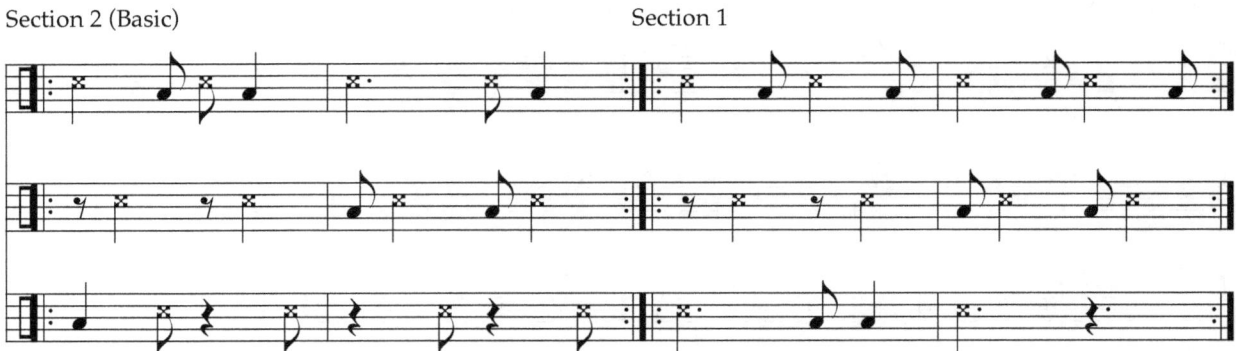

5

Inle

The fifth toque is dedicated to Inle. It has four sections and three calls. The initial call is the basic pattern for Section 1. I have included an iyá variation in Section 1 that may be played ad lib. Call 1 leads to Section 2 where there is another unanswered variation that may be played ad lib. Call 3 leads to Section 4. Here the time signature changes to 7/4. The iyá and itótele play in the new meter while the pattern for the okónkolo remains in 4/4. Inle segues directly into Iyakotá at the end of Section 4 when the iyá player makes the initial call at a slightly slower tempo into that toque.

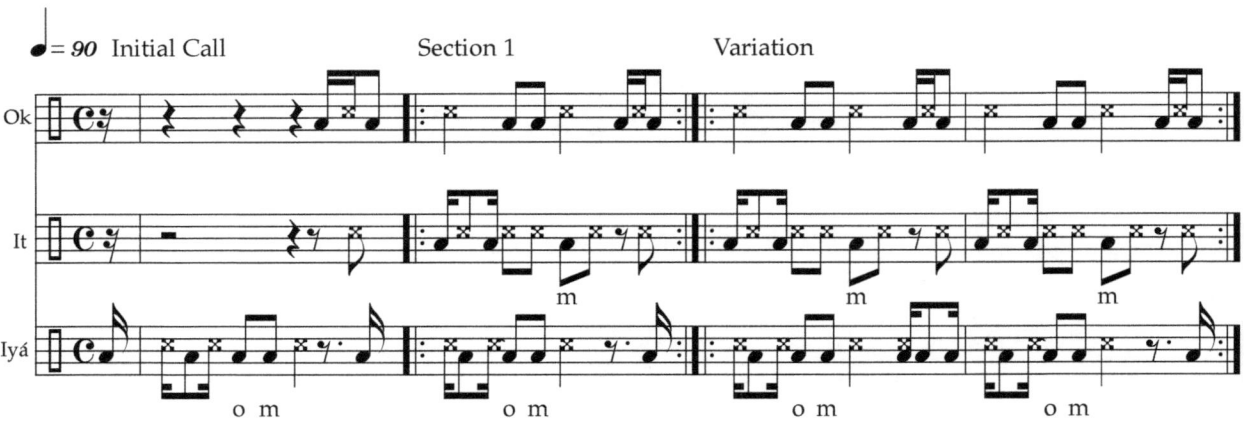

* Can be played any time within Section 2.

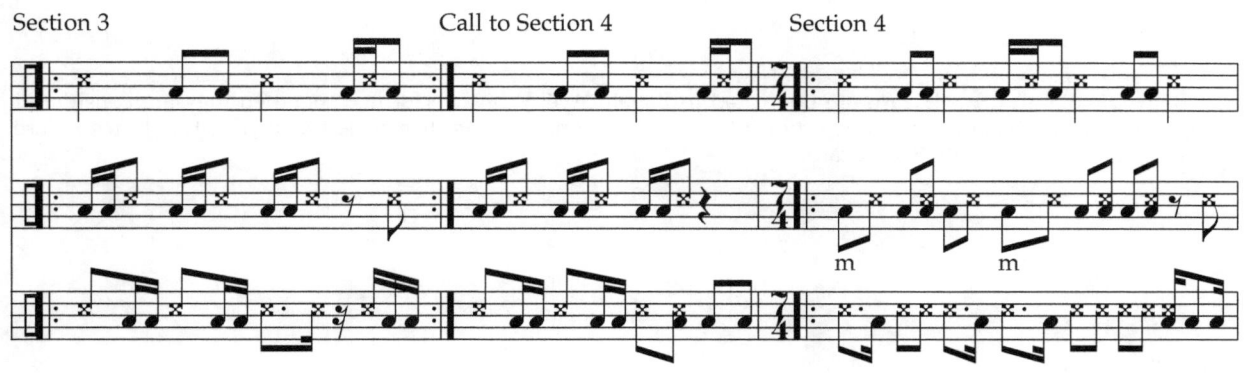

6

Iyacotá

Both Iyakotá and San Lazaro are dedicated to Babalú Ayé. While performed together, they are considered separate toques. Iyakotá has one section with no variations or calls. It can be repeated a few times before making the transition into San Lazaro.

This toque transitions directly into San Lazaro.

San Lazaro

* This is the last note of Iyakotá. Do not play it twice, but you would start from here when playing San Lazaro alone.

This toque segues directly into Osain by making the last iyá 8th note into the 16th note pickup for that toque.

8

Osain

The eighth toque is dedicated to Osain. It has four sections and three calls. The toque begins when the iyá starts its pattern for Section 1. The itótele and okónkolo enter as written. Call 1 leads to Section 2 which changes meter to 4/4 but retains the same tempo. Call 2 leads to Section 3 where I have included an iyá variation which can be played ad lib. Note the optional okónkolo pattern. Call 3 leads to Section 4. The iyá can repeat that call which is answered by the itótele. This toque segues directly into Ósun.

Section 1

Osain, 2

Osain, 3

Section 4   Call and response

9

Ósun

The ninth toque is dedicated to Ósun. It has two sections. After the initial call, the group plays Section 1 ad lib before the iyá calls into Section 2 which is played twice before transitioning into either Rezo de Obatalá or Obatalá.

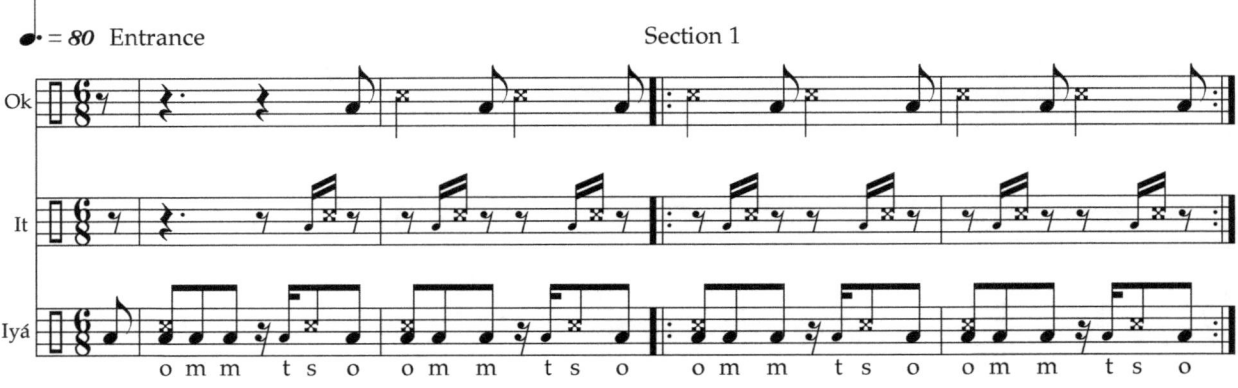

* Play at least 2 X then transition directly into Rezo de Obatalá.

Ósun, 2

Transition to Rezo de Obatalá or Obatalá

10a
Rezo de Obatalá

This toque is optional but can be included if the ceremony is in honor of Obatalá. After the basic pattern is established, the iyá calls twice. The first is answered by the itótele and okónkolo, then the group returns to the basic pattern. The second call initiates the segue into Obatalá.

* This pickup note is also the last note of Ósun, so only play it once when making the segue.

10b

Obatalá
Jeguá Baba Jeguá o

The toque dedicated to Obatalá has five sections. The iyá makes the initial call. In Section 1, play each written repeat ad lib. Repeat Section 3 (playing the 2nd ending last X) then play the transition which leads to Section 4. Repeat Section 4a three times before going into Section 5, Cochicambo. Repeat Section 5 ad lib until ready, then take the second ending. This toque segues directly into Dadá.

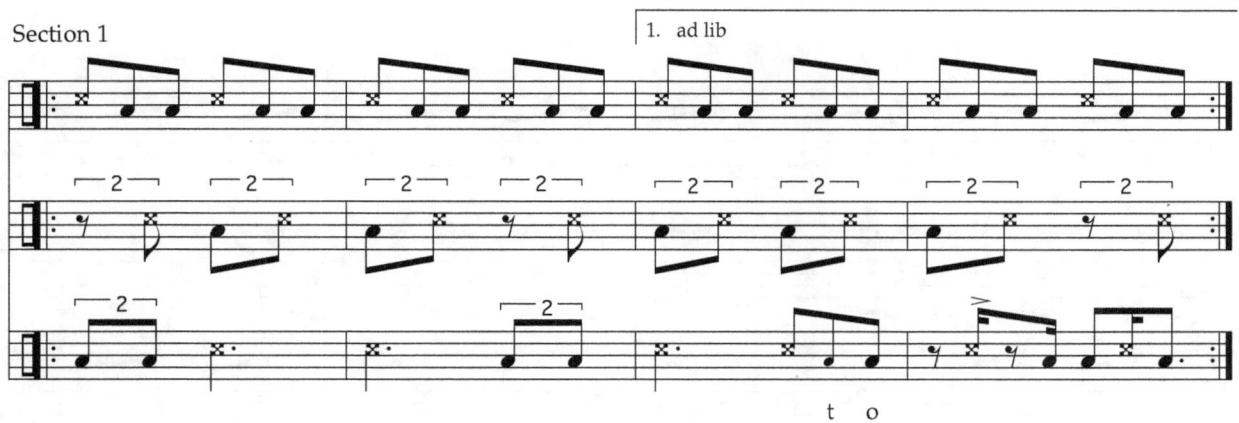

136

Obatalá, 2

*The iyá makes this call 3X before the itótele answers.

Obatalá, 3

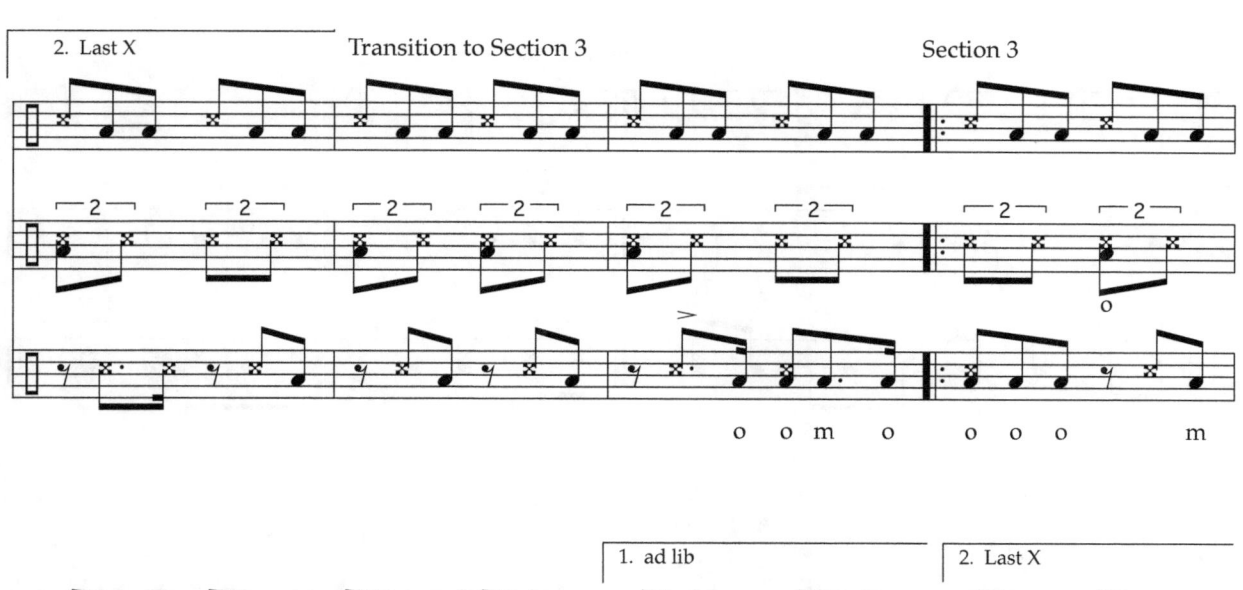

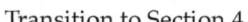
Transition to Section 4

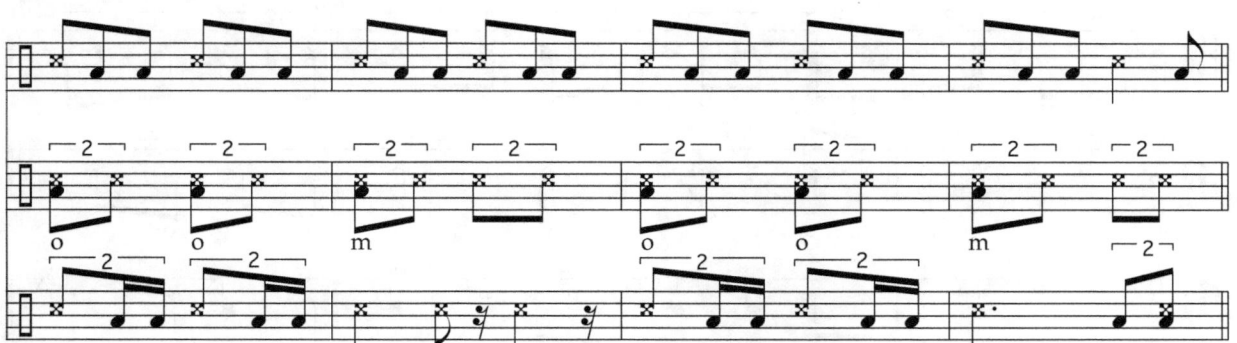

Obatalá, 4

Section 4

Section 4a. Repeat 3X

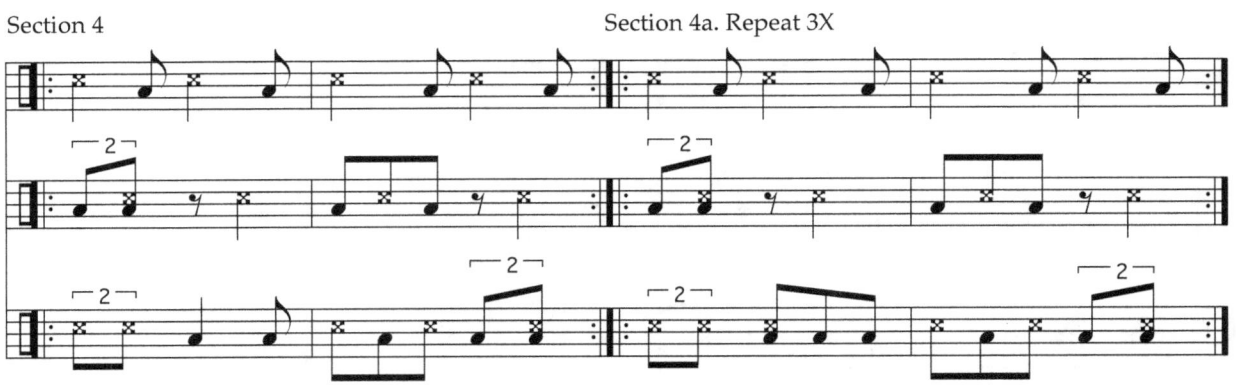

Section 5. Cochicambo *

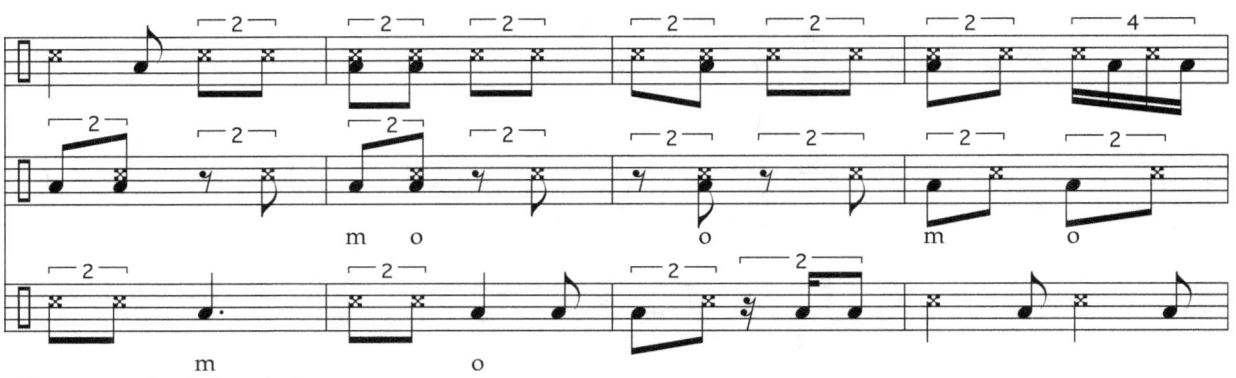

* Spiro names this "Ochicambo."

Obatalá, 5

Section 5a

11a

Dadá

The toque dedicated to Dadá (11a) and the toque dedicated to Óke (11b) are counted and played together, so I have lettered them a and b to differentiate between them. After the initial call, play the call and response twice before going on to Section 2. Play the first ending of Section 2 ad lib before taking the second ending, which is the transition into Óke.

Dadá, 2

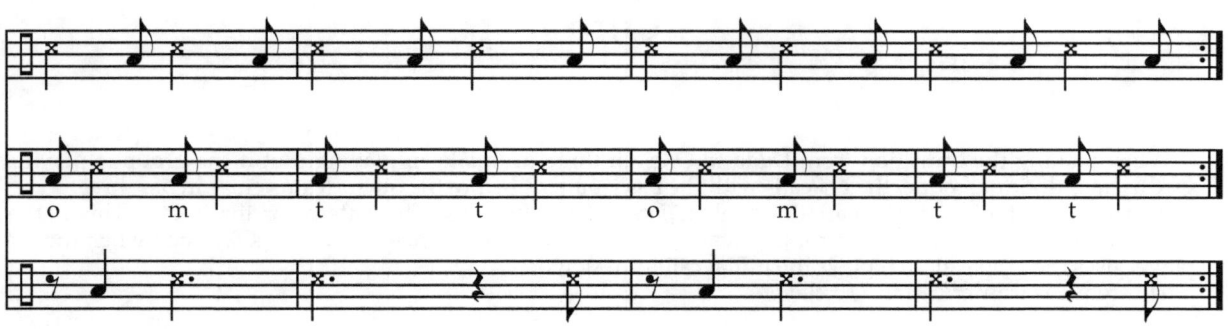

Call to Section 2   Section 2   1. ad lib *   2. Transition into Óke

* From Section 2 you can return to Section 1 or take the 2nd ending to transition into Óke.

This toque segues directly into Óke.

11b

Óke

When making the transition from Dadá to Óke, all three drums keep playing. But if the group is playing Óke as an individual toque, the iyá calls with the basic pattern before the other drums enter in bar three.

During Óke, the iyá plays variations called *floreos*. Note the alternate pattern for the itótele. This is the more traditional of the two patterns. Óke starts at m.m. 96 to 100 but then speeds up. Óke ends when the iyá player uses the Stop call then plays the initial call into Agayú.

This toque is transcribed in 2/3 clave.

Óke. Iyá Floreos

These variations are transcribed in 2/3 clave. Notes in parentheses are pickups to the next variation and should only be played as part of V 3 or V 4.

Alternate itótele pattern

12

Agayú

The twelfth toque of the Oru Seco is dedicated to Agayú. It has two sections. Make the initial call that leads to Section 1 which contains a call and response that can be played ad lib. During Section 2, the call and response is played again to return to Section 1. This toque ends when the iyá plays the initial call into Titilaro.

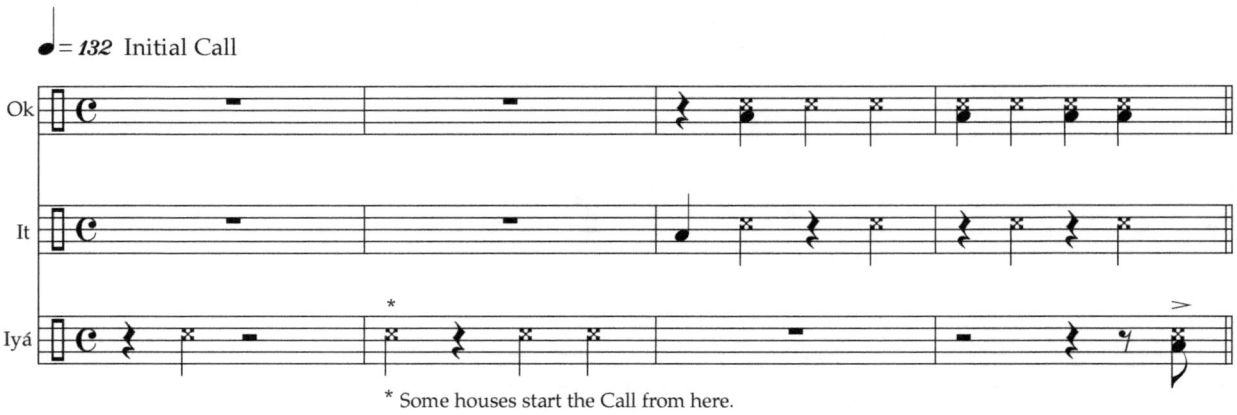

* Some houses start the Call from here.

Agayú, 2

Section 1

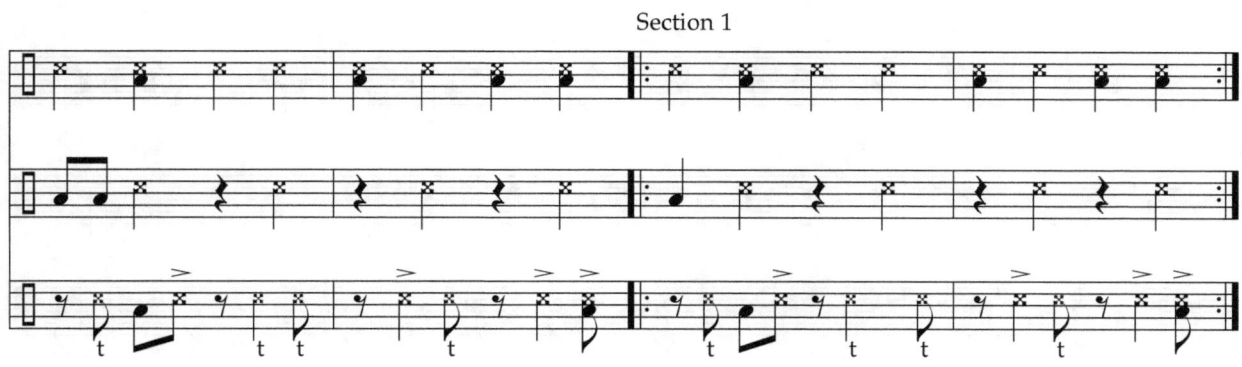

Transition to Section 2   Section 2

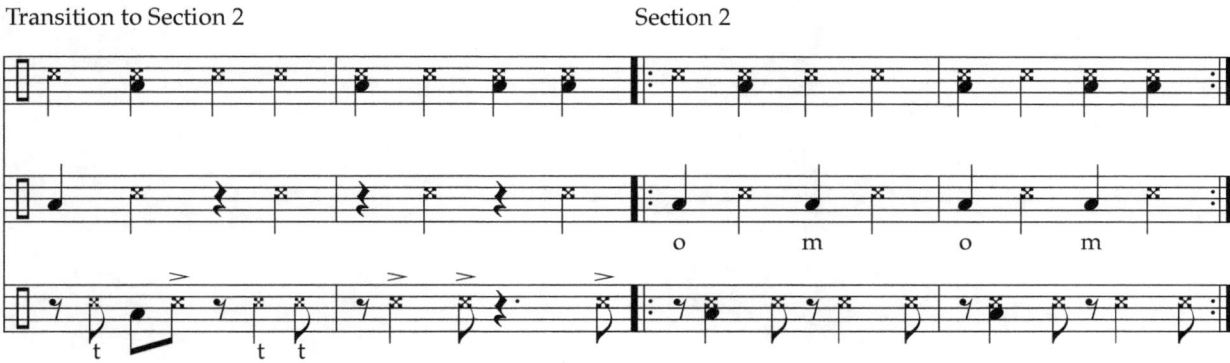

Call to Section 1

Agayú, 3

Section 1

13a

Titilaro

The thirteenth toque in the Oru Seco is the first of two possible salutes to Changó. Section 1 has two parts. The first includes a set of variations listed on the last page of the transcription. Section 1a sets up the call to Section 2, which is a little faster. The call to Section 3 sets up a meter change to six-eight time. The group plays Section 3 ad lib before the iyá calls into Section 4 by changing to its rhythm. Note the okónkolo variation on the last page. It is used occasionally to change the sound of Section 2. It should not be considered an alternate to the basic pattern. Titilaro ends when the iyá plays the Stop call then starts the basic pattern for either Meta or Orisha Oko.

* This itótele pattern is "in fix" and should almost sound like broken triplets until Section 1a where it is played as straight eighth notes. Some houses play this pattern as quarter note triplets until Section 1a.

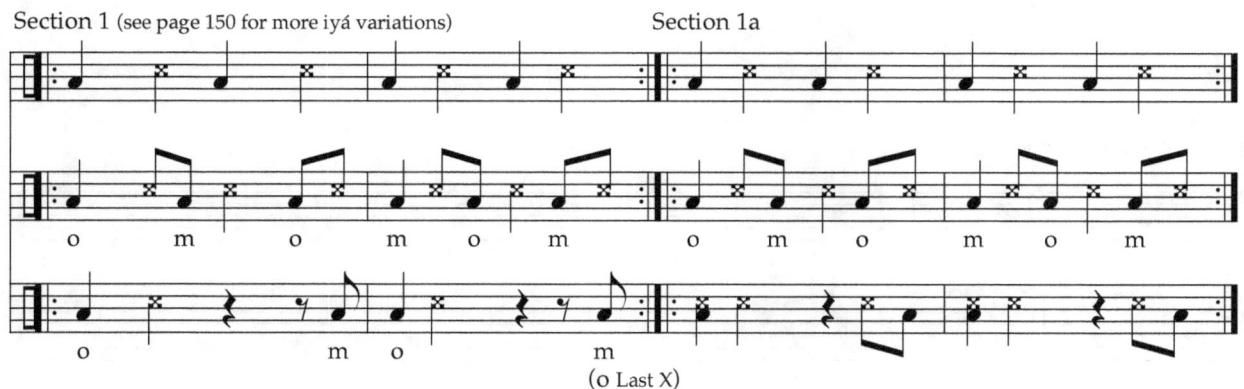

Titilaro, 2

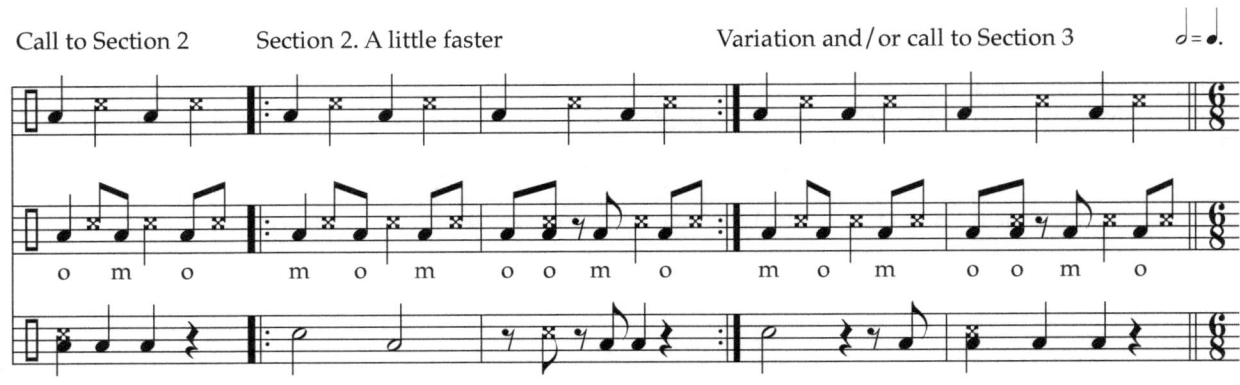

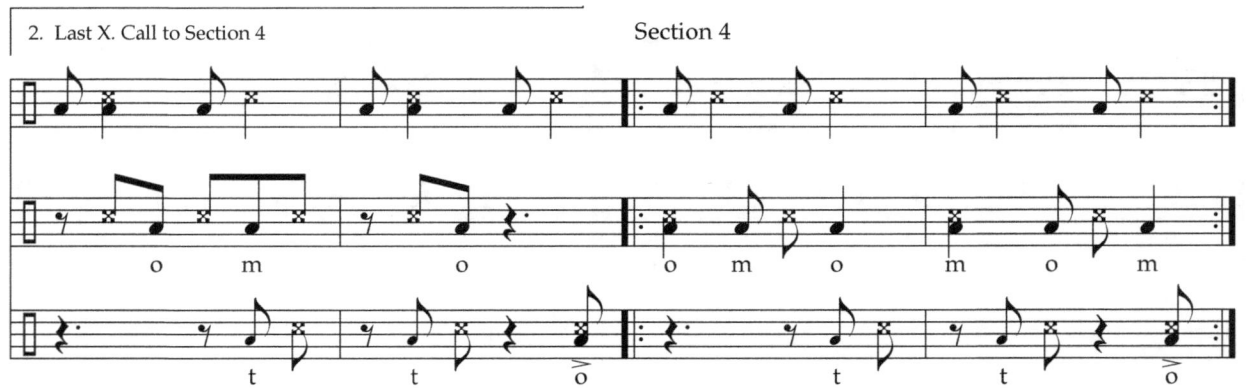

Iyá Variations for Titilaro

Section 1

Section 2. V 1

Okonkolo variation for Section 2

13b

Meta

Although optional, Meta can be included in the Oru Seco if the ceremony is dedicated to Changó. Note that bar 2 of Section 1 is the basic pattern. Bar 1 is only played once or twice to set up the rhythm. The three conversations in Section 1 can be played in any order and as many times as the Iyá player chooses. The order I transcribed here is one that Alejandro uses. All repeated sections are open vamps unless indicated. Meta ends when the iyá plays the stop call, then starts the basic pattern for Orisha Oko.

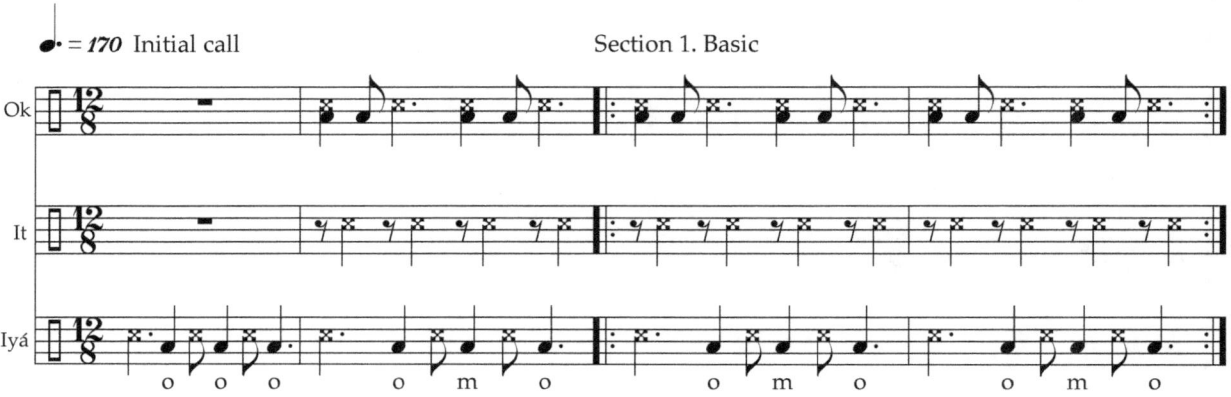

Meta, 2

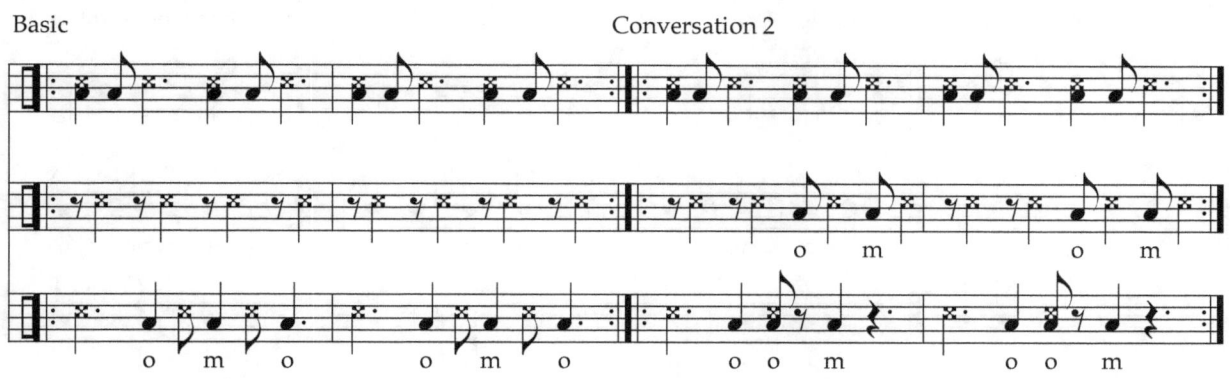
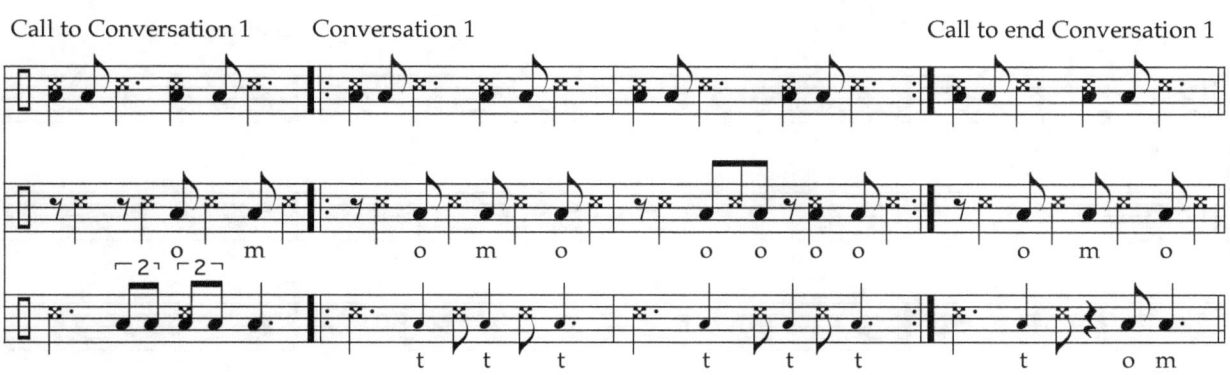
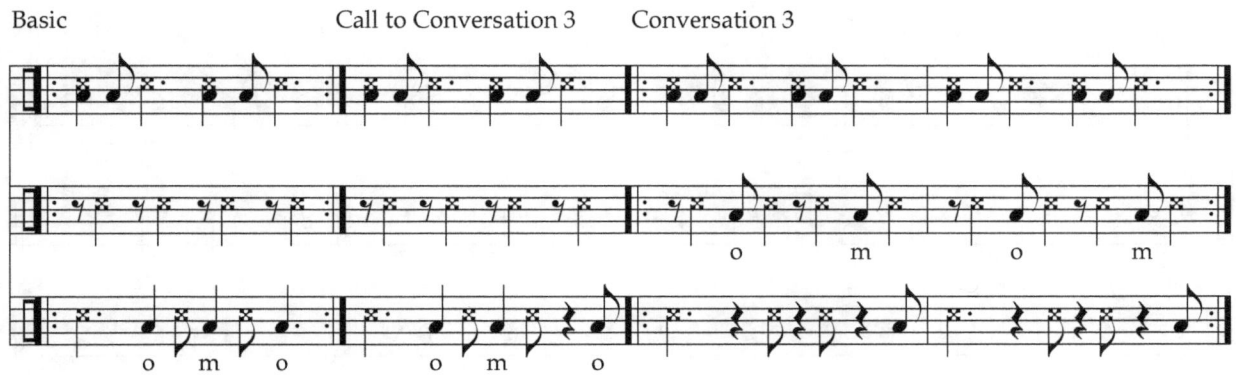

Meta, 3

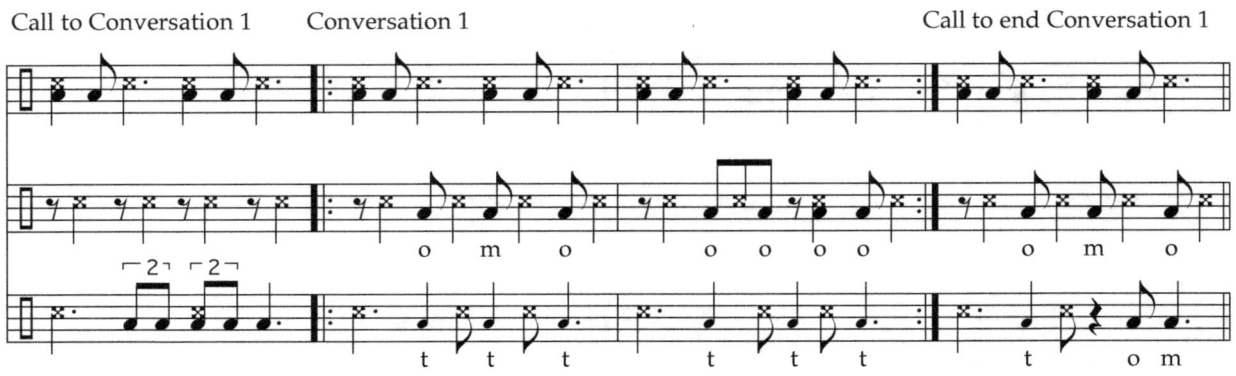

Meta, 4

Conversation

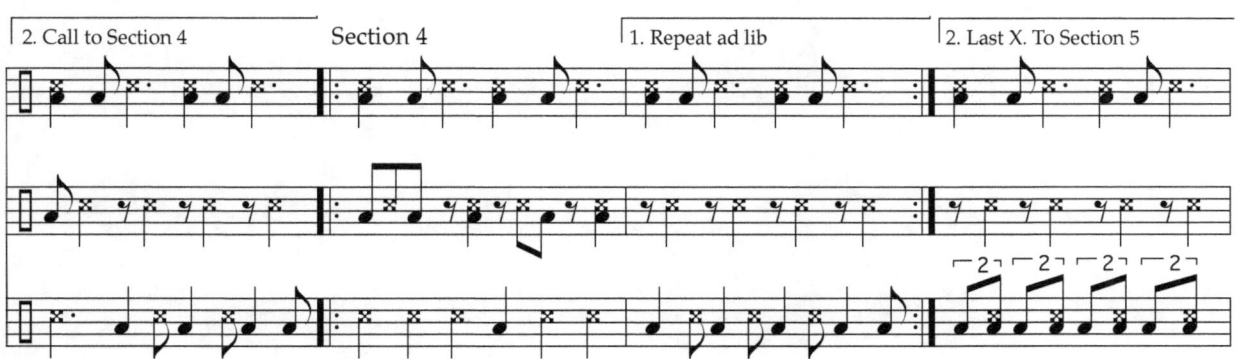

Meta, 5

Pause

14

Orisha Oko

The fourteenth toque of the Oru Seco is dedicated to Orisha Oko. It has three repeated sections in this order: Section 1, Section 2, Section 1, Section 3, then Section 2 which leads into the viro to Ibeyi. The 9/8 bar in Section 2 is a good example of why it is difficult to play clave in some toques. This toque segues directly into Ibeyi.

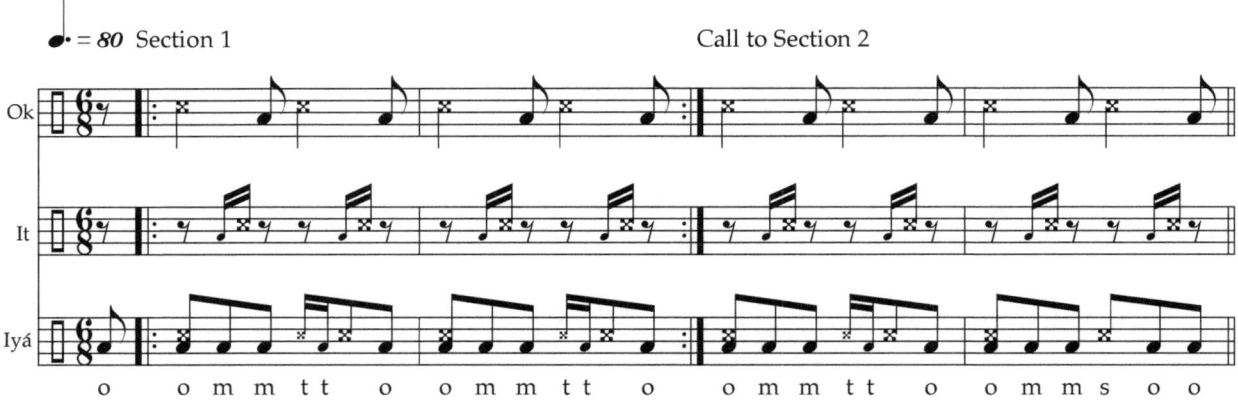

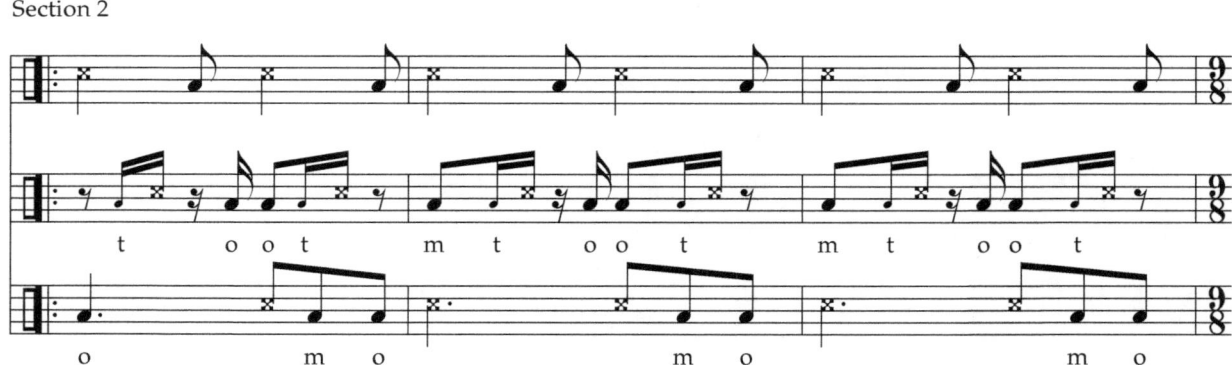

Orisha Oko, 2

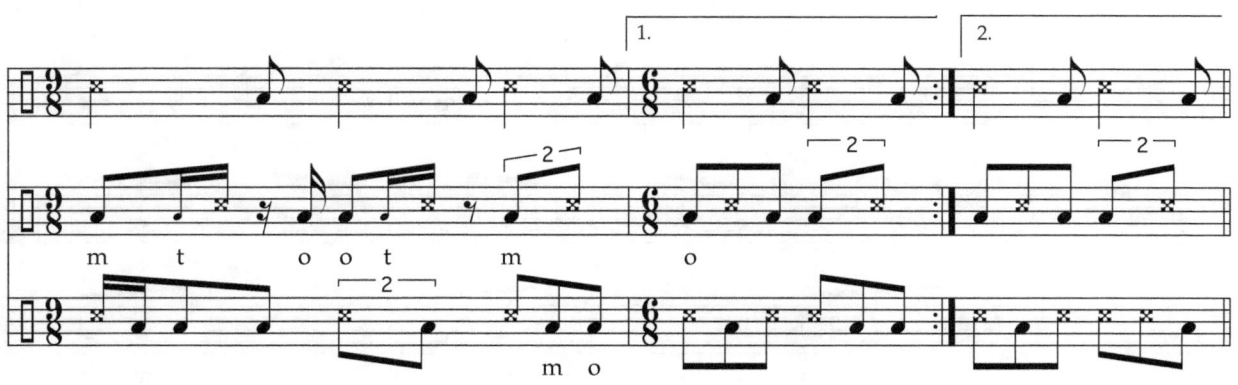

Section 1   Section 3. Conversation

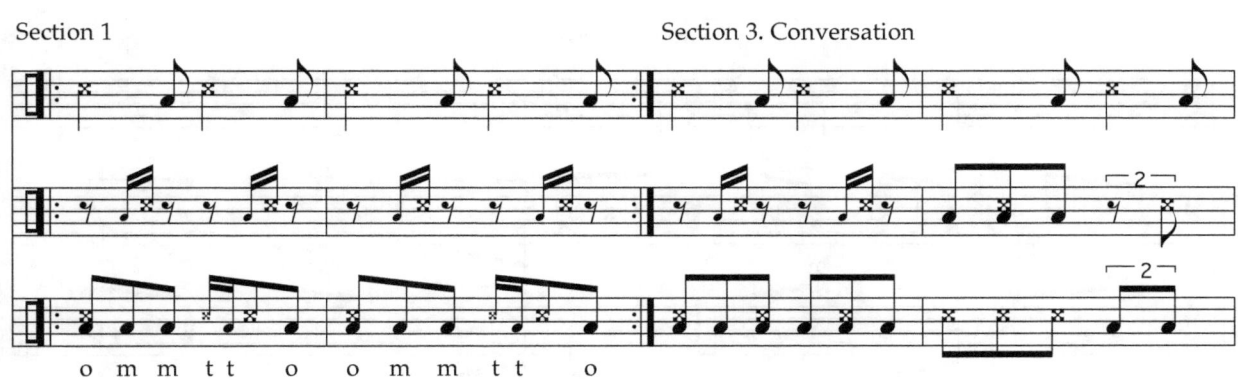

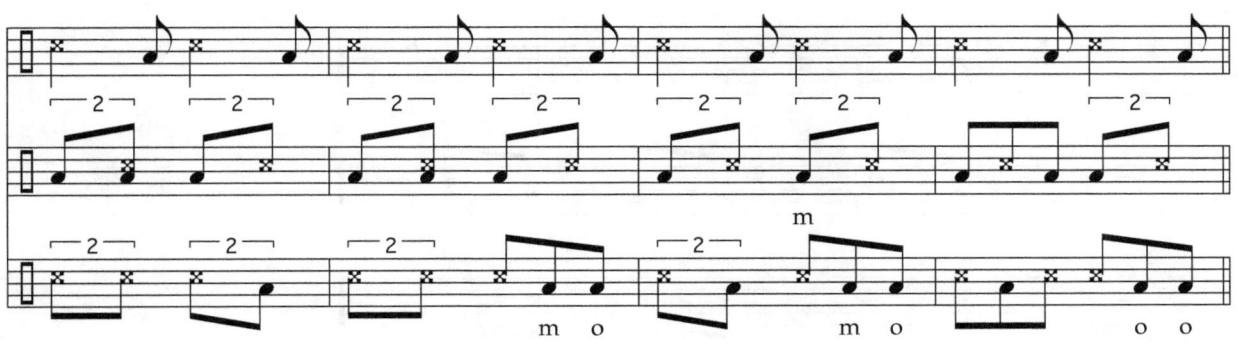

Orishaoco, 3

Section 2

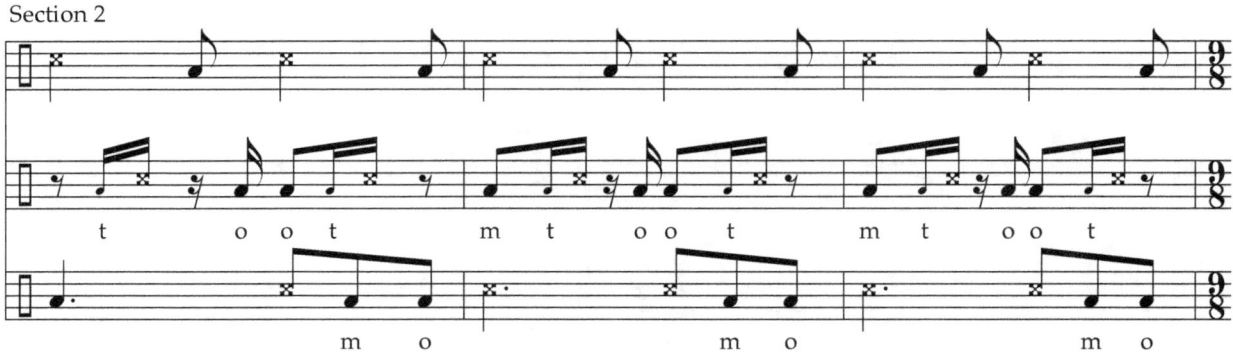

Viro into Ibeyi

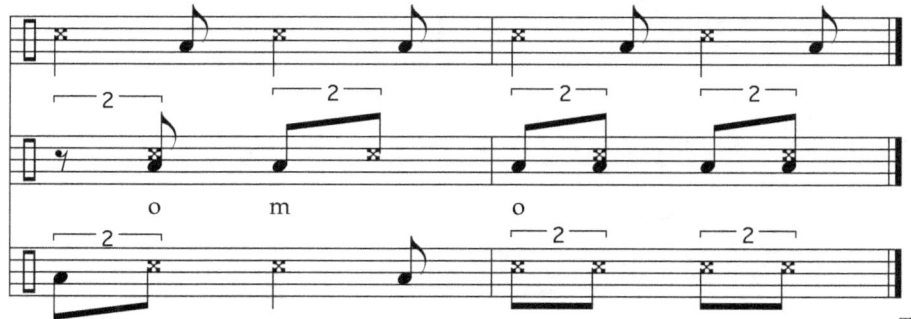

This toque segues directly into Ibeyi

Ibeyi

15

The toque dedicated to the Ibeyi is a simple four-bar pattern with one iyá variation. Play the Basic twice, the Variation once, and the Basic once more before making a direct transition into Yeguá when the iyá plays the initial call into that toque. Note that some songs for this toque begin on bar four, so practice it starting from there as well.

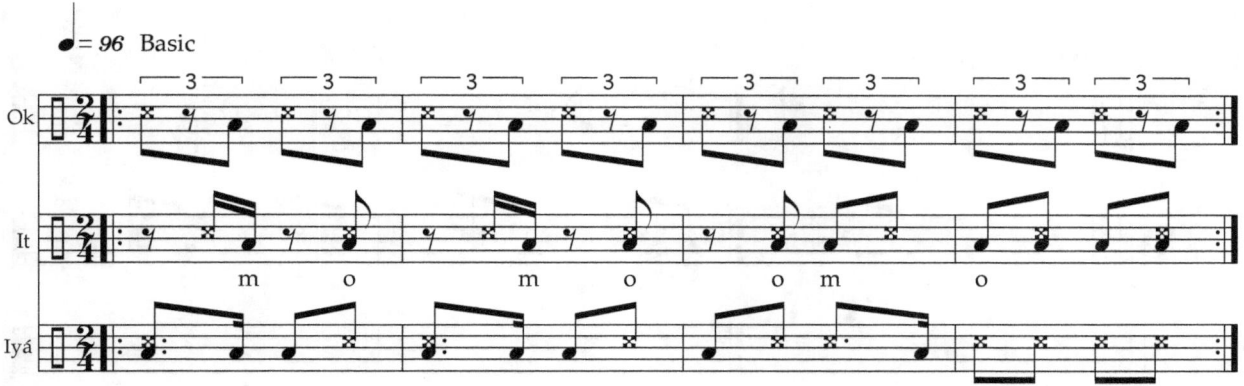

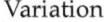

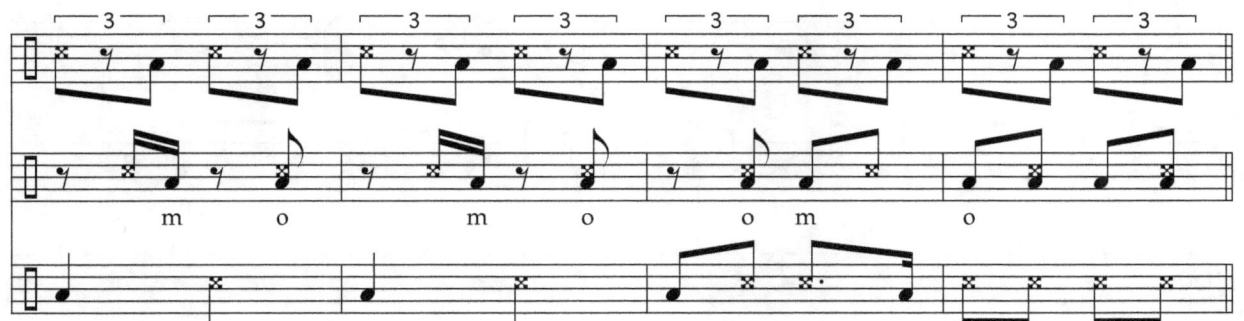

This toque segues directly into Yeguá.

16

Yeguá

The sixteenth toque is dedicated to Yeguá. It starts at m.m. 126 but can speed up gradually. The conversation is played three times before returning to Section 1 at a slightly faster tempo. Play Section 1 again before making the transition to Section 2. Section 2 has a variation I have labeled 2a. When the iyá plays two open tones in every bar, the itótele answers by adding an extra open to its pattern. Once the iyá returns to the basic pattern, so does the itótele. The iyá uses the stop call to end the toque before going on to Oyá.

Transition to conversation

Yeguá, 2

Conversation (3X)

Section 1   Transition to Section 2

Section 2   Section 2a

* Play lower note 2X on repeat

Yeguá, 3

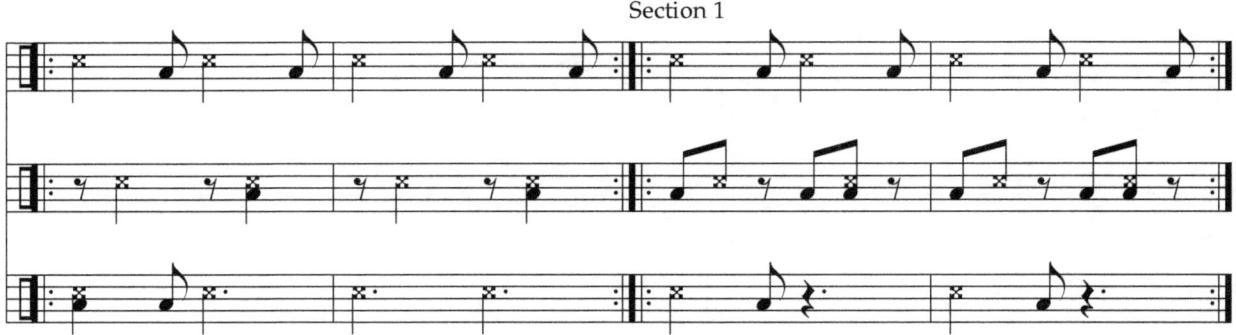

There is a short pause before starting Oyá.

17

Oyá

The toque dedicated to Oyá is very slow, but its intricate rhythms give it an almost double-time feel. In Section 5, the meter changes to six-eight while the pulse stays the same. I have included an iyá variation which can be added during Section 5a before the iyá makes the stop call to complete the toque.

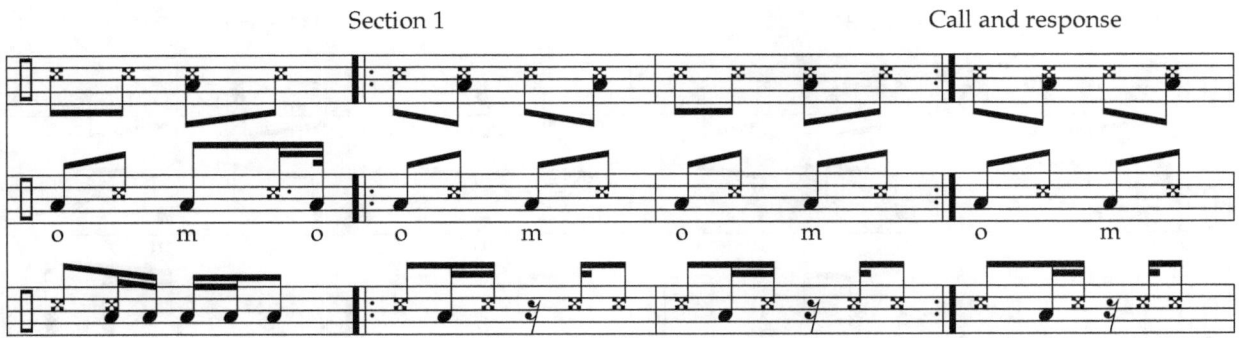

Oyá, 2

Call to Section 2

Section 2   Call to Section 3

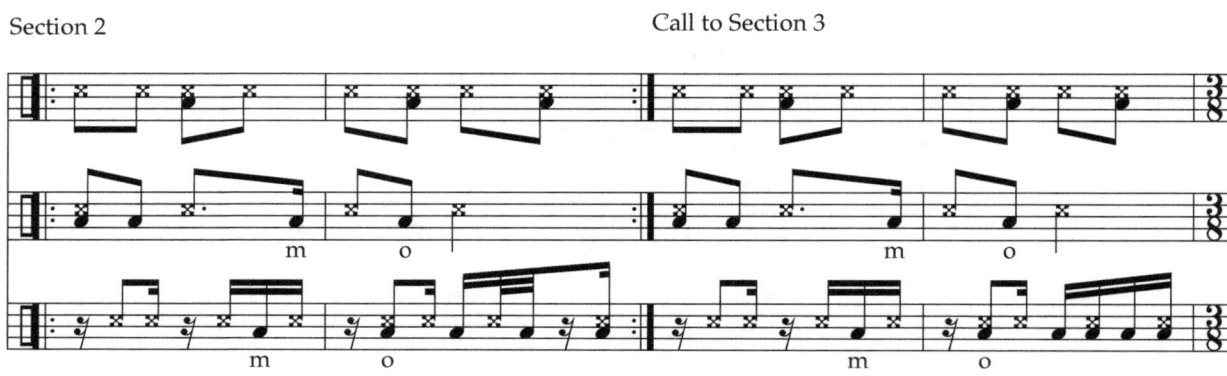

Section 3   Call to Section 2

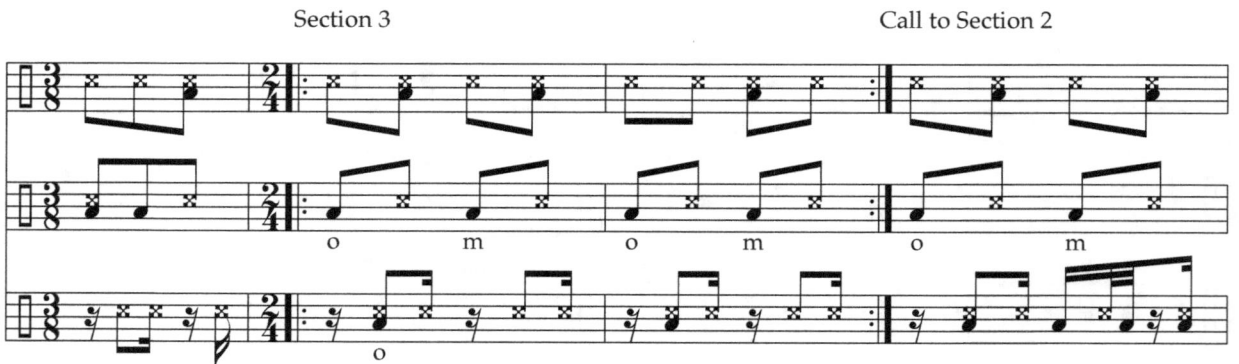

Oyá, 3

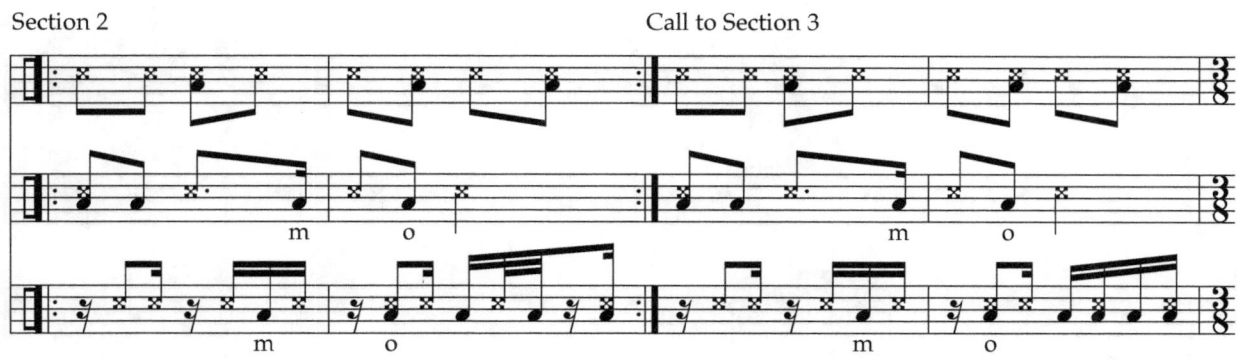

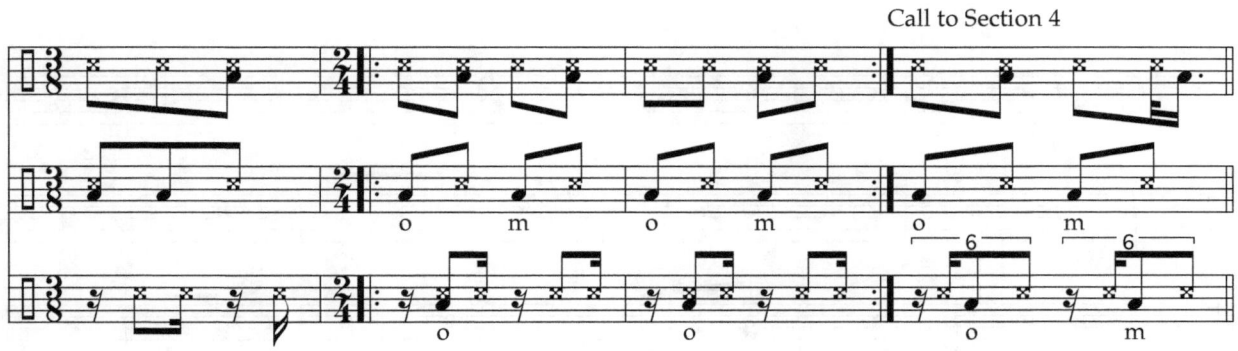

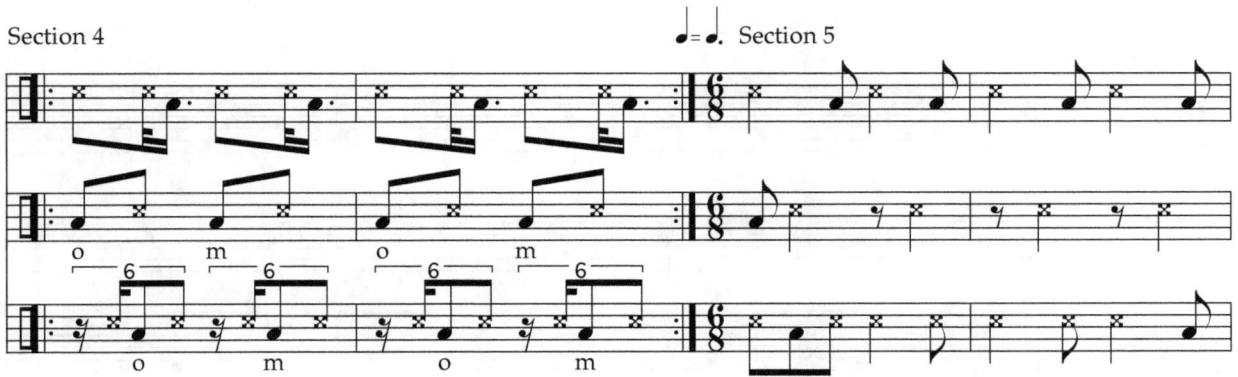

Oyá, 4

Section 5a

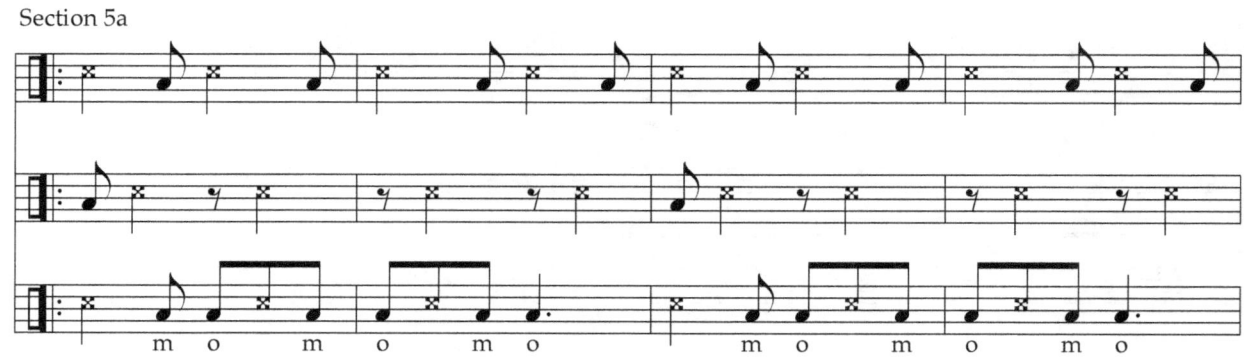

Oyá, 5

*Iyá variation

* The iyá player can include this variation during Section 5a and can play the basic rhythm again before making the Stop call.

Stop call last X only

18

Aro

Aro is dedicated to Yemayá. It is the longest, fastest, and most taxing toque in the Oru Seco. It starts slowly but accelerates quickly starting in Section 3. Although the rate of acceleration can vary, I have included metronome markings within the score to give the performers a sense of how fast they should be at that point in the music.

The initial call sets up Section 1 where the iyá plays a set of variations (see page 175) before transitioning to Section 2. The iyá makes the call into Section 3 where it then plays the call to accelerate to speed up the tempo. The iyá can use this call several times until the tempo reaches m.m. 190, then it plays the Section 3 variations listed on page 175. Once the iyá starts the variations, it does not go back to the basic pattern but makes the call into Section 4. During Section 13, the iyá can use the optional call one or more times to increase the tempo before the direct transition into Section 14. Aro ends when the iyá uses the stop call to create a pause before starting Rezo de Ochún.

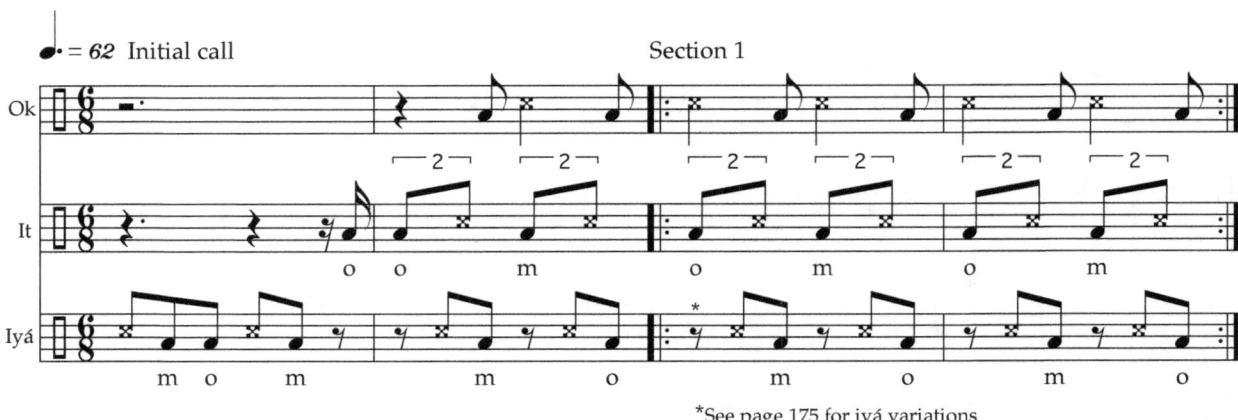

*See page 175 for iyá variations

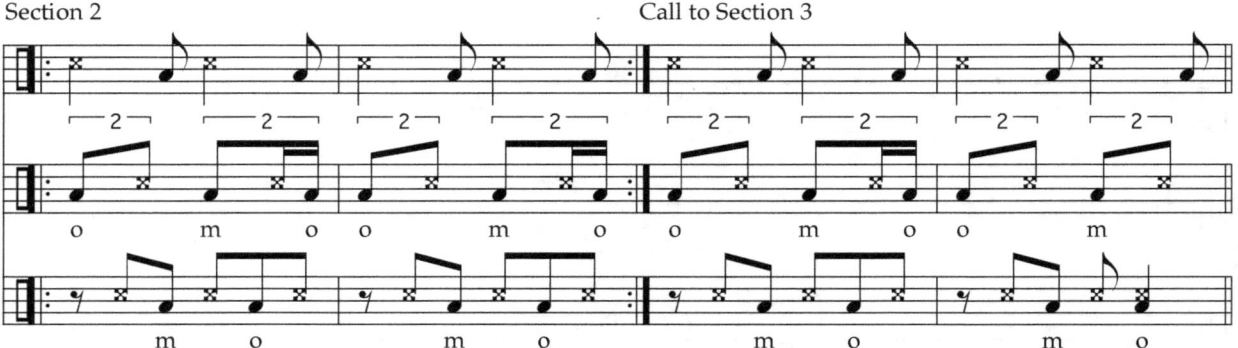

Aro, 2

Section 3. Accel poco a poco

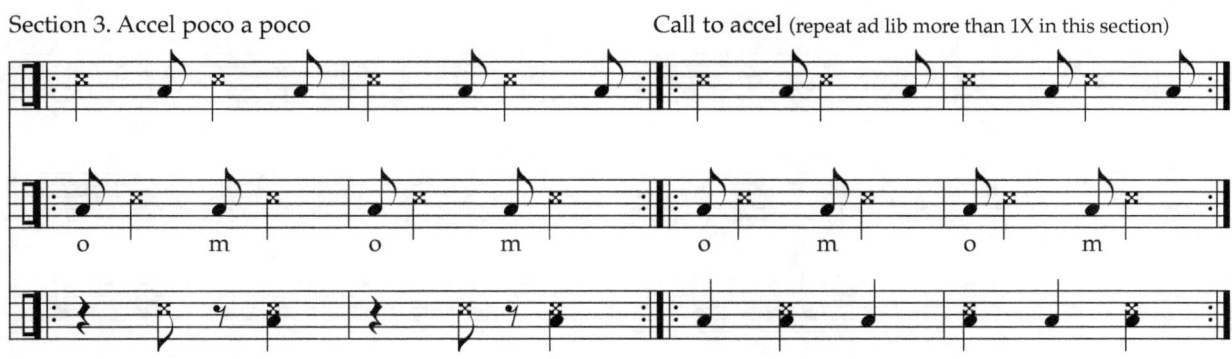

Call to accel (repeat ad lib more than 1X in this section)

Call to Section 4

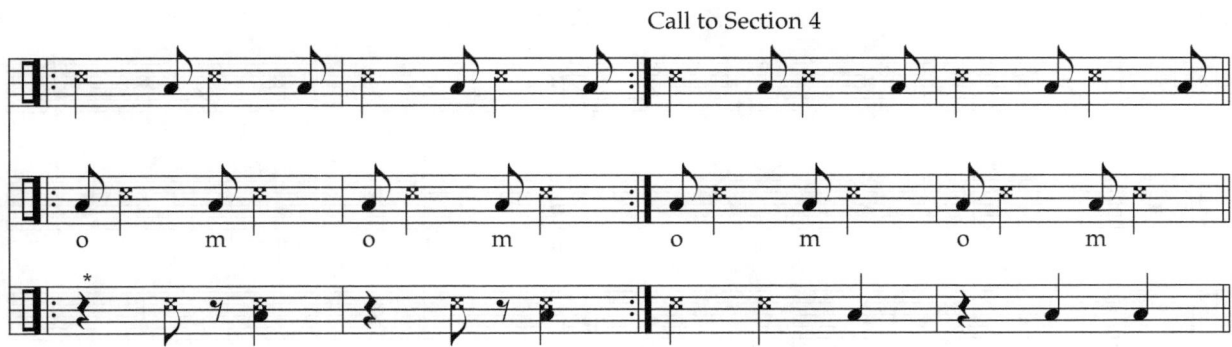

*See page 175 for Iyá variations

$\bullet. = 190$ Section 4

Call to Section 5

Section 5   **Call to Section 6**

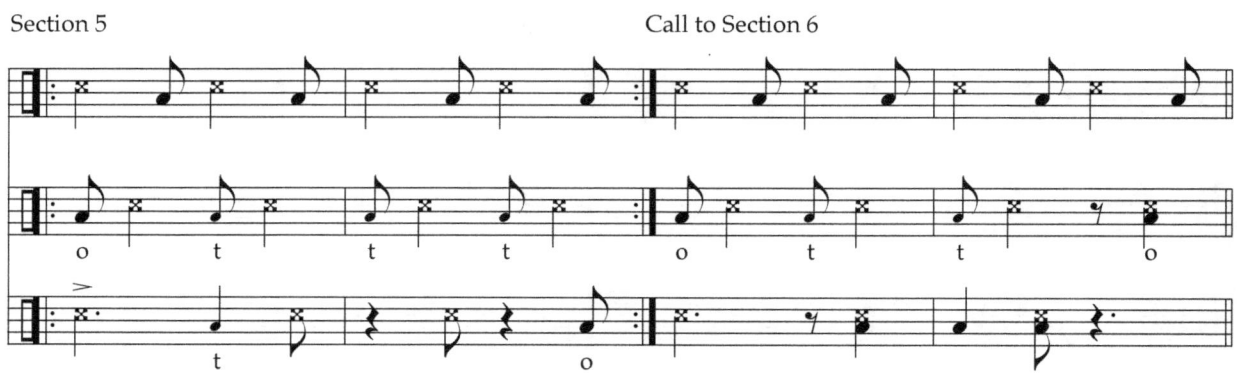

Section 6

Aro, 4

Call to Section 7

Section 7   Section 8

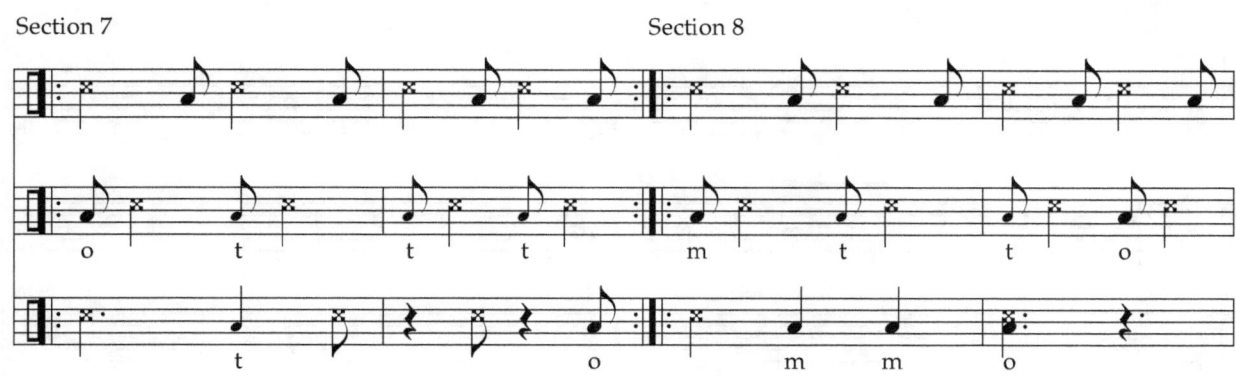

1. Vamp   2. Call last X. To Section 9

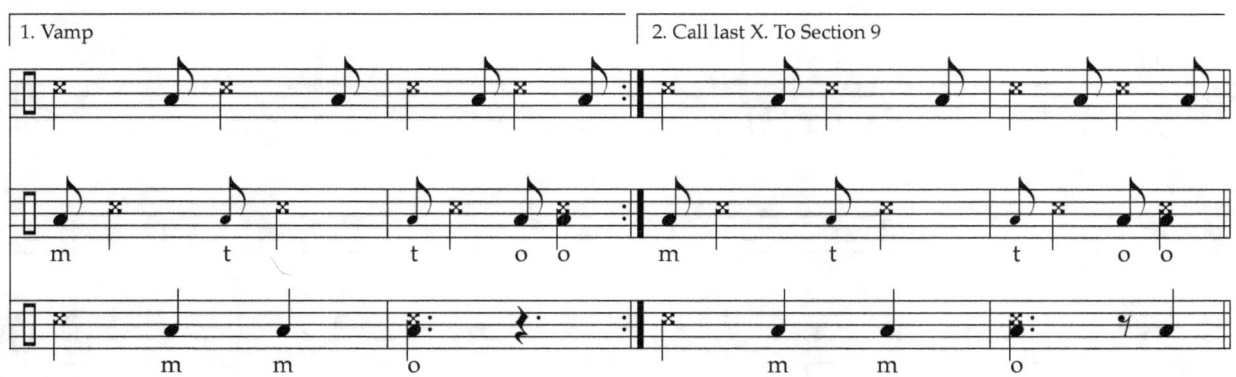

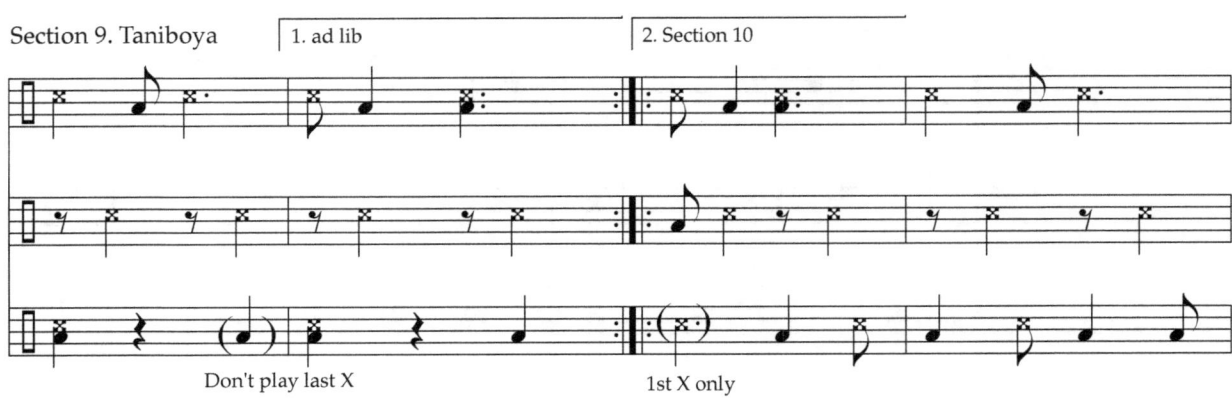

Aro, 6

Section 12

3. Transition to Section 13

Section 13

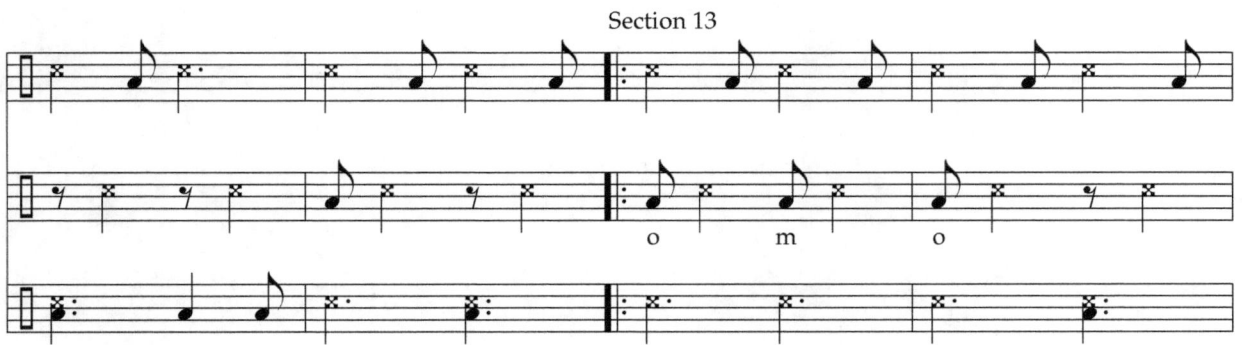

173

Aro, 7

Section 14. Faster

* Optional call to increase tempo before Section 14

174

Aro. Iyá Variations

Variations for Section 1

Variations for Section 3

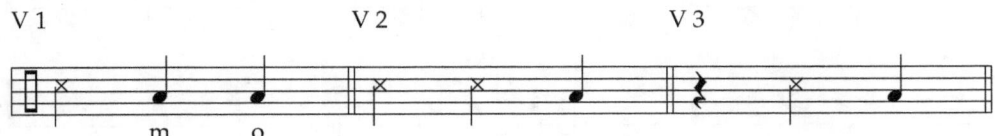

19

Rezo de Ochún

The nineteenth toque in the Oru Seco is a prayer to Ochún. The short, two-bar pattern is preceded by a distinctive initial call. Alejandro chose to include three iyá variations which can be played ad lib, and one iyá call that is answered by the itótele. This toque segues directly into Obba.

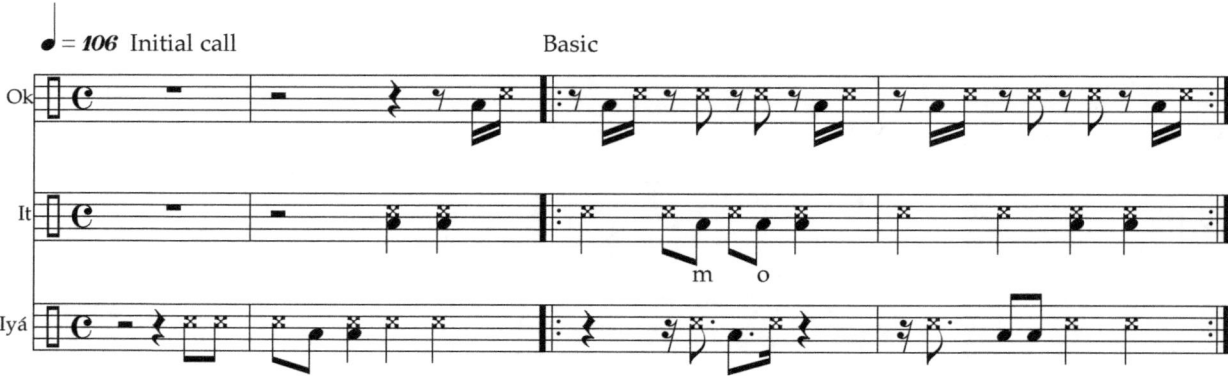

Rezo de Ochún. Iyá variations.

20

Obba

The toque for Obba has five sections. It begins with the iyá playing the basic pattern for Section 1. When ready, the iyá calls to Section 2. Once in Section 5 there are many different variations and conversations played by different groups, but since none of these are part of the traditional version, I have omitted them. The iyá makes the stop call before playing the initial call into Orunla.

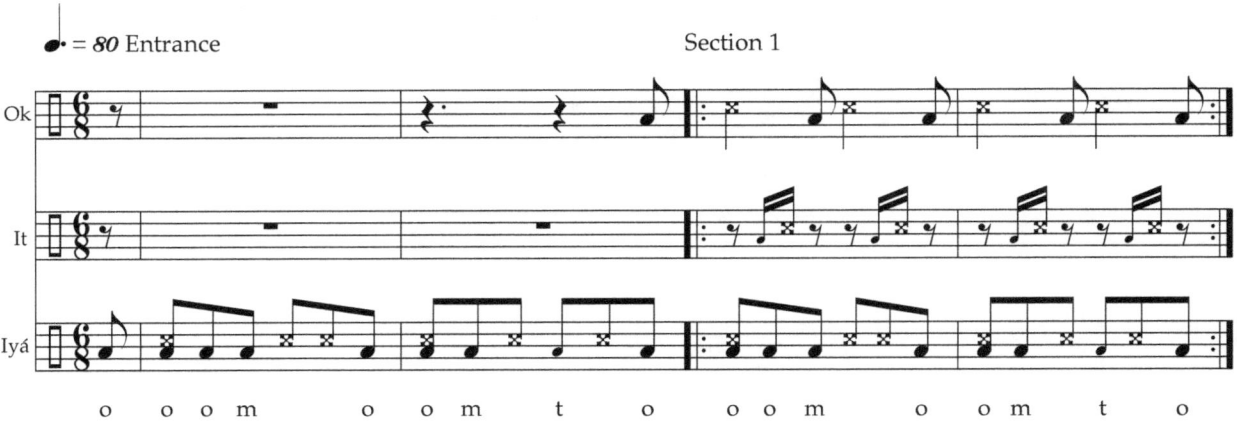

Obba, 2

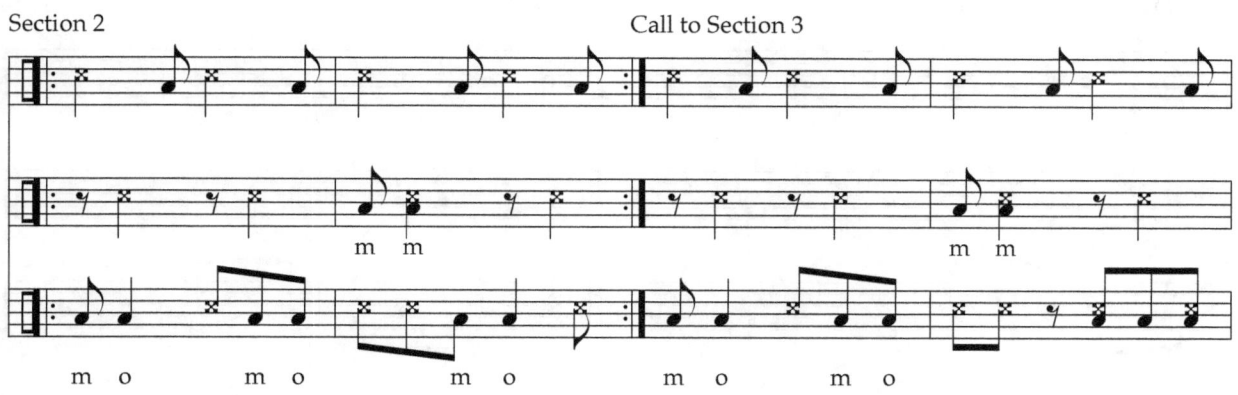

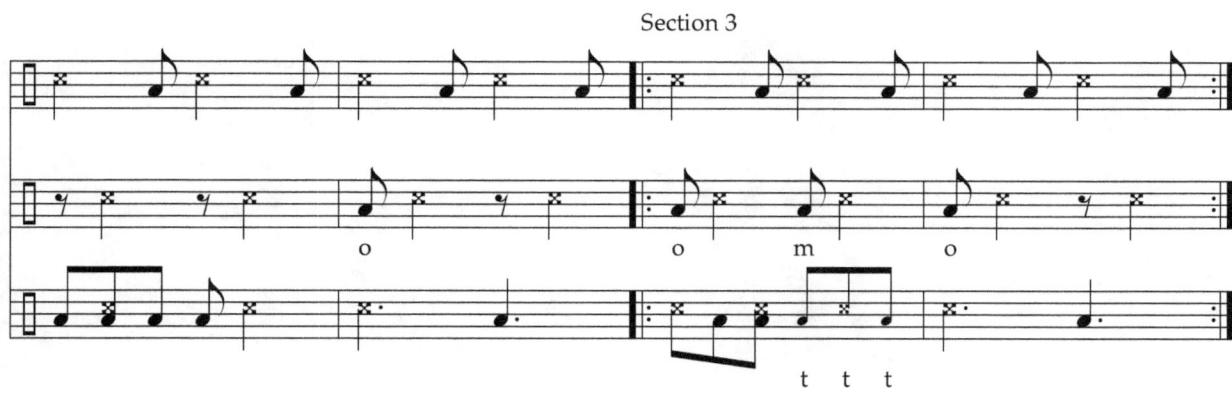

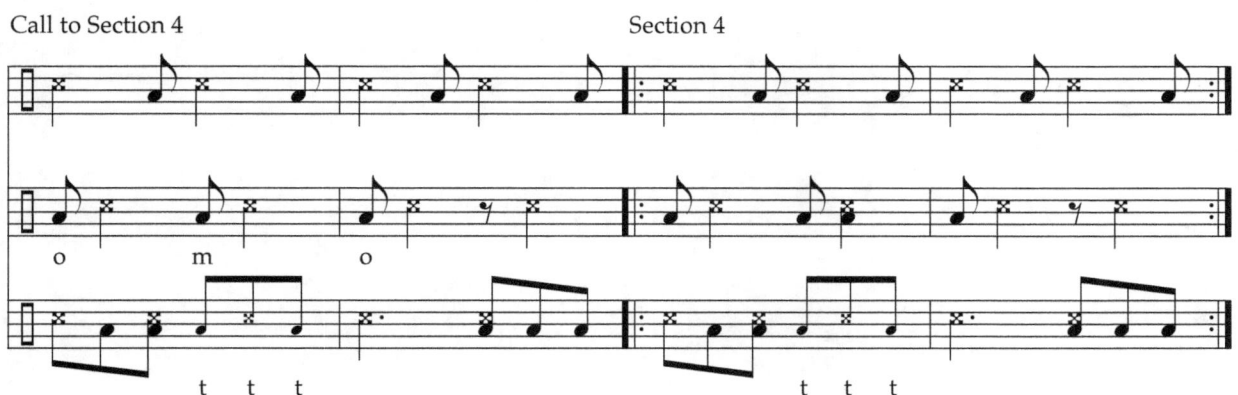

Obba, 3

Call to Section 5   Section 5

There is a short pause before the beginning of Orunla

21

Orunla

The toque for Orunla has three sections. Each is an open vamp. After Section 3, the iyá calls back to Section 2. Pause before starting Oduwa. Note that some houses place this toque after Agayú in the order of the Oru Seco.

* This toque ends the 2nd X through Section 2   Pause

22

Oduwa

The last toque is dedicated to Oduwa. It consists of a basic pattern and a conversation which is performed twice. The roadmap: basic, conversation (repeated three times), basic, then the conversation (repeated twice). The third repeat of the conversation is a coda which calls the drummers to the end of the Oru Seco.

* This conversation can be played more than once simply by making the transition to conversation.

Oduwa, 2

Transition to basic

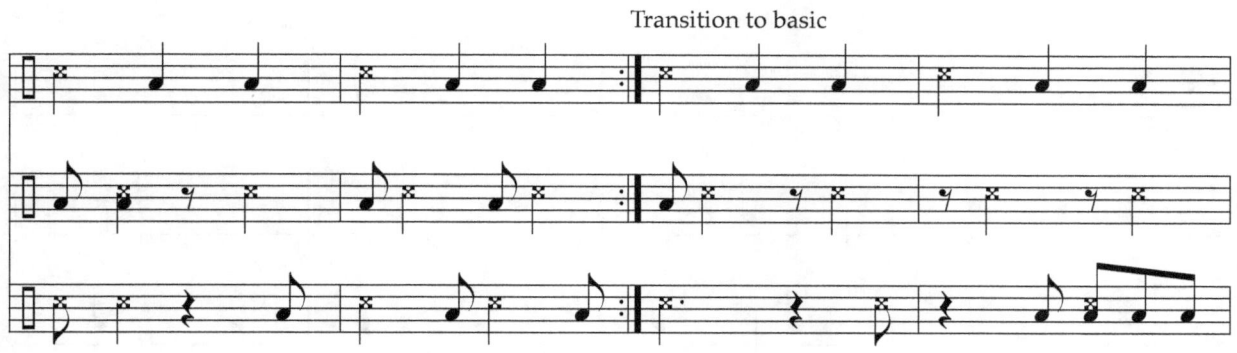

Basic

Transition to conversation (last X) Conversation (repeat 1X then go to the coda)

Oduwa, 3

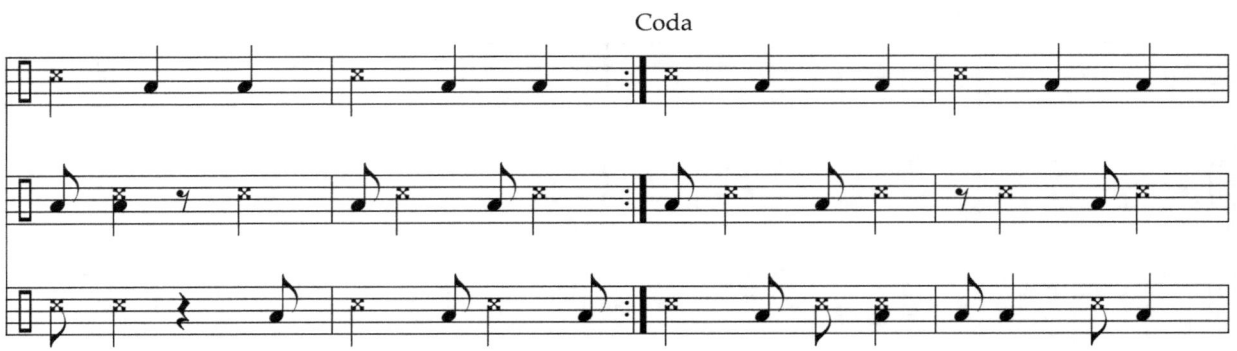

End of the Oru Seco.

Chapter Eleven

Epilogue: Music and Change

> New World it is, for those who became its peoples remade it, and in the process, they remade themselves.
>
> Sidney W. Mintz and Richard Price
> *The Birth of African-American Culture*

One bright February morning, I stood high on the ramparts of Morro Castle, the sixteenth-century guardian of Havana Harbor. Leaning on the cold parapet, I gazed out to the clear waters of the Caribbean, then back across the channel to the crumbling buildings of Old Havana. In my mind, the city was young again, and I was a Spanish soldier nervously watching a British frigate closing to fire—I was a Cuban merchant relieved to see one of my slave ships safely sailing into the canal, laden with black gold—I was a passerby stopping at the dock to assess a group of slaves who had chains on their wrists and fear in theirx eyes—I was an African man, alone, with no words on my tongue to tell others of the wonder in my heart at this new and unfamiliar world.

I have been told I have an overactive and somewhat romantic imagination. This is an asset for a novelist and a hindrance for a journalist. But flights of fancy, when clearly labeled, obscure the subject less than do well-meaning but biased scientific assumptions. Anthropology suffers, at least historically, from two underlying presuppositions that alter the way it collects and views information. The first is a nineteenth-century concept, conceived by misreading Rousseau, that the "native" is a pure, and consequently static, being, and that the search for data on this indigenous being is actually a quest for truth. And, of course, truth is eternal, so some older ethnographic studies read like stone tablets from the mount: "This is how they act. This is what they believe." But in fact there is no eternal ethnographic truth. People change. After hearing Cuban batá drummers play, an old Yoruban man living in New York said that the rhythms were of his grandfather's time and could no longer be heard in his country (Ortiz, 1996: 183). Traditional African drumming is evolving, as is Cuban. But the ethnographer often writes his findings as distinct from the continuum that created them. The danger is that it implies a static truth—"This is the way the santeros play. This is the way the paleros sing"—when in reality all culture is in constant adaptation. This is the way they played and sang *that day*.

The other assumption, which goes hand in hand with the first, is that these pure societies are being destroyed by the soulless cultural imperialism of the West, and that they must be recorded before the flood of western contamination extinguishes their natural goodness. One of the positive results of cultural relativism, now that western culture is no longer considered as the paradigm by which others are measured, is that it can no longer be perceived as meritless either. All cultures can be seen as equal. The new televisions that alter traditional ways of life in Native American communities cannot be seen as cultural imperialism because TV altered western culture as much as it did Native American. Both cultures change and both are now victims or victors, depending on your point of view. This is true in Cuba as well. The process of transculturation that created the various meta-ethnic traditions, black and white, continues today. While some traditions are being weakened or extinguished, they are also being translated into evolving contributions of contemporary art and thought. Roberto Vizcaino says that Pedro Izquerdo (Pello el Afrokán) created *mozambique* by adapting Obanlá from batá to congas. José Quintana (Changuito) borrowed from mozambique to develop *songo*, and the funky feel of songo can still be felt in the *timba* grooves of Charanga Habanera. Instead of looking back towards the Garden of Eden, we might well look forward. Entropy is balanced by creativity, and the only way to gain insight into its dynamic is to try and view the process from a less angled perspective.

Cultural loss is inevitable if society is to continue growing. All music played before the invention of the phonograph has been, in one sense, lost. Writing it down or teaching it to someone does not save the original performance. More was lost when 78 rpm became standard, and much of that vanished when only some of those recordings were transferred to 33 rpm. And thousands of 33 rpm albums are not available on CD. I once came across a dumpster filled with old 78s and have been haunted ever since by the possibility that a rare performance was lost to humanity when that dumpster was hauled off. Today on that site there is a recording engineering school. It seems to me that we need dumpster pickers as much as we need engineering students, if for no other reason than to show them the roots of the art they hope to augment. Those records were not in that dumpster because they were trash, but because they were perceived as being economically useless. By the time their value is recognized, they will have been lost in the landfill for many years. You can't know where you are if you don't know where you've been, and it is painful to realize that not everything can be saved. I have gleaned as much information as I could from my sources, as they did from theirs, and all of it is a handful of sand on a very long beach. Others, far more thoroughly than I, are doing the same. And musicians, beneficiaries of a rich tradition, are using these rhythms as part of the foundation for new musics that express yesterday's cultural roots in tomorrow's musical styles.

Two of the main currents in Cuban music were the folkloric Afro-Cuban traditions that developed into rumba and comparsa, and the son tradition that evolved into contemporary popular music. Each had some traits in common with the other (and with other genres as well), and both continually borrowed, sharing until they were transformed, fusing together to create new styles while still retaining their own identities. Contemporary Cuban music also absorbs aspects of jazz, funk, rock, and rap, but its sophisticated harmonies and home-boy vocal stylings are built on an Afro-Cuban rhythmic foundation that evolved from within while embracing European harmonic and melodic structures, then later, the chord progressions, orchestrations, and song forms of jazz, as well as the back beat that so dominates North American popular music. But to say that the African, European, and American influences have contributed more or less equally to Cuban music, while possibly true, completely ignores the fact that the stylistic hand on the wheel, the driving force in its evolution, the collective artistic will that molded the sound, is Cuban.

So in the end, much of the original African dance, language, and music have been lost in the creation of new artistic expressions. What the folkloric traditions have lost has been replaced, transculturated into forms that are intrinsically part of Cuban music and dance: rumba and comparsa, and newer forms, not so traditional perhaps, but at the edge of the music's evolution. Yet much remains that can be traced back to these roots. One can see the function of the *katá* in Palo evolving into the *guagua* of rumba then into the *cáscara* of timbales. The rich harmonic structures of jazz have brought a new aspect to the complicated rhythms that revolve around the clave. The original African call and response can be found in the montunos of songo and timba, creating new musics from traditional ones. And groups such as Irakere have reversed the process by starting with a contemporary jazz framework and bringing folkloric elements like batá and orisha song into a modern musical architecture. Anyone who wishes to unravel this complicated tangle of modern and traditional, innovative and folkloric, sacred and sacrilegious, must pick a place and make a start, sorting and resorting to achieve small victories of understanding in a sea of non-comprehension.

For a non-Latino musician attempting to gain some proficiency in the vast, confusing world of Cuban music, the quest becomes one of time and place, and of people. By traveling back historically and out geographically, first over a little strait then across a fathomless ocean, one is immersed in the stories of millions of people, a rainbow of skin color, and a roaring flood of uprooted lives. It is a history movie run in reverse, a slowly rethreading spool of film that, for me, began at a toque in Regla and ended up on the beach with Columbus as the first natives walked down to the shore to greet him. And so the circle is complete.

References Cited and Other Resources

Abbreviations

CIDMUC Centro de Investigación y Desarrollo de la Música Cubana.

AMAC *Antología de la Música Afrocubana*. EGREM-Areíto. 9 Vols. The AMAC is the definitive source of Afro-Cuban field recordings and has excellent liner notes in Spanish. Released starting in 1981 on 33 rpm LPs but now out of print, it was rereleased on cassette without the liner notes, but retaining the same catalog numbers as the originals, except that the letters LD were replaced by C, so LD 3325 is C 3325 on the cassettes. It was rereleased again as a boxed CD set in 2005 by Egrem, with liner noters in English and Spanish.

Printed Sources

Alén Rodríguez, Dr. Olavo. 1981. Liner notes to AMAC. Vol. 7. *Tumba Francesa*. EGREM-Arieto. LD-3606.

--------. 1986. *La Música de las Sociedes de Tumba Francesa en Cuba*. Havana: Casa de las Americas.

--------. 1994. *De lo Afro Cubano a la Salsa*. Havana: Ediciones Artex S.A.

--------. 2006. *Pensamiento Musicológico*. Havana: Editorial Letras Cubanas.

Alén Rodríguez, Dr. Olavo. and Ana Casanova Oliva. 1999. Liner notes to *Official Retrospective of Cuban Music*. CIDMUC. Tonga Productions. TNG4CD 9303.

Altman, Thomas. ND. *Cantos Lucumí a los Orichas.* Self-published.

Amat Medina, José Eladio, and Curtis Lanoue. 1998. *Afro-Cuban Percussion Workbook*. Unpublished.

Amira, John and Steven Cornelius. 1992. *The Music of Santería*. Crown Point: White Cliffs Media.

Arce Burguera, Arisel, and Armando Ferrer Castro. 2002. *The World of the Orishas.* Havana: Editorial José Martí.

Argüelles Mederos, Aníbal and Ileana Hodge Limonta. 1991. *Los Llamados Cultos Sincreticos Y El Espiritismo.* Havana: Editorial Academica.

Averill, Gage. 1995. Liner notes to *Rhythms of Rapture: Sacred Musics of Haitian Vodou.* Washington: Smithsonian Folkways Records. SF CD 40464.

Barnet, Miguel. [1981] 1998. *La Fuente Viva.* Havana: Editorial Letras Cubanas.

--------. 1995. *Cultos Afrocubanos: La Regla de Ocha, La Regla de Palomonte.* Havana: Ediciones UNIÓN.

--------. {1967] 2001. *Cimarrón: Historia de un Esclavo.* Madrid: Ediciones Siruela.

Barz, Gregory F. and Timothy J. Cooley. 1997. *Shadows in the Field.* New York: Oxford University Press.

Bascom, William. [1969] 1984. *The Yoruba of Southwestern Nigeria.* Prospect Heights: Waveland Press.

Bebey, Francis. [1969] 1975. *African Music: A People's Art.* Brooklyn: Lawrence Hill Books.

Bockie, Simon. 1993. *Death and the Invisible Powers.* Bloomington: Indiana University Press.

Bolívar Aróstegui, Natalia. 1994. *Los Orishas en Cuba.* Havana: PM Ediciones.

Bolívar Aróstegui, Natalia, and Carmen González Díaz de Villegas. 1998. *Ta Makuende Yaya y Las Reglas de Palo Monte.* Havana: Ediciones UNIÓN.

Brandon, George. 1993. *Santeria from Africa to the New World.* Bloomington: Indiana University Press.

Brown, David H. 2003. *The Light Inside: Abakuá Society, Arts, and Cuban Cultural History.* Washington and London: Smithsonian Books.

Burkholder, Mark A., and Lyman L. Johnson. 1998. *Colonial Latin America*. Third edition. New York: Oxford University Press.

Cabrera, Lydia. [1954] 1996. *El Monte*. Havana: Editorial SI-MAR.

--------. 1958. *La Sociedad Secreta Abakuá*. Havana: Ediciones C.R.

--------. 1986. *Reglas de Congo: Mayombe Palo Monte*. Miami: Ediciones Universal.

Carpentier, Alejo. [1946] 1989. *La Música en Cuba*. Havana: Editorial Pueblo y Educación.

Casanova, Manuel Martínez, and Nery Gómez Abréu. No date. *La Sociedad Secreta Abakuá*. Villa Clara: Grupo de Etnología y Folklore Universidad Central de Las Villas.

Castellanos, Jorge. 2003. *Pioneros de la Etnografía Afrocubana*. Miami: Ediciones Universal.

Castellanos, Jorge, and Isabel Castellanos. 1988. *Cultura Afrocubana 1, El Negro en Cuba, 1492-1844*. Miami: Ediciones Universal.

--------. 1990. *Cultura Afrocubana 2, El Negro en Cuba, 1845-1959*. Miami: Ediciones Universal.

--------. 1992. *Cultura Afrocubana 3, Las Religiones y las Lenguas*. Miami: Ediciones Universal.

--------. 1994. *Cultura Afrocubana 4, Letras, Música, Arte*. Miami: Ediciones Universal.

Chernoff, John Miller. 1979. *African Rhythm and African Sensibility*. Chicago: University of Chicago Press.

CIDMUC. 1997. *Instrumentos de la Música Folclórico-Popular de Cuba*. 2 vols. Havana: Editorial de Ciencias Sociales.

Clifford, James, and George E. Marcus. eds. 1986. *Writing Culture: the Poetics and Politics of Ethnography*. Berkeley: University of California Press.

Coburg, Adrian. 2004. *Oru Cantado: Cantos Yoruba y Arara*. Bern: Self-published.

--------. [2002] 2004. *Oru Seco: Bata Scores*. Bern: Self-published.

--------. 2002. *Toques Especiales: Bata Scores*. Bern: Self-published.

Courlander, Harold. 1996. *A Treasury of African Folklore*. New York: Marlowe & Company.

Cutié Bressler, Alberto. 2001. *Psiquiatría y Religiosidad Popular*. Santiago de Cuba: Editorial Oriente.

Davidson, Basil. 1980. *The African Slave Trade*. Boston: Little, Brown and Company.

Durant, Will, and Ariel Durant. 1967. *Rousseau and Revolution*. The Story of Civilization. Vol. 10. New York: Simon and Schuster.

Ekpe Akpabot, Samuel. 1975. *Ibibio Music in Nigerian Culture*. Michigan State University Press.

Elliott, John Huxtable. 1989. *Spain and its World 1500-1700*. New Haven and London: Yale University Press.

Entralgo, Elías. 1953. *La Liberación Étnica Cubana*. Havana: University of Havana Press.

Epega, Afolabi A., and Philip J. Neimark., trans. and eds. 1995. *The Sacred Ifa Oracle*. New York: Harper Collins.

Fariñas Gutierrez, Daisy. 1995. *Religión en las Antillas*. Havana: Editorial Academia.

Fernandez, Robert. 2007. *The Afro-Cuban Folkloric Musical Tradition*. Sylmar: Leisure Planet Music.

Fleurant, Gerdès. 1995. Liner notes to *Rhythms of Rapture: Sacred Musics of Haitian Vodou*. Washington: Smithsonian Folkways Records. SF CD 40464.

Floyd, Jr. Samuel A. 1995. *The Power of Black Music*. New York: Oxford University Press.

Franco, José Luciano. 1985. *Comercio Clandestino de Esclavos.* Havana: Editorial de Ciencias Sociales.

Garcia, Nanette, and Maurice Minichino. ND. *The Sacred Music of Cuba: Bata Drumming Matanzas Style.* Mdantone Publishing.

García-Carranza, Araceli. Norma Suárez-Suárez and Alberto Quesada Morales. 1996. *Cronología Fernando Ortiz.* Havana: Fundación Fernando Ortiz.

Gately, Iain. 2001. *Tobacco: A Cultural History of How an Exotic Plant Seduced Civilization.* New York: Grove Press.

Gómez, Zoila. ed. 1984. *Musicologia en Latinoamerica.* Havana: Editorial Arte y Literatura.

--------. and Victoria Eli Rodríguez. 1995. *Música Latinoamericana y Caribeña.* Havana: Editorial Pueblo y Educación.

González-Wippler, Migene. 1984. *The Santeria Experience.* Englewood Cliffs: Prentice Hall, Inc.

--------. 1994. *Santeria: The Religion.* St. Paul: Llewellyn Publications.

Guanche, Jesús. 1983. *Procesos Etnoculturales de Cuba.* Havana: Editorial Letras Cubanas.

--------. 1996. *Componentes Etnicos de la Nación Cubana.* Havana: Ediciones UNIÓN.

Guillermoprieto, Alma. 2004. *Dancing with Cuba: A Memoir of the Revolution.* New York: Pantheon Books.

Hagedorn, Katherine J. 2001. *Divine Utterances: The Performance of Afro-Cuban Santería.* Washington and London: Smithsonian Institution Press.

Hanger, Kimberly S. 1996. *A Medley of Cultures: Louisiana History at the Cabildo.* New Orleans: Louisiana Museum Foundation.

James, Joel. José Millet. and Alexis Alarcón. 1998. *El Vodú en Cuba.* Santiago de Cuba: Editorial Oriente.

Johnson, Jerah. 1992. "Colonial New Orleans." In *Creole New Orleans*. Edited by Arnold R. Hirsch and Joseph Logsdon. Baton Rouge: Louisiana State University Press.

Klein, Herbert S. 1986. *African Slavery in Latin America and the Caribbean*. New York: Oxford University Press.

Lanier, Oilda Hevia. 1996. *El Directorio Central de las Sociedades Negras de Cuba 1886-1894*. Havana: Editorial de Ciencias Sociales.

León, Argeliers. 1981. Liner notes to AMAC. Vol. 3. *Música Iyesá*. EGREM-Arieto. LD-3747.

--------. 1984. *Del Canto y El Tiempo*. Havana: Instituto Cubano Del Libro.

--------. [1951] 1993. Prologue to Fernando Ortiz. *Los Bailes y el Teatro de los Negros en el Folklore de Cuba*. Havana: Editorial Letras Cubanas.

Linares, María Teresa. 1981a. Liner notes to AMAC. Vol. 2. *Oru de Igbodú*. EGREM-Arieto. LD-3995.

Loomis, John A. 1999. *Revolution of Forms: Cuba's Forgotten Art Schools*. New York: Princeton Architectural Press.

Martínez Furé, Rogelio. 1979. *Diálogos Imaginarios*. Havana: Editorial Arte y Literatura.

Mason, Michael Atwood. 2002. *Living Santeria: Rituals and Experiences in an Afro-Cuban Religion*. Washington: Smithsonian Books.

Mbiti, John S. [1969] 1990. *African Religions and Philosophy*. Portsmith: Heinemann.

McArthur, Tom. Editor. 1992. *The Oxford Companion to the English Language*. New York: Oxford University Press.

Merriam, Alan P. 1964. *The Anthropology of Music*. Evanston: Northwestern University Press.

Métraux, Alfred. [1959] 1972. *Voodoo in Haiti*. New York: Schocken Books.

Midlo Hall, Gwendolyn. 1992. "The Formation of Afro-Creole Culture." In *Creole New Orleans*. Edited by Arnold R. Hirsch and Joseph Logsdon. Baton Rouge: Louisiana State University Press.

Mintz, Sidney W. and Richard Price. [1976] 1992. *The Birth of African-American Culture*. Boston: Beacon Press.

Moore, Robin D. 1997. *Nationalizing Blackness: Afrocubanismo and Artistic Revolution in Havana, 1920 -1940*. Pittsburgh: University of Pittsburgh Press.

-------- . 2006. *Music and Revolution: Cultural Change in Socialist Cuba*. Berkeley: University of California Press.

Moreno, Dennis. 1988. *Un Tambor Arará*. Havana: Editorial de Ciencias Sociales.

Moreno Fraginals, Manuel. 1978. *El Ingenio: Complejo Económico Social Cubano del Azúcar*. 3 vols. Havana: Editorial de Ciencias Sociales.

Murphy, Joseph M. [1988] 1993. *Santería: African Spirits in America*. Boston: Beacon Press.

Nketia, J.H. Kwabena. 1974. *The Music of Africa*. New York: Norton.

Orovio, Helio. [1981] 1992. *Diccionario de la Música Cubana*. Havana: Editorial Letras Cubanas.

Ortiz, Fernando. [1947] 1963. *Contrapunteo Cubano del Tabaco y el Azúcar*. Havana: Consejo Nacional de Cultura. Contains chapters excluded from the English translation.

------- . 1975. *Nuevo Catauro de Cubanismos*. Havana: Instituto Cubano del Libro.

------- . 1986. *Los Negros Curros*. Havana: Editorial de Ciencias Sociales.

------- . 1987. *Los Negros Esclavos*. Havana: Editorial de Ciencias Sociales.

------- . 1991. Compiled by Isaac Barreal Fernández. *Estudios Etnosociológicos*. Havana: Editorial De Ciencias Sociales.

------- . [1921] 1992. *Los Cabildos y la Fiesta Afrocubanos del Día de Reyes*. Havana: Editorial De Ciencias Sociales.

------- . [1950] 1993a. *La Africanía de la Música Folklórica de Cuba*. Havana: Editorial Letras Cubanas.

------- . [1951] 1993b. *Los Bailes y el Teatro de los Negros en el Folklore de Cuba*. Havana: Editorial Letras Cubanas.

------- . [1947] 1995. *Cuban Counterpoint, Tobacco and Sugar*. Durham: Duke University Press.

------- . [1906]1995a. *Los Negros Brujos*. Havana: Editorial de Ciencias Sociales.

------- . [1952] 1996. *Los Instrumentos de la Música Afrocubana*. 2 vols. Madrid: Editorial Música Mundana Maqueda S. L. This is a reissue of Ortiz's 5 vol. work. It is complete, but note that the page numbers do not correspond to those in the original edition.

------- . 2000. *La Santería y la Brujería de los Blancos*. Havana: Fundación Fernando Ortiz.

Paz, Octavio. 1982. *Sor Juana Inés de la Cruz*. Mexico City: Fondo de Cultura Económica.

Pedroso, Lázaro. 1995. *Obbedi, Cantos a Los Orishas: Traducción e Historia*. Havana: Ediciones ARTEX.

Pérez de la Riva, Juan. 1975. *El Barracón y Otros Ensayos*. Havana: Editorial de Ciencias Sociales.

Raboteau, Albert J. 1978. *Slave Religion: The "Invisible Institution" in the Antebellum South*. New York: Oxford University Press.

Ramos Venereo, Zobeyda. 1989. *La Música Popular Traditional en la Provincia Holguín*. Mechanical reproduction. Havana: CIDMUC.

Rodríguez, Victoria Eli and Zoila Gómez García. 1989. *Haciendo Música Cubana*. Havana: Editorial Pueblo Y Educación.

Rouget, Gilbert. [1980] 1985. *Music and Trance*. Chicago: University of Chicago Press.

Scott, Rebecca J. 1985. *Slave Emancipation in Cuba: The Transition to Free Labor, 1860-1899*. Princeton: Princeton University Press.

Shilgi, Jerry *et al*. 1994. *Orisha. Rumba. Song Anthology*. Mechanical reproduction. Originally released anonymously, this work is now credited to Mr. Shilgi and his collaborators in the San Francisco area.

Sosa Rodríguez, Enrique. 1982. *Los Nañigos*. Havana: Casa de las Americas.

-------. 1984. *El Carabalí*. Havana: Editorial Letras Cubanas.

Spiro, Michael. 2006. *The Conga Drummer's Guidebook*. Petaluma: Sher Music Co.

Sublette, Ned. 2004. *Cuba and its Music: From the First Drums to the Mambo*. Chicago: Chicago Review Press.

Sued-Badillo, Jalil. ed. 2003. *General History of the Caribbean. Volume One: Autochthonous Societies*. Paris: UNESCO Publishing.

Summers, Bill and Neraldo Duran. 2007. *Bata Rhythms from Matanzas, Cuba; Transcriptions of the Oro Seco*. Matanzas: Kabiosile. Companion book to the DVD, *El Lenguaje del Tambor*.

Thomas, Hugh. 1993. "Cuba, c. 1750-c. 1860." In *Cuba, A Short History*. Edited by Leslie Bethell. New York: Cambridge University Press.

------- . 1997. *The Slave Trade*. New York: Simon & Schuster.

------- . [1971] 1998. *Cuba or The Pursuit of Freedom*. New York: Da Capo Press.

Vélez, María Teresa. 2000. *Drumming for the Gods*. Philadelphia: Temple University Press.

Vinueza Gonzáles, Maria Elena. 1988. *Presencia Arará en la Música Folclórica de Matanzas*. Havana: Casa de las Americas.

Vinueza Gonzáles, Maria Elena and Ana V. Casanova. No date. *Algunas Consideraciones Sobre el Aporte Yoruba a la Cultura Musical Cubana*. Mechanical reproduction. Havana: CIDMUC.

Vinueza Gonzáles, Maria Elena and Carmen Maria Sáenz. 1992. " El Aporte Africano en la Formacíon de la Cultura Musical Cubana." In *Folklore Americano*. #53. Instituto Panamericano de Geografía e Historia.

Webster's New Universal Unabridged Dictionary. 2nd ed., s.v. "creole."

Wilcken, Lois. 1992. *The Drums of Vodou*. Tempe: White Cliffs Media Co.

Williams, Eric. [1970] 1984. *From Columbus to Castro: The History of the Caribbean 1492-1969*. New York: Vintage Books.

-------- . [1944] 1994. *Capitalism and Slavery*. Chapel Hill: University of North Carolina Press.

University of Chicago Spanish Dictionary. 4th ed., s.v. "cabildo."

Yih, David. 1995. Liner notes to *Rhythms of Rapture: Sacred Musics of Haitian Vodou*. Washington: Smithsonian Folkways Records. SF CD 40464.

Interviews, Lectures, and Lesson Tapes Cited in Text

Alén Rodríguez, Dr. Olavo. 1999a. Interview tape by author, 10 February.

-------- . 1999b. Interview tape by author, 17 February.

------ . 2000a. Interview tape by author, 2 February.

------ . 2000b. Interview tape by author, 4 February.

Izquierdo, Pedro. 1999a. Lesson tape by Bob Murphy, 13 February.

-------- . 1999b. Lesson tape by author, 20 February.

López, Luis Ramón. 2000. Lesson tape by author, 31 January.

-------. 2000b. Lesson tape by author, 2 February.

Pablo, Pedro. 2001a. Lesson tape by author, 19 April.

-------. 2001b. Lesson tape by author, 21 April.

Terry Gonzáles, Eladio. 1997. Lesson tape by author, 6 February.

-------. 1999. Lecture tape by author, 16 February.

-------. 2000. Interview tape by author, 28 January.

Vinueza Gonzáles, María Elena. 1994. Lecture tape by author, 15 February.

-------. 1996a. Interview tape by author, 2 February.

-------. 1996b. Interview tape by author, 3 February.

Vizcaino, Roberto. 1998. Lesson tape by author, 21 February.

-------. 1999. Lesson tape by author, 18 February.

Discography

Abbreviations

AMAC.   *Antología de la Música Afrocubana*. EGREM-Areíto. 9 vols. The AMAC is the definitive source of Afro-Cuban field recordings and has excellent liner notes. Released starting in 1981 on 33 rpm LPs but now out of print, it was rereleased on cassette without the liner notes, retaining the same catalog numbers as the originals, except that the letters LD have been replaced by C, so LD 3325 is C 3325 on the cassettes. It has now been released in a CD boxed set with the liner notes by Egrem (col. 0011).

Audio Recordings

Aché. ND. Merceditas Valdes. EGREM-Artex. CD 010.

Aché IV. 1994. Merceditas Valdes. EGREM. C 4692.

Cantos Afrocubanos. 1996. Merceditas Valdes con los Tambores de Jesus Pérez. EGREM. C224. Contains the same recordings of Lucumí chants on her A.S.P.I.C. release but without the other material.

Cantos de Santería. 1994. Artex. CA 212. Contains batá, güiro, and bembé.

CUBA - Merceditas Valdes y Los Tambores Batá de Jesús Pérez. No date. A.S.P.I.C. Editions Suisse. X55512. Contains Lucumí chants as well as contemporary arrangements and songs not directly of Yoruba origin.

Fiesta de Bembé. AMAC. Vol. 6. EGREM-Arieto. LD-3997 (C-3997).

Fundamento Yoruba 1. 1998. Papo Angarica. EGREM. CD 0253.

Havana & Matanzas, Cuba ca. 1957: Batá, Bembé, and Palo Songs. 2003. Smithsonian Folkways Recordings. SFW CD40434. Historic field recordings by Lydia Cabrera and Josefina Tarafa.

Ito Iban Echu. 1996. Los Muñequitos de Matanzas. Qbadisc. QB9022.

Música Iyesá. AMAC Vol. 3. EGREM-Arieto. LD-3747 (C-3747).

Música Yoruba. 1996. Conjunto Folklórico Nacional de Cuba. Bembé Records. CD 2010-2.

Obbedi, Cantos a Los Orishas: Traducción e Historia. approx. 1995. Lázaro Pedroso. The companion tape to the book of the same name. Presumably released by Artex, but my copy is hand recorded.

Olorún. 1994. Lázaro Ros. Green Linnet Records. Xenophile. GLCD 4022.

Orisha Aye. Oggún. 2001. Lázaro Ros. Unicornio Producciones Abdala. UN-CD6008.

Orisha Aye. Oyá. 2001. Lázaro Ros. Unicornio Producciones Abdala. UN-CD6010.

Oru de Igbodú. AMAC. Vol. 2. EGREM-Arieto. LD-3995 (C-3995).

Orumilla Obbi Wao. 2007. Miguel Valdés. Ediciones Pentagrama. APCD-629.

Osun Lozun. 2003. Papo Angarica. Egrem. CD 0568.

Sacred Rhythms. 1995. Grupo Ilú Añá. Fundamento Productions.

Sacred Rhythms of Cuban Santería. 1995. Smithsonian Folkways Recordings. SF CD 40419.

Santisimo. 1996. Emilio Barreto, Orlando Rios, and Amelia Pedroso. Luz Productions. LUZ0001CD.

Spirit Rhythms. 1996. Orlando "Puntilla" Ríos & Nueva Generación. Music of the World. LAT50603.

Songs for Eleguá. 1996. Lazaro Ros & Olorún. Ashé Records. CD 2001.

Tambor Yoruba, Aggayú. 1999. Abbilona. Caribe Productions, Inc. CD 9549.

Tambor Yoruba, Aggayú II 2001. Abbilona. Caribe Productions, Inc. CD 9603.

Tambor Yoruba, Changó. 1999. Abbilona. Caribe Productions, Inc. CD 9550.

Tambor Yoruba, Changó II 2001. Abbilona. Caribe Productions, Inc. CD 9604.

Tambor Yoruba, Elegguá, Oggún y Ochosi. 1999. Abbilona. Caribe Productions, Inc. CD 9546.

Tambor Yoruba, Elegguá, Oggún y Ochosi II. 2001. Abbilona. Caribe Productions, Inc. CD 9600.

Tambor Yoruba, Obatalá. 1999. Abbilona. Caribe Productions, Inc. CD 9545.

Tambor Yoruba, Obatalá II. 2001. Abbilona. Caribe Productions, Inc. CD 9599.

Tambor Yoruba, Ochún. 1999. Abbilona. Caribe Productions, Inc. CD 9547.

Tambor Yoruba, Ochún II. 2001. Abbilona. Caribe Productions, Inc. CD 9601.

Tambor Yoruba, Orisha Oko, Oddua, Ibeyis, Olókun, y Otros. 1999. Abbilona. Caribe Productions, Inc. CD 9552.

Tambor Yoruba, Orisha Oko, Oddua, Ibeyis, Olókun, y Otros II. 2001. Abbilona. Caribe Productions, Inc. CD 9606.

Tambor Yoruba, Oyá. 1999. Abbilona. Caribe Productions, Inc. CD 9551.

Tambor Yoruba, Oyá. II. 2001. Abbilona. Caribe Productions, Inc. CD 9605.

Tambor Yoruba, Yemayá. 1999. Abbilona. Caribe Productions, Inc. CD 9548.

Tambor Yoruba, Yemayá II. 2001. Abbilona. Caribe Productions, Inc. CD 9502.

Toque de Güiros. AMAC. Vol. 8. EGREM-Arieto. LD-4483 (C-4483).

Various

A Carnival of Cuban Music. 1990. Compilation. Rounder Records. CD 5049. Has one example each of batá, comparsa, and rumba, as well as other styles.

Cuba. 1998. Compilation. Air Mail Music. SA 141024. A collection of field recordings by Francois Jouffa of various folkloric and son traditions, including Tumba Francesa.

CUBA, Chants et rythmes afro-cubains. 1988. Compilation. Arion. ARN 64057. Contains a variety of field recordings, including examples of rumba and comparsa.

De lo Afrocubano a la Salsa. 1994. Artex. No catalog number. Two cassettes. The companion cassettes to Alén Rodríguez's book are an excellent introduction to the panorama of Afro-Cuban and Cuban genres leading up to salsa.

Drum Jam. 2000. Grupo Exploración. Bembé Records. 2026-2. Contains excellent, well-recorded examples of columbia, guarapachangeo, iyesá, vodú, batá, and conga oriental, among others.

Hacia el Amor. No date. John Santos and the Coro Folklórico Kindembo. Xenophile Records. XENO 4034. Although recorded in the United States, this CD was well produced and is worth a listen. Contains batá, rumba, arará, and comparsa.

Official Retrospective of Cuban Music. 1999. Dr. Olavo Alén Rodríguez and Lic. Ana Casanova Oliva. CIDMUC. Tonga Productions. TNG4CD 9303. The only single source for field recordings of batá, güiro, bembé, iyesá, arará, makuta, yuka, kinfuiti, palo, maní, abakuá, tonada trinitaria, yambú, guaguancó, columbia, and conga.

Raíces Africanas. 1998. Grupo AfroCuba de Matanzas. Shanachie. 66009.

Viejos Cantos Afrocubanos. AMAC. Vol. 1. EGREM-Arieto. LD-3325 (C-3325) Contains field recordings of various songs and drumming groups of the Lucumí, Arará, Congos, and Carabalí.

Related

Yoruba Drums from Benin, West Africa. 1996. Smithsonian Folkways Recordings. SF CD 40440.

Video Recordings

AfroCuba de Matanzas. 1995. Caribbean Music & Dance Programs.

Conjunto Folklórico Nacional de Cuba. ND. Mundo Latino.

Everyday Art. 1994. The Cinema Guild, Inc.

El Lenguaje del Tambor: Bata Rhythms and Techniques from Matanzas, Cuba. 2007. Kabiosile.

La Fuerza del Tambor: Batá, Bembé, y Güiro en Matanzas, Cuba. 2006. Kabiosile.

Rumbambeo. No date. Boogalu Productions.

Rumbon Tropical. No date. Boogalu Productions.

Sworn to the Drum: A Tribute to Francisco Aguabella. 1995. Flower Films.

Vamos al Tambor: Presentations in Matanzas, Cuba. 2003. Kabiosile.

Don Skoog (*omó aña*) is an independent musician, teacher, and writer who lives in Oak Park, Illinois. He performs on drumset, Latin percussion, marimba, and flamenco cajón. His teachers include James Dutton, Vida Chenoweth, Gordon Stout, Karl Husa, Roberto Vizcaino, José Eladio, Rich Gajate, and Alejandro Carvajal. He has taught percussion at the American Conservatory of Music, Sherwood Music School, and the Contemporary Music Project, which he founded in 1982. Mr. Skoog has given demonstrations and clinics at Northwestern University, Valparaiso University, Vandercook College, Kansas State University, Colorado State University, Illinois Wesleyen University, the Nashville Jazz Workshop, and the PAS Illinois Day of Percussion, as well as hundreds of presentations in grade and high schools through the International Music Foundation. He was lead artist for the Gallery 37 Latin Big Band from 1993 to 2002, and has traveled to Cuba many times to study and conduct tours. Mr. Skoog is also director of the Cuba in Chicago program in Oak Park, Illinois.

Alejandro Carvajal Guerra is a renowned, babalawo, batalero (*omó aña*), abakuá, palero, and rumbero whose musical and family roots go back to the Yorubas of Africa. Trained in the tradition as a child by his father and by his padrino, Papo Angarica, Mr. Carvajal is now recognized as one of the most knowledgeable bataleros in Cuba. He has taught at the *Instituto Superior de Arte* and the *Centro Nacional de Escuelas de Arte*, and is currently a faculty member at the *Escuela Nacional de Arte* in Havana. He has performed with (*mi tío*) Ángel Bolaños, Jesús Pérez, Regino Jiménez, Fermín Nane, Mario Jaure, Carlos Aldama, Alfonso Aldama, Santiaguito, Pedro Aspirina, *"y les agradezco por todo lo aprendido a todas aquellas personas que están hoy conmigo y a las que ya están ibaes (muertas). Les debo mis conocimientos."*

The Contemporary Music Project publishes percussion music, books, and recordings, and provides musical groups for schools and other educational presenters.

The Contemporary Music Project
P.O. Box 1070
Oak Park, IL 60304
708 524-8605
don@contemporarymusicproject.com

www.contemporarymusicproject.com

www.ingramcontent.com/pod-product-compliance
Lightning Source LLC
Chambersburg PA
CBHW080548230426
43663CB00015B/2755